Landmarks Preservation
and the Property Tax

Landmarks Preservation and the Property Tax

Assessing Landmark Buildings for Real Taxation Purposes

David Listokin
with
Alan Neaigus
Jessica Winslow
and
James Nemeth

THE CENTER FOR URBAN POLICY RESEARCH
Rutgers University
Building 4051, Kilmer Campus
New Brunswick, New Jersey 08903

NEW YORK LANDMARKS CONSERVANCY
330 West 42nd Street
New York, New York 10036

Landmarks Preservation and the Property Tax is co-published by the Center for
Urban Policy Research of Rutgers University and the New York Landmarks Conservancy. The Conservancy, a not-for-profit organization, sponsored the study
with funds raised from the New York State Council on the Arts and the James A.
Macdonald Foundation.

The statements and conclusions contained herein are those of the authors and do not
necessarily reflect the views of the Conservancy, the funding sources, the members
of the Advisory Board, or the organizations which they represent. No warranty,
express or implied, or responsibility for the accuracy or completeness of the
information contained herein is assumed by the aforementioned organizations or
individuals.

Library of Congress Publication Data

Listokin, David.
      Landmarks preservation and the property tax.

      Bibliography: p.
      1. Real property tax—Law and legislation—United States.
2. Historic sites—Law and legislation—United States. 3. Real
property tax—Law and legislation—New York (N.Y.) 4. Historic
sites—Law and legislation—New York (N.Y.) I. Rutgers University.
Center for Urban Policy Research. II. Title.

KF6784.L58	343.7305'4	82-1263
ISBN 0-88285-077-6	347.30354	AACR2

To Yair and Siona

Contents

Exhibits

CHAPTER THREE: PROPERTY-TAX ASSESSMENT OF LANDMARK BUILDINGS: PREVAILING PRACTICE AND IMPLICATIONS 55

CHAPTER FOUR: POLICY AND PROCEDURAL RECOMMENDATIONS FOR ASSESSING NEW YORK CITY LANDMARKS 114

APPENDIX ONE 156

FOREWORD

Landmarks Preservation and the Property Tax is the result of an extensive inquiry into the effect of tax assessment policy upon the owners of landmarks. The study focuses on New York City, but its findings are drawn from the experience of assessors from towns and cities throughout the country. The project was sponsored by the New York Landmarks Conservancy, a private, not-for-profit organization chartered in New York State to promote the preservation of architecturally, historically, and culturally significant properties. In order to ensure that the findings of the study are both meaningful and practicable, the Conservancy and the authors worked closely with agencies of the City of New York on this project. The Department of Finance, the Tax Commission, and the Corporation Counsel participated in the study.

As a result of communications consequent on the formulation of *Landmarks Preservation and the Property Tax*, the Bureau of Real Property Assessment and the Landmarks Preservation Commission established a successful new system for sharing information. Meetings of representatives of the City agencies and the study team produced a working model program for assessment of landmark property. Draft policy on the subject has been put forward by the Department of Finance. Senior field assessors debated proposed recommendations based on the findings of the study with the authors and the Conservancy. The representatives of the Bureau of Real Property Assessment became a "sounding board" for the study's major points. *Landmarks Preservation and the Property Tax* has benefited greatly from the active participation of the assessors. Significant progress has been made in understanding the complexities of the assessment of landmark property since the Conservancy convened a symposium on "Historic Preservation and the Law," which included a session on the "Valuation of Historic Properties," in September of 1978 at The Association of the Bar of the City of New York. The work of *Landmarks Preservation and the Property Tax* is an outgrowth of that earlier forum, and it represents the finest of constructive partnerships between public agencies and a private organization concerned with a mutual goal.

The knowledgeable and equitable assessment for tax purposes of property that is subject to a landmark designation or encumbered by a preservation restriction, a conservation easement, or a restrictive covenant, is only an element of a much larger problem. The issues of assessing landmarks are complex, yet they are but a small part of a greater set of questions surrounding the assessment for tax purposes of any property in New York State. *Landmarks Preservation and the Property Tax* has given the City of New York a stronger basis upon which to promulgate its policy concerning the assessment of landmarks.

Mendes Hershman
Co-Chairman
Study Advisory Board
New York Landmarks
  Conservancy

Edgar A. Lampert
Co-Chairman
Study Advisory Board
New York Landmarks
  Conservancy

ACKNOWLEDGMENTS

The preparation of this study would have been impossible without the assistance and cooperation of many individuals. Dr. George Sternlieb, director of the Center for Urban Policy Research, must be singled out for his patience and guidance. Ms. Carol Clark, associate director of the New York Landmarks Conservancy, served an invaluable role in shaping the analysis and establishing contacts with government officials, property owners and others knowledgeable about New York City's landmarks. The final scope and direction of this monograph is a tribute to Ms. Clark's constant input over an eighteen month period.

Staff members of the Center for Urban Policy Research assembled background data and wrote draft sections of the report. Dr. Alan Neaigus researched the property tax records of the case study properties and participated in describing New York City's property tax assessment system. Dr. Neaigus also was involved in the national statutory search. On this latter task he was joined by Jessica Winslow—an able, dedicated and careful researcher. Ms. Winslow assisted with writing Appendix one of the study. Appendix two—the survey of practice—is a tribute to the perseverance and energy of James Nemeth. Mr. Nemeth called hundreds of local tax assessors throughout the United States to determine how landmark buildings are valued for taxation purposes.

The author also wishes to extend his gratitude for the financial support offered by the New York Landmarks Conservancy in sponsoring the project, and the suggestions given by the Conservancy's past executive

director, Susan Henshaw Jones, as well as its current director, Laurie
Beckelman. In addition, appreciation is extended to the financial assistance
provided by the James A. Macdonald Foundation and the New York State
Council on the Arts.

A key role was played by the study's Advisory Board assembled by the
New York Landmarks Conservancy. The Advisory Board members are
listed on an accompanying page. All provided advice, leads and guidance.
A special debt of gratitude is owed to the Board's co-chairmen, Mendes
Hershman and Edgar A. Lampert, for their recommendations and com-
ments on numerous drafts. Their insistence that the research be keyed to
practical policy has been realized. Special thanks must also be extended to
other advisory board members: Philip Click, for describing New York
City's assessment process; John Costonis, for his legal and policy input;
Walter J. Handelman, for enunciating the special problems faced by the
nonprofit landmark property owner; Mary E. Mann, for special insight into
the issues; Dorothy Miner, for a comprehensive review of an initial study
draft as well as needed advice throughout the analysis; Eugene J. Morris,
for sharing his vast experience in tax assessment practice; Donald Schnabel,
for pointing to the reality of New York City realty; and Edith I. Spivack, for
her insistence that the interests of both New York City and landmark
owners be balanced in the study's recommendations.

A number of New York City's governmental officials not previously
mentioned also deserve special thanks. The Chairman of the Landmarks
Preservation Commission, Kent L. Barwick, lent needed insight into the
issues and reviewed the study's policy recommendations. Ms. Lenore
Norman, executive director of the Commission, was helpful as always.
Commissioner Philip R. Michael of the Department of Finance commented on and improved the policy recommendations. William Block,
assistant commissioner of the Department of Finance, provided background detail on the landmark case studies and reviewed the policy outline.

Many other individuals helped guide the analysis. Roger M. Darby, MAI,
provided the insight of an experienced appraiser. William J. Murtagh, of
the Historic Preservation Program at Columbia University, gave a national
perspective of the landmark assessment issue. Arthur Zabarkes, Executive
Director of the Citizens Housing and Planning Council, discussed the
complexity of the assessment task. William Ginsberg of Hofstra University
overviewed New York City's assessment process. Richard Almy of the
International Association of Assessing Officers reviewed basic assessment
concepts and practices. Frank Gilbert of the National Trust for Historic
Preservation commented on landmark assessment challenges, both nationally and in New York City.

Mrs. Mary Picarella, Mrs. Joan Frantz, Mrs. Lydia Lombardi, and Mrs.

Arlene Pashman, the mainstays of the Center for Urban Policy Research's administrative and typing staff, all performed valuable duties in preparing the manuscript. Ms. Barbara Tieger and Arlene Pashman assisted its editing and final publication. Ms. Jean Acker and Mrs. Joan Dalton also warrant thanks for their publication efforts.

The author assumes responsibility for any errors or misinterpretations that remain.

David Listokin

Landmarks Preservation and the Property Tax
Study Advisory Board

Co-Chairmen

Edgar A. Lampert, Esquire, Director, Housing Initiative, New York City
Partnership, Inc.
Mendes Hershman, Esquire, Rosenman Colin Freund Lewis & Cohen

Members

Philip Click, Real Property Assessment Board, New York City
John Costonis, Esquire, Professor, New York University School of Law
Walter J. Handelman, Esquire, The James A. Macdonald Foundation
Mary E. Mann, President, New York City Tax Commission
Dorothy Miner, Esquire, New York City Landmarks Preservation
Commission
Eugene J. Morris, Esquire, Demov, Morris, Levi & Schein
Donald Schnabel, Senior Vice President and Director, Julian J. Studley,
Inc.
Edith I. Spivack, Esquire, Executive Assistant, Corporation Counsel of
New York City

Board of Directors
New York Landmarks Conservancy

INTRODUCTION AND SUMMARY OF FINDINGS

Study Background and Focus

Historic preservation is an issue of growing importance and public commitment. Federal and state mechanisms have been established to identify and support historic buildings/sites.* Local governments have been especially active in supporting and protecting historic resources. Communities across the country have established designation programs whereby individual buildings or districts of historical-architectural significance are accorded landmark status.* Designation protects the landmark by delaying/prohibiting: inappropriate alterations to the property's facade, unsuitable interior changes (in the case of an interior landmark), and demolition of the structure itself.

Designation activity has been accompanied by growing interest in other local incentives/disincentives to the support of historic buildings. In this regard, the property tax is viewed as both a possible powerful drawback to or catalyst of preservation. This study examines the relationship *between historic preservation and the property tax, focusing on the question of how designated buildings should be assessed for real taxation purposes.* Appropriate valuation is a fundamental tenet of the property tax—an *ad valorem* levy. Assessment of landmark buildings* is a special concern because the very act of designation may ultimately influence property value, and this association is typically ignored by many local assessors.

---

*With the exception of chapter one where federal and state landmark designation mechanisms are discussed, this study's references to "landmark," "historic," or "designated properties" (used interchangeably) all concern buildings/districts designated by a local governmental body with attendant restrictions on alterations/demolition.

Omission of historic status from the assessment equation can have significant implications. Where designation detracts from value and this factor is not considered, the landmark will be overassessed. Such over valuation adds to the landmark's property tax/operating cost burden and may ultimately impede necessary maintenance/rehabilitation. Conversely, where designation enhances value and this linkage is unacknowledged, the landmark will be undervalued for property tax purposes, thereby shortchanging the local taxing jurisdiction.

The study focuses on New York City in considering the effects of historic status on property value and in evaluating current assessment practices. Our policy recommendations are also directed toward New York's Department of Real Property Assessment. While the focus is on New York City, the monograph's findings are transferrable to other communities because the base conditions are similar. Many other cities have designation programs, in some cases modeled, at least in part, on New York City's. In addition, New York's property-tax system and administrative processes resemble those found in communities across the nation. To enhance the transferrability of this study's findings, we frequently refer to the national experience and literature, typically on a side-by-side basis with the New York City counterpart. In short, while our analysis utilizes New York's experience and potential, it has far wider application.

Study Organization

The monograph is organized into four chapters and four appendices:

Chapter one: Historic Preservation, Property Tax, and Landmark Assessment: Background and Issues

Chapter two: Landmark Designation and Property Value: Summary of the Literature

Chapter three: Property-Tax Assessment of Landmark Buildings: Prevailing Practice and Implications

      Appendix 3-A: Assessment of Landmark Properties: New York City Case Studies

      Appendix 3-B: New York City Property Tax: Structure and Administration

Chapter four: Policy and Procedural Recommendations for Assessing New York City Landmarks

Appendix I: Landmark Properties and the Property Tax: National Statutory Survey and Survey of Practice

Appendix II: Landmark Properties and the Property Tax: Annotated
Bibliography

Chapter one presents the background to the landmark-assessment issue.
It summarizes the growing interest in historic preservation in general and
the relationship between preservation and the property tax in particular.
The chapter concludes by examining the underlying reasons for the interest
in proper landmark assessment for real taxation purposes.

Chapter two considers the association between landmark designation
and property value—a key interrelationship, albeit difficult to define, to
the landmark-assessment question. Based on national as well as New York
City studies on this subject, it discusses when and where designation may
influence buyer-seller responses to historic buildings. This literature suggests that depending on property type, use, and other characteristics,
designation may enhance, detract, or be neutral with respect to property
value. Chapter two synthesizes the research on this topic and points to its
strengths and weaknesses.

Chapter three considers how assessors currently react to landmark status
and the implications of their prevailing practice to both the landmark
owner and the local taxing jurisdiction. Landmark assessment state-of-the-
art and consequences are discussed both for New York City as well as for
communities across the nation. Two appendices follow this chapter.
Appendix 3-A details six New York City case studies illustrating the effects
of designation on property value and attendant assessment issues. Appendix 3-B highlights the New York City property-tax structure and administration.

Chapter four turns to policy recommendations. It details how landmarks
should be asssessed, specifying development of an appropriate data base,
application of valuation techniques sensitive to landmark situations, and
preparation of assessor training and other support programs to promote
field-level implementation of the recommendations.

Appendix one summarizes the statutory direction taken by states across
the country concerning landmark assessment as well as other landmark-
property tax relationships. It also highlights the degree and manner to
which these statutes have been implemented. This statutory and administrative overview serves to guide the substance and tone of the policies
proposed in chapter four.

Appendix two annotates the landmark-assessment literature—a source
drawn upon by all the prior chapters, especially chapter two's discussion of
the landmark-property value association and chapter four's recommendations.

Study Scope and Terminology

This study is an exploratory investigation. It concerns itself with the impact of designation—an inherently difficult to isolate effect that has just begun to be explored on an empirical basis. It also deals with real-property assessment—a similarly convoluted process whose operating dynamics are hard to determine. Complicating the investigation is the changing nature of both phenomena. Designation today is still in its gestation period and its scope and emphasis will undoubtedly be modified as it matures. Prevailing assessment practices are also due for change, in part as a consequence of the courts' questioning the legality of the current valuation procedures. In short, our analysis is an early attempt to define and act upon inherently difficult landmark-property value-assessment relationships that themselves have yet to be fully explored or finalized.

A note on terminology is required. Except in chapter one where federal and state designation mechanisms are discussed, this study's references to "landmark," "historic," or "designated properties" (used interchangeably) all concern buildings/districts designated by a local governmental body with attendant restrictions on alterations/demolition. The terms "assessment," "appraisal," and "valuation," also used interchangably, all refer to the determination of property value. While there is a technical distinction between assessment and appraisal (i.e., a property valued at $100,000 will be assessed for $50,000 in a jurisdiction adhering to a 50 percent assessment-to-value ratio), central to both procedures is the estimation of property worth.

CHAPTER ONE

HISTORIC PRESERVATION, PROPERTY TAX, AND LANDMARK ASSESSSMENT: BACKGROUND AND ISSUES

Introduction

This chapter discusses the background to the landmark-assessment issue. It commences with a brief overview of the growing interest in historic preservation and the federal, state, and local mechanisms established to identify and protect historically significant resources. New York City's landmark-designation program—the nation's most extensive one—is described. The chapter then turns to the relationship between landmark buildings and the property tax, focusing on the questions and implications of the assessment of historic properties for real taxation purposes.

Historic Preservation Comes of Age

In recent years interest in historic preservation has been kindled. In 1965, fewer than 100 communities had taken steps to protect neighborhoods of historical or architectural importance; by 1980, almost 1,000 localities had designated one or more historic districts.[1] In 1970, there were approximately 2,000 entries on the National (federal) Register of Historic Places; a decade later there were almost 20,000.[2] Interest in preserving the past is reflected in other ways. Membership in the National Trust for Historic Preservation has grown dramatically. Graduate-level historic preservation programs have been established at Columbia and many other universities. Preservation literature has proliferated; conferences on the subject have become commonplace.[3]

1

The current advocacy for and support of historic preservation is due to numerous, interrelated factors. Urban-renewal excesses in the 1950s and 1960s, particularly widespread demolition, evoked a turning to preserving and building on the past. Dissatisfaction with the uniformity of suburban tract construction in the postwar period has instilled a growing appreciation of the distinctiveness and value of the historic built environment. Preparation for the nation's bicentennial in 1976 sparked further interest in preserving the past—both cultural and physical. And the rapid rise of construction costs in the late 1970s gave new value and attractiveness to the extant residential and nonresidential stock as a lower cost alternative to new development.

Historic preservation is also viewed as not only an end in itself but also as an important means for revitalizing declining urban areas. The theme of preservation has served as an important rallying point for numerous urban restoration activities.[4] Many of the leading examples of residential urban turnabout—Brooklyn Heights and Park Slope in New York City, Society Hill in Philadelphia, and Beacon Hill in San Francisco—have historical motifs. The same is true of numerous nonresidential rehabilitation success stories—Boston's Faneuil Hall, San Francisco's Ghiradelli Square, and Denver's Larimer Square.[5]

Federal, State, and Local Historic Preservation Mechanisms/Programs

Interest in historic preservation has evoked a series of federal, state, and local protective mechanisms and programs.

Federal Historic Preservation Mechanisms/Programs (See Exhibit 1)

Federal historic preservation activity dates from the period following the Civil War when the federal government acted to preserve battlefields. At the turn of the twentieth century, the Antiquities Act of 1906 gave the President the power to declare and set aside national monuments.[6] In 1935, the National Historic Sites Act empowered the Secretary of the Interior to acquire and preserve properties of national historical significance.[7] In 1949, Congress chartered the National Trust for Historic Preservation as a nonprofit corporation to facilitate public interest and participation in preservation.[8]

While the federal government's involvement in historic preservation goes back many years, its most important activities are quite recent. The

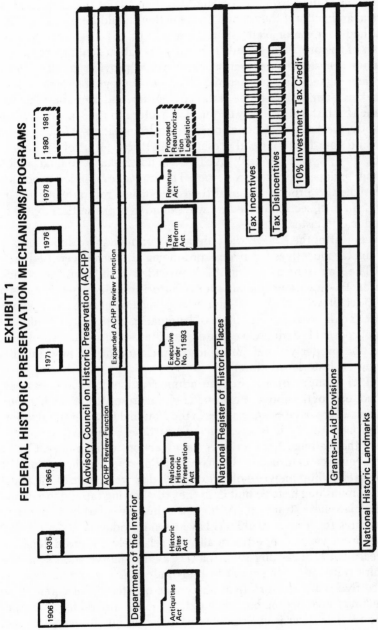

EXHIBIT 1

FEDERAL HISTORIC PRESERVATION MECHANISMS/PROGRAMS

1906   1935   1966   1971   1976   1978   1980   1981

Department of the Interior

Advisory Council on Historic Preservation (ACHP)

ACHP Review Function

Expanded ACHP Review Function

Antiquities Act

Historic Sites Act

National Historic Preservation Act

Executive Order No. 11593

Tax Reform Act

Revenue Act

Proposed Reauthorization Legislation

National Register of Historic Places

Grants-in-Aid Provisions

National Historic Landmarks

Tax Incentives

Tax Disincentives

10% Investment Tax Credit

Source: Economics Research Associates, *Economic Impact of the Multiple Resource Nomination to the National Register of Historic Places of the St. Louis Central Business District.* Report prepared for the St. Louis Community Development Agency (Boston: Economics Research Associates, 1980).

National Historic Preservation Act of 1966 (NHPA)[9] set the tone and mechanisms of the current federal intervention. NHPA declared that "the historical and cultural foundation of the nation should be preserved"[10]; it established four major elements to achieve this goal[11]: (1) the National Register of Historic Places would inventory the nation's cultural resources; (2) National Historic Preservation Fund would provide grants-in-aid to states carrying out the purposes of NHPA (i.e., surveying historic properties, making nominations to the National Register, and providing financial assistance for historic property acquisition/restoration); (3) a new cabinet-level body, the Advisory Council on Historic Preservation (ACHP), would advise and coordinate federal preservation efforts; (4) a review process (section 106), spearheaded by ACHP, would evaluate federal actions affecting National Register properties. This impact evaluation procedure was designed to protect National Register entries from adverse federal activity. (In 1976, section 106 review was extended to properties eligible for the National Register.)

A decade after the NHPA, the federal government provided a series of important tax incentives for income-producing historically certified properties. The Tax Reform Act of 1976[12] provided both "carrot and stick" measures. To encourage rehabilitation of historic buildings, section 2124 of the 1976 act allowed a rapid (60-month) depreciation of renovation expenditures.[13] To discourage demolition of landmarks, section 2124 disallowed for tax purposes (1) deduction of the expenditures incurred in demolishing an historic property[14] and (2) rapid depreciation of the new building replacing the historic structure.[15]

The 1981 changes by the Reagan administration and Congress have modified some of the above-mentioned federal preservation mechanisms/ programs. There have been changes in the National Register nomination/ listing procedure. To illustrate, for the first time, a property cannot be listed on the National Register over the objections of its owner. Certain preservation tax measures have been revised. For example, the section 2124 five-year rehabilitation write-off was repealed as were some of the penalties for demolishing historic buildings (i.e., disallowing rapid depreciation on the replacement structure). At the same time, new and quite generous tax measures for historic buildings have been introduced. Rehabilitation expenditures on such properties qualify for relatively preferred depreciation treatment (concerning such matters as the depreciation schedule, recapture rules, and adjustment to basis), albeit less generous than the repealed five-year write-off. In addition, one-quarter of the expenditures incurred in renovating the historic building can be applied for an income tax credit.[16] The latter is one of the most generous investment provisions provided by the 1981 Economic Recovery Act.

State Historic Preservation Mechanisms/Programs

By enacting enabling legislation, state governments have authorized local preservation activity—the cutting edge of the preservation effort, as we shall see momentarily. For the most part, however, states serve as the operating-arm partners of the federal preservation thrust.[17] With federal assistance, states survey historical properties, nominate eligible buildings to the National Register, and grant aid for the acquisition and/or rehabilitation of historic resources.[18] States also participate in the section 106 review process; their efforts in this regard are expected to assume greater importance under the Reagan administration's shift of regulatory responsibility from the federal to state governments.

Local Historic Preservation Mechanisms/Programs

The most important historic preservation controls are those imposed by local communities. Many localities have enacted procedures whereby architecturally and/or historically significant properties can be designated as landmarks. Typically this process works as follows: A local commission identifies buildings that meet specific criteria of architectural, historical, or cultural significance and are worthy of preservation. These recommendations are submitted to the city council and, after a public hearing, the council decides whether historic status should be accorded. Designation protects the landmark by delaying or prohibiting inappropriate alterations to the property's facade, unsuitable interior changes (in the case of an interior landmark), and demolition of the structure itself. Property changes are allowed only if they conform to the prevailing architectural style, historical motif, and so on[19].

> Local preservation regulation requires the owner of the designated property to obtain approval of the historic preservation commission for any alteration he proposes for his property. The variations in the basic theme are myriad. The ordinance may apply to individually designated landmarks or, as is more often the case, to all properties within a designated historic district. Control may extend to demolition and new construction or be limited to exterior alterations. Failure to obtain permission may prohibit the owner from carrying out his proposal or simply require him to wait.

No comparable controls are found at other levels of government: federal-state regulations may police their own actions threatening historic resources but are not directed at the owners of these resources as are local designation measures. Local units of government are also involved in many other historic preservation efforts, ranging from providing financial assistance for rehabilitation to sponsoring research-demonstration programs. In short, the owner of a historic property is much more likely to be touched by local, as opposed to federal-state, historic preservation regulatory or programmatic activity. The significance of the local preservation thrust is summarized by John Fowler, general counsel to the Advisory Council on Historic Preservation[20]:

> Most of the action in preservation occurs in the private sector controlled by local regulation and often supported by local programs. The real cutting edge of historic preservation is at the local level. Exercising their police power...communities have adopted ordinances to control what the owners of historic buildings can do with their properties.

We can obtain a sense of the local preservation effort by examining the historic regulations and programs found in New York City. In this regard, New York is in the nation's vanguard. No other community has been so active in designating historic properties and districts. Its landmark controls were the subject of the leading court decision concerning the constitutionality of such measures. In *Penn Central Transportation Co.* v. *New York City*,[21] the United States Supreme Court upheld New York's designation of the Grand Central Station. New York City's preservation regulations have been copied by many other communities. And in addition to designation, New York City offers many other supports for historic preservation.

New York City Landmark Designation

Basis and Process

In 1956, New York State enacted enabling legislation allowing cities to provide "special conditions or regulations for [the] protection, enhancement, perpetuation or use...of structures having a special character or special historical or aesthetic interest or value."[22] Approximately a decade later, New York City enacted a local landmarks-preservation act.[23] Chapter 8A of the city's charter and administrative code (added by local law no. 46, enacted April 1965) authorized the creation of the New York City Landmarks Preservation Commission (LPC) and gave it the mandate to designate and regulate buildings of special historical, cultural, or aesthetic value.

LPC consists of eleven members appointed by the mayor for three-year terms. By law, the commissioners must include at least three architects, a realtor, a city planner or landscape architect, and a historian. The work of the Commission is aided by a paid staff.

One of the major LPC duties is designation. According to New York City law, a landmark can be any improvement, any part of which is thirty years or older and has special historical/aesthetic interest or value as part of the development, heritage, or cultural characteristics of the city, state, or nation. In practice, the commission considers, among other things, architectural significance, uniqueness of design, status as the work of a noted architect, the property's place in the continuity of architectural development within the city, and special historical association with events or individuals.

The process of designation involves research by the LPC staff, a public hearing, notices to all affected property owners, and publication of the proposed designation in the *City Record* (see Exhibit 2.) The Commission decides whether landmark status shall be accorded. After designation by the Commission, which takes effect as soon as it is adopted, the matter is submitted to the Board of Estimate. Within five days, the board refers the item to the City Planning Commission, which has thirty days in which to report on its conformity with the city's land use directives and regulations. Thereafter, the Board of Estimate may affirm, modify, or disapprove the designation. The latter action has been taken only once, however.

Four categories of designation are specified (see notes for statutory definitions)[24]:

Historic District. An area that has a special character or special historical/or aesthetic interest representing one or more architectural styles or periods that constitutes a distinct section of the city.

Landmark. A structure that represents or reflects elements of the city's cultural, social, economic, political,or architectural history.

Interior Landmark. An interior of a structure, in whole or part, which is customarily open and accessible to the public and which has special qualities of design.

Scenic Landmark. A landscape feature that is of special character or historical/aesthetic interest. It must be located on city-owned property.

Following designation, the owner of the property accorded historic status has an affirmative obligation to keep it "in good repair." Much more significant are restrictions to alterations/demolition. A designated property cannot be altered, demolished, or reconstructed in any way (including such minor changes as adding a new sash, door, air conditioner, business sign, etc.) without first obtaining from LPC an appropriate certificate.[25] There are three types of certificates: (1) Certificate of No Effect on Protected Architectural Features (CNEE); (2) Permit for Minor Work (PMW); and (3) Certificate of Appropriateness (C of A).

CNEE—Property alterations (typically involving a building permit) not affecting protected landmark traits are issued a Certificate of No Effect on

EXHIBIT 2

NEW YORK CITY LANDMARK DESIGNATION PROCESS

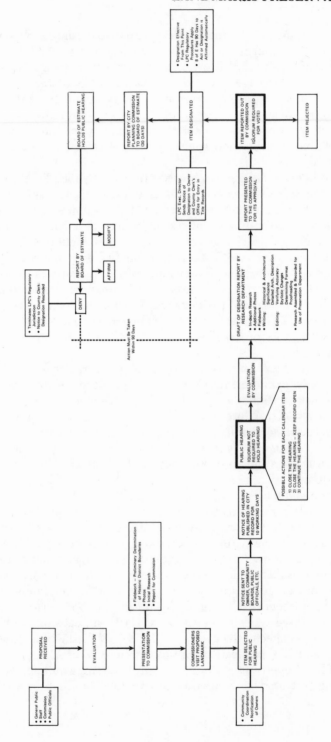

Source: New York Landmarks Preservation Commission.

Protected Architectural Features. Protected landmark traits vary by the designation categories. Publicly viewable portions of the facade are protected in the case of landmarks or buildings in historic districts. The CNEE, if applicable, is issued upon application. It would be granted if only interior changes (i.e., replacing a boiler) are planned to a landmark, or conversely if an interior is designated and changes are to be made only to the exterior.

PMW—Property alterations affecting protected architectural features, yet minor in nature (typically not necessitating a building permit, i.e., maintenance, or small repairs/alterations/restoration), require a Permit for Minor Work. Examples are painting a landmark's facade, replacing sashes or doors, or installing awnings or storm windows. A PMW is granted upon application by the property owner, and site visit/review by the LPC to ascertain the nature of the proposed changes.

C of A—Property alterations requiring a building permit and affecting protected landmark features can proceed only if the LPC grants a Certificate of Appropriateness. New construction on vacant lots in the historic districts similarly requires a C of A. This permit involves extensive review by the LPC. In considering what is "appropriate," the commission takes into account the effect of the proposed alteration/new construction to the prevailing architectural, historical, and aesthetic style/motif/quality. A public hearing is conducted for C of A requests in which the public at large, as well as community boards/groups, may voice their opinions. If approved, the C of A is issued with a detailed set of LPC-specified construction materials and standards.

The LPC's refusal to grant permission to alter or demolish is binding,[26] although the owner of the landmark can plead financial hardship, namely, that the landmark as it currently stands is incapable of earning a reasonable return (defined by statute as a 6 percent return on the property's assessed value).[27] In that case the following procedures are activated[28]

> Upon such a showing of insufficient return...the commission is empowered to devise a plan which may include exemption from or reduction of, real property taxes. If no such compromise plan is formulated or if it is rejected by the owner, the commissioner may recommend...that the city acquire an interest in the landmark. If the city does not purchase or condemn such interest, the owner is permitted to alter or demolish his building.

While this hardship procedure is specified by statute it has been used only a handful of times. In effect, the owner of a New York City landmark can alter his/her property only if issued an appropriate certificate by the LPC.

Scope and Diversity

New York City's designation activity is the most extensive and diverse in the country. As of 1981, LPC had designated 41 historic districts (containing about 16,000 buildings), about 600 individual landmarks, and approximately 30 interior/scenic landmarks.[29] Their diversity is evident from the following glimpse at the historic districts. These areas vary significantly in size. Greenwich Village, Park Slope, and Brooklyn Heights are large neighborhoods of 50 to 100 blocks each; Sniffern Court, Turtle Bay Gardens, and Treadwell Farm are enclaves of no more than one or two blocks (see Exhibit 3). The districts display significant differences in economic and social profile. As of 1978 average townhouse prices ranged from over $300,000 in Sniffern Court to $40,000 and under in both Mount Morris Park and Mott Haven.[30] The latter two designated neighborhoods were, in fact, experiencing housing abandonment, in contrast to vigorous rehabilitation in the other historic areas. The districts, as well as the individual landmarks, also differ in their density, land-use mix, architectural style, and other features, as is evident from Exhibits 4 through 7.

Beyond Designation: Further
Local Support for Landmarks

Communities have turned to designation and attendant restraints to demolition and alterations as an important means for protecting historic properties. There is growing realization, however, that further support is necessary if the goal of preservation is to be achieved. Numerous preservation conferences and publications[31] have emphasized the significance of comprehensive assistance, including public financial aid in the form of loans and grants, encouragement of local preservation organizations, improved public services in the historic districts, and so on.[32]

New York City has aspired for a comprehensive preservation support package. In addition to its ambitious designation activity, LPC offers many other aids. It provides grants to low-and moderate-income property owners in historic districts to enable them to repair/restore their building's facade including stoops, cornices, doors, windows, and ironwork. In addition, LPC monitors city actions affecting historic resources, funds preservation research and public education programs, and fosters community organization and monitoring efforts. In addition, the law allows owners of individually designated properties to sell their authorized yet unused development (air) rights to adjacent property holders. (The property value-assessment implications of air rights are discussed in chapter four.)

EXHIBIT 3
NEW YORK CITY HISTORIC DISTRICTS
LOCATED IN MANHATTAN AND OTHER BOROUGHS

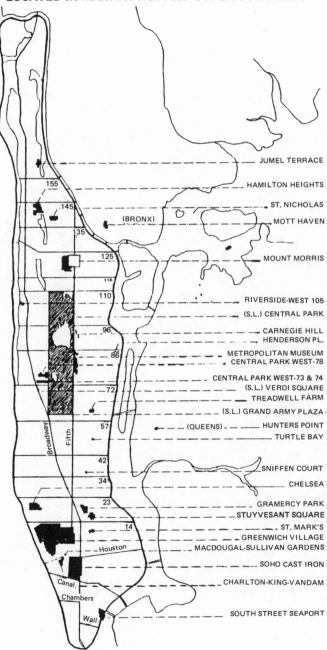

JUMEL TERRACE

HAMILTON HEIGHTS

ST. NICHOLAS

MOTT HAVEN

MOUNT MORRIS

RIVERSIDE-WEST 105

(S.L.) CENTRAL PARK

CARNEGIE HILL
HENDERSON PL.

METROPOLITAN MUSEUM
CENTRAL PARK WEST-78

CENTRAL PARK WEST-73 & 74

(S.L.) VERDI SQUARE

TREADWELL FARM

(S.L.) GRAND ARMY PLAZA

(QUEENS) ─── HUNTERS POINT

TURTLE BAY

SNIFFEN COURT

CHELSEA

GRAMERCY PARK

STUYVESANT SQUARE

ST. MARK'S

GREENWICH VILLAGE

MACDOUGAL-SULLIVAN GARDENS

SOHO CAST IRON

CHARLTON-KING-VANDAM

SOUTH STREET SEAPORT

NOTE: Map is a partial listing.

EXHIBIT 4
EXAMPLE OF NEW YORK CITY DESIGNATED LANDMARK PROPERTY:
ST. BARTHOLOMEW'S CHURCH

EXHIBIT 5
EXAMPLE OF NEW YORK CITY DESIGNATED LANDMARK PROPERTY:
McGRAW-HILL OFFICE BUILDING

EXHIBIT 6
EXAMPLE OF NEW YORK CITY DESIGNATED LANDMARK PROPERTIES:
TOWNHOUSES, GREENWICH VILLAGE HISTORIC DISTRICT

EXHIBIT 7

EXAMPLE OF NEW YORK CITY DESIGNATED LANDMARK PROPERTIES: INDUSTRIAL/COMMERCIAL BUILDINGS, SOHO-CAST IRON DISTRICT

Landmark Properties and the Property Tax

In the search for ways by which local communities can support historic preservation, increasing attention is being paid to the relationship between landmark buildings and the local property tax. To understand the landmark-property tax association it is important first briefly to consider the nature and process of the property-tax levy.

Local Property-Tax System: An Overview

The property tax is one of the oldest means of raising government revenue and remains one of the main supports for local government services, albeit its importance has diminished in the past two decades.[33] It is levied on property, in some cases only real, in others, both real and personal. The magnitude of the levy is usually expressed as a rate, typically in mills or as a dollar amount per hundred dollars of valuation. The property tax is "applied to assessed value...which ideally reflects the value of the property involved."[34] Value, in turn, is derived by local assessors via three approaches[35]: sales of comparable property (sales method); cost of reproducing the property (cost method); and capitalized income derived from the property (income method; see chapter four of this study for a detailed discussion of these techniques).

To illustrate, the New York City property tax, imposed only on real property, is one of this community's most important revenue sources. As of 1980, it yielded over 3 billion dollars—about one-quarter of the city's total income from all sources. In that year, the property tax rate was about $9.00 per $100 of assessed value. Since properties were assessed at only a fraction of their real value (about 40 percent), the real or equalized rate was about $4.00. Assessments are determined by city assessors utilizing the three traditional sales, cost, and income approaches (see Appendix 3-B to this study for a full description).

While the property tax is relied upon by nearly all local units of government, it is subject to increasing critical scrutiny. Its administration is attacked as arbitrary and as often violating constitutionally imposed standards.[36] New York joins numerous other states where prevailing property-assessment practices have been declared illegal on these grounds (See Appendix 3-B). The property tax is also criticized as being regressive,[37] imposing a disproportionate burden on the poor; failing to secure adequate quality of local services, especially education[38]; and fueling unwarranted increases in local government expenditures by unfairly capturing inflationary gains in housing prices.[39]

Urban planners also warily view the property tax. Numerous studies on the plight of America's cities point to the property levy as a destructive influence on older urban neighborhoods and buildings.[40] Inequitable assessment practices, whereby better neighborhoods are favored over slums, hasten the decline of the latter locations.[41] The property tax is also seen as a severe restraint to rehabilitation for properties undergoing renovation are penalized by an increased assessment and higher tax obligation.[42] To curb these harmful effects, urban planners advocate numerous reforms. These range from addressing the negative impacts (i.e., instituting more uniform and equitable assessment procedures so as to not penalize deteriorating neighborhoods), to turning the property tax into an urban ally by offering special rehabilitation tax incentives. The latter strategy has become commonplace in New York and many other cities.

The Relationship between Landmark Properties and the Property Tax

Preservationists similarly view the property tax as both a possible deterrent to, and a potential support for landmark buildings. As discussed by one observer[43]:

> The U.S. property tax, bulwark of local government finance, alternatively is enlisted as an ally in the cause of land-use policies or is castigated for having caused their failure. It is natural then that as sentiment for the preservation of cultural artifacts builds, interest in the effects of the property tax on historic preservation also grows.

There are a number of ways in which the property tax can interact with landmarks. Fear of upward reassessment can discourage the rehabilitation of such buildings. In a positive vein, the property tax can serve to bolster preservation. Landmarks owned by local historic groups can be declared exempt from property-tax obligations. Property-tax relief can be given to designated buildings confronting financial hardship. Rehabilitation of landmarks can be encouraged by offering property-tax incentives. To illustrate, assessment of renovated properties can be frozen despite the fact that the rehabilitation may add to value. An even more generous provision would reduce the extant property taxes of the landmarks undergoing upgrading.

Concern that the property tax be applied in a landmark-supportive fashion has resulted in the adoption of numerous special property-tax programs for historic buildings. Appendix one to the study indicates that about half the states have taken such action. To illustrate:

Indiana, Ohio, New Mexico, Washington, and many other states exempt landmarks owned by nonprofit and/or historic organizations from property taxation.

Connecticut authorizes municipalities to enact ordinances to reduce real property taxes where the current level of taxation is a material factor threatening a landmark's existence.

Alabama reduces the property taxes of certain landmark buildings by one-half.

Maryland provides that counties may elect to allow a credit against local property taxes of up to 10 percent of an owner's rehabilitation costs.

New Mexico reduces the landmark property-tax assessment by the amount expended for restoration, preservation, and maintenance.

New York City provides some property-tax relief for landmarks, albeit to a lesser extent than other jurisdictions (see Appendix one). As discussed, chapter 8-A authorizes the LPC to extend full or partial exemption of property taxation to financially strapped landmarks (this provision has not been operative). New York also offers a J.51 program, which, while not targeted specially for landmarks, provides one of the most generous packages of property-tax incentives for rehabilitation in the country. For twelve years following the rehabilitation of a multifamily or other eligible property, J.51 freezes the building's assessment. In addition, the extant property taxes prevailing before renovation may be substantially reduced. These and related programs are discussed in Appendix one to this study.

Assessment of Landmark Buildings: Why the Issue?

The approaches mentioned above all involve special cases—the nonprofit historical society, economically distressed building, or owner engaged in upgrading. In recent years, attention has turned to the more encompassing case, namely, how in general should landmark properties not involving atypical attributes of ownership, financial status, and so on be valued for real-property-taxation purposes. The question arises because *assessors are charged with determining property value and landmark status may influence value. This landmark-value association is not only overlooked by some assessors but furthermore its exact effect is difficult to define. In addition, designation sometimes strains the applicability of numerous assessment assumptions/procedures.*

One of the principal tenets of the property tax is that it is an *ad valorem* levy—it is based on the value of the real/personal property subject to taxation. Landmark designation, in turn, can affect property value. By imposing limitations to the alteration/demolition of the building accorded historic status, designation may detract from value. Conversely, the prestige and other benefits resulting from designation may enhance selling prices. If designation can affect property value, then assessors charged with determining this very element should factor landmark status. Such sensitivity, however, is typically absent, according to many informed observers. As discussed by Richard Almy, research director of the International Association of Assessing Officers[44]:

> Professional practice has yet to incorporate the application of designation. Some assessors may acknowledge landmarks; [however] this usually reflects a special sensitivity on their part.

It is important to realize that the landmark-assessment issue is not one that arises simply because assessors may not enter historic status into the assessment equation. There are further complications. It is difficult to define the effects of designation on property value, in part due to landmark's inherent countervailing influences[45]:

> When historic district recognition involves placing controls on the ways that parcels...may be altered, additions are made to existing government regulations, on right of use or occupancy. What is owned and can be sold is less, as a result, than it was before. But effective controls directed to the preservation and enhancement of the normally perceived environment, can sustain and increase the amenities of use and occupancy.

What is the trade-off?

Chapter two of this study points to numerous other difficulties in attempting to determine the association of designation and property value. These range from ambiguities in the practical extent of landmark's alteration/demolition restrictions to more fundamental questions concerning the cause-and-effect relationship of landmark status and property-value changes. These uncertainties complicate the landmark-assessment question.

Even if the market impacts of designation were easier to define, another problem of assessing landmarks is that this class of property challenges the applicability of numerous commonly accepted assessment assumptions. To cite some examples: Assessment theory associates building age with depreciation—a factor lessening value—yet in the landmark case, age may add to value. Similarly, assessment theory views certain obsolescent building features (high ceilings, older bathrooms/kitchens, and so on) as deterrents to value, yet these very same traits may be value- enhancing in a landmark situation. Assessment practice stresses valuing properties on the basis of sales of comparable properties ("comps"). By definition, however, landmarks are often characterized by special architectural, historical, or cultural characteristics, thus confounding the search for "comps." Even if more assessors realized that designation should enter the valuation equation, they would be hard-pressed as to the exact manner such factoring should be accomplished.

Assessment of Landmark Buildings: Significance of and Interest in the Issue

The question of appropriate designated property assessment is far from an academic one. It has significant practical implications both to the landmark owner and to the taxing jurisdiction where the historic property is located. These consequences are explored at length in chapter three of this study. In brief, if the landmark is incorrectly assigned an assessment greater than its real worth, then it is burdened with an unfairly high tax obligation. Such overassessment is more than inequitable (as well as illegal), for over time it can contribute to financial pressures discouraging the landmark's rehabilitation and even possibly essential maintenance. If the landmark is undervalued, this underassessment means that the local taxing authority is being denied revenue due it. Communities may have the right to extend preferred tax treatment to landmarks, or any other class of property possibly deserving special support. However, such assistance should be accorded explicitly, as a result of a policy decision, and not accomplished inadvertently as a consequence of unintended flaws in the assessment process.

Given these significant consequences, it is no wonder that there is a growing interest in landmark assessment.[46] At a 1975 conference sponsored by the International Association of Assessing Officers (IAAO), Frank Gilbert, then executive director to the New York City Landmarks Preservation Commission (LPC), pointed out instances where LPC-designated properties were unfairly assessed.[47] Gilbert stressed the need for New York City assessors to familiarize themselves with the aftereffects of landmark designation.

Gilbert's call was not heeded. A recent New York City conference on "Historic Preservation and the Law," sponsored by the New York Landmarks Conservancy and the Association of the Bar of the City of New York, included as one of its panels a session on the "Valuation of Historic Properties." The panel members—Mary E. Mann, president of the New York City Tax Commission, Eugene J. Morris, a distinguished certiorari attorney, and others knowledgeable about historic preservation—stressed the importance for New York City assessors to confront the landmark-valuation issue. As summarized by Eugene Morris[48]:

> Now it may reasonably be anticipated that the preservation movement will strike out more boldly and begin to encompass, on a much wider scale, private property operated for profit. This, in turn, will give rise to a host of new legal problems.... One of these areas involves the question of how to assess for local real estate tax purposes privately owned property which has been designated for historic preservation—a problem which must be confronted although until now it has largely been swept under the rug.

Interest in landmark asessment is not confined to New York City. A national literature has developed. (See Appendix two of this study for an annotation of these studies.) An early discussion on landmark assessment is found in John J. Costonis' 1974 analysis, *Space Adrift*.[49] This monograph analyzes the transfer of development rights as a mechanism for preserving historic properties. As part of its overall examination, it considers the impact of landmark restrictions on property value, as well as attendant assessment issues. Costonis examines both the principles and practice of real-estate taxation, notes when and where landmarks may be penalized by prejudicial assessment, and recommends various reform strategies.

A more recent discussion is found in the 1980 National Trust publication, *Tax Incentives for Historic Preservation*.[50] The significance of the landmark-assessment question is forcefully summarized in the monograph's lead article on property taxation:

> When Chief Justice Marshall stated the now familiar principle that the power to tax is the power to destroy, the applicability of taxation to historic preservation was doubtless far from anything he then had in mind. Yet, he was perhaps a better prophet than he intended. In preservation terms, the question is whether the potentially destructive power of taxation of which Justice Marshall spoke can be reversed to become a positive power for the protection of historic buildings.

Concern over landmark assessment has evoked a flurry of legislative activity in the past few years. California, Colorado, Maryland, North Carolina, Oregon, Virginia, and many other states have enacted statutes alerting assessors to landmark status, and/or specifying a special assessment treatment sensitive to landmark effects (see Appendix one for details).

The question of landmark's influences has also become a subject of increasing attention in the appraisal literature. Appraisers, charged with the professional responsibility of valuing properties, have realized that historic status should enter their calculations. Numerous articles in *The Appraisal Journal, Real Estate Appraisal,* and other publications, have considered how designation may affect buyer and seller responses, and in turn how landmark status should be incorporated into appraisal routines (see appendix two of this study). Interest in the valuation of landmarks has prompted the American Institute of Real Estate Appraisers to prepare a handbook on this subject that should be available shortly.

Conclusion

There is a growing interest in and literature on the landmark assessment/ valuation issue. This study is inspired by the recognition that in the interests of both the landmark owner and the taxing jurisdiction, landmark assessment deserves closer scrutiny. The monograph draws on and builds from the literature on this subject. Chapter two reviews national and New York City studies evaluating the relationship between designation and property value. Similarly, chapter three's evaluation of prevailing landmark assessment practices, and the policy recommendations contained in chapter four, are guided by the prior writings of assessors/appraisers.

Notes

1. Advisory Council on Historic Preservation, *Report to the President and the Congress of the United States, 1979* (Washington, D.C.: Government Printing Office, no date).
2. Ibid.
3. For a sampling of the wide range of literature on historic preservation, see Arthur P. Ziegler, Jr., Leopold Adler II, and Walter C. Kidney, *Revolving Funds for Historic Preservation: A Manual of Practice,* (Pittsburgh: Ober Park Associates, Inc., 1975). Charles B. Hosmer, Jr., *Presence of the Past: A History of the Preservation Movement in the United States before Williamsburg,* (New York: G.P. Putnam's Sons, 1965). United States Conference of Mayors, *With Heritage So Rich,* Special Committee on Historic Preservation (New York: Random House, 1966). National Trust for Historic Preservation, *A Guide to Federal Programs: Programs and Activities Related to Historic Preservation,* 1978 ed. (Washington, D.C.: National Trust for Historic Preservation, 1978). Marsha Glenn, *Historic Preservation: A Handbook for Architecture Students,* Washington, D.C.: American Institute of Architecture, 1974). Richard L. Tubesing, "Architectural Preservation in the United States, 1965-1974: A Bibliography of Federal, State, and Local Government Publications," Monticello, Ill, 1975. "Historic Preservation: Saving the Past for the Future," in *Nation's Cities,* 12 (May 1974): 14; Kathleen Agena, "Historic Preservation—A Matter of Dollars and Sense," *ASPO Planning* April 1972), p. 63.
4. Robert W. Burchell and David Listokin, *The Adaptive Reuse Handbook* (New Brunswick, New Jersey: Center for Urban Policy Research, 1980).
5. Ibid.

6. The Antiquities Act of 1906, 16 U.S.C. §§431 et seq. (1976). See Mendes Hershman, "Critical Legal Issues in Historic Preservation," *The Urban Lawyer* 12, no. 1 (Winter, 1980): 19.

7. The Historic Sites Act, 16 U.S.C. §461 (1976).

8. 16 U.S.C. §468 (1976).

9. 16 U.S.C. §420 et seq. (1976).

10. Ibid.

11. John M. Fowler, "Historic Preservation and the Law Today," *The Urban Lawyer* 12, no. 1 (Winter 1980): 3.

12. P.L. 94-455. 90 Stat. 1519.

13. Ibid., §2124 (a).

14. Ibid., §2124 (b)(c).

15. Ibid.

16. Pub. L. 97-34 (August 13, 1981), Economic Recovery Tax Act of 1981. 95 Stat. 172.

17. Fowler, "Historic Preservation and the Law Today," page 10.

18. Ibid.

19. Ibid.

20. Ibid., pp. 10-11.

21. 438 U.S.C. §104 (1978).

22. Laws of 1956, Ch. 216, New York Laws, formerly N.Y. Gen. City Law §20 (25-a) (McKinney 1968). See Glen, S. Gerstell, "Needed: A Landmark Decision", *The Urban Lawyer* 8, no. 2 (Spring 1976): 219. For further discussion of landmarks activity-historic preservation in New York City, see "Development Rights Transfer in New York City," *Yale Law Journal* Vol. 82, (December 1972): 838, Frank B. Gilbert, "Historic Preservation—Legal Aspects Preservation Law: The Grand Central (New York City) Case," *Preservation News*, (February 1976), p. 12; Mendes Hershman, "Beauty as the Subject of Legislative Control," *Practical Lawyer* 15 (February 1969): 20; "Historic Preservation in the American City: A New York Case Study," *Law and Contemporary Problems*, 36 (1971): 362, Ada Louise Huxtable, "To Keep the Best of New York," *New York Times Magazine*, §10, 1971, pp. 44-45; Charles Kleinhaus, "Architectural Control, Urban Environment and the Law," *Columbia Journal of Law and Social Problems* 1 (1965): 26; "Landmark Problems in New York," *NYU Intgra L. Rev.* 22 (January 1967): 99. New York Charter and Administrative Code, 8A §§205-1.0 to 207-21.0 (1973) (added by Local Law no. 46, April 27, 1965).

23. New York Charter and Administrative Code, 8A §§205-1.0 to 207-21.0 (1973) (added by Local Law no. 46, April 27, 1965).

24. New York City Landmarks Preservation Commission, "Try to Imagine New York City without Central Park, the...Brooklyn Bridge....St. Nicholas Historic Districts," no date. The four categories of designation are defined by statute (see footnote 23) as follows:

Historic District. Any area which:
(1) contains improvements which:
    (a) have a special character or special historical or aesthetic interest or value; and
    (b) represent one or more periods or styles of architecture typical of one or more eras in the history of the city; and
    (c) cause such area, by reason of such factors, to constitute a distinct section of the city; and

(2) has been designated as a historic district pursuant to the provisions of this chapter.

Landmark. Any improvement, any part of which is thirty years old or older, which has a special character or special historical or aesthetic interest or value as part of the development, heritage or cultural characteristics of the city, state or nation and which has been designated as a landmark pursuant to the provisions of this chapter.

Interior landmark. An interior, or part thereof, any part of which is thirty years old or older, and which the public is customarily open or accessible to the public, or to which the public is customarily invited, and which has a special historical or aesthetic interest or value as part of the development, heritage or cultural characteristics of the city, state or nation and which has been designated as an interior landmark pursuant to the provisions of this chapter.

Scenic landmark. Any landscape feature or aggregate of landscape features any part of which is thirty years or older, which has or have a special character or special historical or aesthetic interest or value as part of the development, heritage or cultural characteristics of the city, state or nation and which has been designated a scenic landmark pursuant to the provisions of this chapter.

25. New York City Landmarks Preservation Commission Interviews, September, 1981.

26. Gerstell, "Needed: A Landmark Decision," p. 220.

27. N.Y.C. Code §§207-8.0 (a) (1) (a), 207-1-0 (c), (q).

28. Gerstell, "Needed: A Landmark Decision," pp. 220-221. Charities, religious organizations and other owners of tax-exempt landmarks that wish to alter or demolish their properties must meet the following standards. They must establish that: (1) they have entered into an agreement to sell or lease the landmark for at least twenty years, and that such agreement is conditioned on approval to alter or demolish; (2) the structure would have been incapable of earning a reasonable return had it not been tax-exempt; (3) the building is no longer suited to carrying out the purposes of the owner; and (4) the prospective purchaser or tenant intends to demolish and construct a new facility, or to alter or reconstruct the existing structure. If a tax-exempt owner establishes these four conditions the Landmarks Preservation Commission has six months to find another prospective buyer or tenant whose acquisition or lease is not conditioned upon approval to alter or demolish the landmark. The owner must sell or lease to the substitute purchaser or tenant found by the commission, assuming equivalent terms and conditions. If no substitute purchaser or tenant is discovered, or if no agreement to sell or lease is consummated, the commission may recommend to the mayor that the city acquire an interest in the landmark. If such an interest is not recommended or acquired, the requested certificate of appropriateness to alter or demolish is granted to the owner. See Gerstell, "Needed: A Landmark Decision."

29. See Christopher Gray, "Landmarks Preservation Comes of Age," *New York Affairs* 6, no. 3 (1980): 46.

30. Data provided by the New York City Landmarks Preservation Commission.

31. See, for example, National Trust for Historic Preservation *Economic Benefits of Preserving Old Buildings* (Washington, D.C.: Preservation Press, 1976); National Trust for Historic Preservation, *Preservation: Toward an Ethic in the 1980's* (Washington, D.C.: Preservation Press, 1980); *Program Summary—Conference on Neighborhood Conservation* (New York City, September 24-26, 1975); Brownstone Revival Committee, *Back to the City: A Guide to Urban Preservation,*

Proceedings of the Back to the City Conference, New York City, September 13-16, 1974 (New York: Brownstone Revival Committee, 1975).

32. John E. Zuccotti, "Planning for Preservation," in Brownstone Revival Committee, *Back to the City*, p. 26.

33. Arnold H. Raphaelson, "The Property Tax," in J. Richard Aronson and Eli Schwartz (eds.), *Management Policies in Local Government Finance* (Washington, D.C.: International City Management Association, 1981), p. 123.

34. Ibid., p. 124.

35. Steven David Gold, *Property Tax Relief* (Lexington: D.C. Heath, 1979).

36. Ibid. See also Raphaelson, "The Property Tax."

37. Richard A. Musgrave, "Is a Property Tax on Housing Regressive?," *American Economic Review* 64, no. 2 (May 1974): 222; Tax Institute of America, *The Property Tax: Problems and Potentials* (Princeton, N.J.: Tax Institute of America, 1967); Karl E. Case, *Property Taxation: The Need for Reform* (Cambridge, Mass.: Ballinger Publishing Co. (1978); Dick Netzer, *Economics and Urban Problems*, 2d ed. (New York: Basic Books, 1974), pp. 256-58.

38. U.S. Advisory Commission on Intergovernmental Relations, *Financing Schools and Property Tax Relief—A State Responsibility*, A-40 (Washington, D.C.: Government Printing Office, 1973).

39. William H. Oakland, "Proposition XIII 32, Genesis and Consequences," *National Tax Journal* no. 2 (June 1979 Supplement): 387; Michael Boskin, "Some Neglected Economic Factors Behind the Recent Tax and Spending Limitation Movement," *National Tax Journal* 32, no. 2 (June 1979 Supplement): 37.

40. See, for example, U.S. National Commission on Urban Problems, *Building the American City* (Washington, D.C.: Government Printing Office, 1968).

41. Classical studies include Mason Gafney, *Property Taxes and the Frequency of Urban Renewal* (paper presented at National Tax Association Annual Conference, Pittsburgh, September 17, 1964); Alvin L. Schorr, *Slums and Social Insecurity* (Washington, D.C.: Government Printing Office, 1963). For more recent studies see Price, Waterhouse, and Company. *A Study of the Effects of Real Estate Property Tax Incentive Programs upon Property Rehabilitation and New Construction* (Washington, D.C.: Government Printing Office, 1972); Norman Alpert, "Property Tax Abatement: An Incentive for Low Income Housing," *Harvard Journal of Legislation* 2, no. 1 (1973): 1; Kenneth K. Baar, "Property Tax Assessment Discrimination Against Low-Income Neighborhoods," *The Urban Lawyer* 13, no. 3 (Summer 1981): 333.

42. Ibid.

43. Richard Almy, "Considerations in Creating Property Tax Relief for Historic Preservation," in Gregory E. Andrews (ed.), *Tax Incentives for Historic Preservation* (Washington, D.C.: National Trust for Historic Preservation, 1980).

44. Center for Urban Policy Research telephone interview, December 1980.

45. John B. Rackham, "Values of Residential Properties in Urban Historic Districts," *Information from the National Trust for Historic Preservation* (Washington, D.C.: Preservation Press, 1977).

46. For further discussion of landmarks and the property tax, see National Trust for Historic Preservation, *Economic Benefits of Preserving Old Buildings*; Gregory E. Andrews, (ed.), *Tax Incentives for Historic Preservation* (Washington, D.C.: Preservation Press, 1980); International Association of Assessing Officers, *Property Tax Incentives for Preservation: Use-Value Assessment and the Preservation of Farmland, Open Space and Historic Sites* (Chicago: International Association of

Assessing Officers, 1976).

47. Frank B. Gilbert, "When Urban Landmarks Commissions Come to the Assessor." In IAAO, *Property Tax Incentives for Preservation*.

48. Eugene J. Morris, "Appraisals of Realty for Taxation," in Eugene C. Cowan, *Historic Preservation and the Law* (Washington, D.C.: Preservation Press, 1978), p. viii/3.

49. John J. Costonis, *Space Adrift* (Urbana: University of Illinois Press, 1974).

50. Andrews, *Tax Incentives for Historic Preservation*.

CHAPTER TWO

LANDMARK DESIGNATION AND PROPERTY VALUE: SUMMARY OF THE LITERATURE

Introduction

A major underlying issue of how landmarks are to be assessed for real-taxation purposes is the relationship between historic designation and property value. This chapter examines the market influences of landmark status. It commences with a brief review of national reports on this subject, followed by focus on a number of evaluations conducted in New York City. The national and New York studies are then compared and their findings are synthesized (see Exhibit 1). Based on these investigations, the chapter concludes that landmark status appears to exert mixed effects with respect to property value: prices may be enhanced by the prestige, protective, and other support features accorded by designation; a downward price pressure may result from landmark-induced facade-maintenance expenses, regulatory costs, and alteration/demolition restrictions. Possible variables influencing the presence/strength of these differing effects are then identified.

The literature referred to in this chapter represents initial attempts to define the inherently complex relationship between historic status and property value. The studies are characterized by methodological and other drawbacks common to such exploratory efforts. Thus, it identifies major influences, yet falls short in fully describing the many-sided designation effects.

EXHIBIT 1

STUDIES CONSIDERING THE ASSOCIATION OF HISTORIC DESIGNATION AND PROPERTY VALUE

Study Characteristics	Landmark Studies						
	Scribner[1]	Rackham[2]	Booz, Allen and Hamilton, Inc.[3]	Costonis[4]	ERA[5]	Heudorfer[6]	RPPW[7]
Year Study Conducted	1976	1977	1979	1974	1980	1975	1977
Historic Districts Examined	Old Town (Alexandria) Capitol Hill (Washington D.C.)	Georgetown (Washington D.C.)	Historic districts in Alexandria, Galveston, Savannah and Seattle	Focus on Chicago, but other areas cited	Proposed designation of St. Louis Central Business District	Mt. Morris Park Riverside Drive-West 105th St. Central Park West-76th Street Chelsea	Park Slope, Mount Morris Park, West 76th Street
Methodology	Overviews prior studies, examines gross property value changes over time	Gross property value changes; some comparison to comparable non-historic areas (Washington D.C. overall)	Gross property value changes; some comparison to comparable non-historic areas	Detailed economic analysis applied to hypothetical case studies (building economic profiles were derived from actual cases)	Alternative economic scenarios are studied	Analysis of gross socio-economic/housing changes over time; comparison to four control areas (non-designated neighborhoods)	Gross socioeconomic changes; comparison to control areas
Time Period	Varies by district; a 10-year period was considered in the Capitol Hill case	1967-1976	Varies by district, from 1960-1977 to 1974-1977	See Methodology	1980	Varies, mostly 1960 to mid-1970's	Varies, mostly 1970 to mid-1970's
Findings	Property values are higher in historic districts	Property values significantly higher in historic districts	Designation has a beneficial impact on property values and many other socio-economic traits	Designation can incur DAMAGES (reductions in property value); a detailed and influential air rights program was proposed to neutralize any such losses	Designation's impact varies by building, market, federal tax provision variables, etc.	Designation's support of property values difficult to document; some anecdotal support for designation-value association	Designation does not exert a measurable property value effect but does support numerous subjective variables which in turn can bolster landmark selling prices

Sources:

[1] David Scribner, Jr., "Historic Districts As an Economic Asset to Cities," *The Real Estate Appraiser* (May-June, 1976).

[2] John B. Rackham, "Values of Residential Properties in Urban Historic Districts: Georgetown, Washington, D.C. and Other Selected Districts," *Information: From The National Trust for Historic Preservation* (Washington, D.C.: Preservation Press, 1977).

[3] Booz, Allen and Hamilton, Inc., *The Contribution of Historic Preservation to Urban Revitalization* (Washington, D.C.: Government Printing Office, 1979), study prepared for the Advisory Council on Historic Preservation.

[4] John Costonis, Space Adrift: *Saving Urban Landmarks Through the Chicago Plan* (Urbana, University of Illinois Press, 1974)

[5] Economics Research Associates, *Economic Impact of the Multiple Resource Nomination to the National Register of Historic Places of the St. Louis Central Business District*, Report prepared for the St. Louis Community Development Agency (Boston: Economics Research Associates, 1980).

[6] Bonnie Smyth Heudorfer, *A Quantitative Analysis of the Economic Impact of Historic District Designation*, Masters Thesis, Pratt Institute, 1975.

[7] Raymond, Parish, Pine and Weiner, Inc., *The Impacts of Historic District Designation–Summary*, study conducted for the New York Landmarks Conservancy, November 16, 1977.

National Studies

Landmark Status Associated with Increasing Property Value

Many studies report that designation enhances property desirability and price. In some cases there is a dramatic association, such as the simple presence of a plaque proclaiming landmark status increasing the value of buildings with such markers[1]:

> Owners of historic buildings were given the opportunity to acquire plaques, attesting to the special status of the structures. The plaques were popular, and have proven to be a good investment as well. Various estimates note that the presence of the early building plaque on a house facade increases the potential selling price by $1,000-$3,000.

The Advisory Council on Historic Preservation even reports owners suing for the placement of an historic plaque under the belief that this action would benefit them financially[2]:

> In Alexandria, Virginia, a developer sued the Historic Alexandria Foundation when it refused to give him historical plaques for six houses he was redoing mainly because real estate agents told him that such recognition added $10,000 to the value of each property in that area. The developer lost the suit.... The monetary value of the plaque was never questioned.

A plaque is a dramatic attribution of landmark status. Its presence, however, is not required for designation to bolster property prices. The very fact of designation, especially in the context of an entire area being accorded historic status, is often in itself a positive market influence. Numerous studies have demonstrated landmark's market-shoring ability. David Scribner, in a 1976 review[3] of the overall economic benefits of designation, found:

> In the Old Town historic area of Alexandria, Virginia the value of unrestored buildings has increased about 3.5 times in 20 years.... Today the unrestored buildings in Old Town [are worth] approximately 2.5 times ...similar ones outside of the historic district.

Scribner discovered similar patterns in examining historic properties in the Capitol Hill area of Washington, D.C.[4]:

> The value of unrestored buildings "on the Hill" are worth approximately four times more than those "off the Hill." Unrestored buildings that are

just "on the Hill" have increased about 40 percent in value; unrestored buildings nearby, but "off the Hill" have declined 25 percent over the same period.

John Rackham, in a 1977 analysis conducted for the National Trust for Historic Preservation, reached similar conclusions.[5] Focusing on the Georgetown historic district in the District of Columbia, Rackham concluded that location within this historic neighborhood was in itself an important factor commanding a premium. This historic district price advantage was present for almost all the classes of properties analyzed by the author (see Exhibit 2). Comparable historic district-property value linkages were observed in other cities[6]:

Houses in the Winston-Salem (North Carolina) historic district sold for double the price of comparable homes located elsewhere in the city.

In St. John's Church Historic District (Richmond, Virginia) restored houses sold for considerably more than physically similar properties located just over the district's boundaries.

Since the Old Towne section of Portsmouth (Virginia) was declared a historic district, residential buildings there increased in value at a rate more than double that of the average of such properties in Portsmouth as a whole. Houses within the district sold for three to four times more than comparable structures located elsewhere in the city.

Similar "well-above-average to extraordinary" property-value increases were evident in other historic areas, including Philadelphia's Society Hill, New Orleans' Vieux Carre and the historic districts in Annapolis, Maryland, and Charleston, South Carolina.

The most recent and comprehensive study showing property-value trends in historic districts was conducted by Booz, Allen and Hamilton, Inc. (BAH) in 1979 for the Advisory Council on Historic Preservation.[7] Four historic neighborhoods were examined: Alexandria's (Virginia) Old Town Historic District, Galveston's (Texas) Strand neighborhood, Savannah's (Georgia) National Landmark area, and Seattle's (Washington) Pioneer Square. Comparison of property selling prices within and outside these areas lead the consultant to conclude[8]:

Significant increases in the real estate value of properties in the historic districts have occurred.... Sales figures reflect a direct link between location in an historic district and a higher value.

To illustrate, Booz, Allen and Hamilton compared property prices in Alexandria's historic district to those just outside this neighborhood (see

EXHIBIT 2
COMPARISON OF AVERAGE MARKET VALUES OF RESIDENTIAL PROPERTIES
GEORGETOWN HISTORIC DISTRICT VERSUS DISTRICT OF COLUMBIA OVERALL

Property Type	Average Market Values for Indicated Years				Average Annual 1967-1976 Percentage Increase in Value
	1967	1970	1973	1976	
Single Family Dwellings					
Georgetown	$ 65,792	$ 68,402	$83,118	$118,783	+ 8.1%
D.C. Overall	22,496	23,055	27,855	37,409	+ 6.6%
Semidetached Houses					
Georgetown	80,838	84,523	103,218	145,149	+ 8.0%
D.C. Overall	23,442	24,289	30,309	39,096	+ 6.7%
Detached Houses					
Georgetown	148,554	153,158	186,827	230,682	+ 5.5%
D.C. Overall	37,728	39,469	53,037	65,065	+ 7.2%

EXHIBIT 2
COMPARISON OF AVERAGE MARKET VALUES OF RESIDENTIAL PROPERTIES
GEORGETOWN HISTORIC DISTRICT VERSUS DISTRICT OF COLUMBIA OVERALL

| Property Type | Average Market Values for Indicated Years | | | | Average Annual 1967-1976 Percentage Increase in Value |
	1967	1970	1973	1976	
Multifamily Dwellings					
Flats					
Georgetown	59,648	69,042	71,627	145,563	+14.0%
D.C. Overall	25,709	25,013	23,463	33,008	+ 2.8%
Garden Apartments					
Georgetown	304,435	No Sales	440,823	-	-
D.C. Overall	157,369	131,212	131,096	176,655	+ 1.2%

Source:

John B. Rackham, "Values of Residential Properties in Urban Historic Districts: Georgetown, Washington D.C., and Other Selected Districts." *Information: From the National Trust for Historic Preservation* (Washington, D.C.: Preservation Press, 1977).

Exhibits 3 and 4). Over a three-decade period, the designated buildings enjoyed appreciation of about 40 percent annually—a sharper increase compared to price trends exhibited on comparable blocks located outside the district (see Exhibit 3). Property values in Alexandria's historic areas were also more robust as compared to the gains recorded in the Washington Standard Metropolitan Statistical Area (SMSA) as a whole (see Exhibit 4)[9]:

> The significance of the increase emerges when the average value for each sample block is indexed against that for the Washington SMSA . . . . The average value of the sample single-family homes in the historic district were as much as 45 percent lower than in the SMSA in 1949-1950...67 to 81 percent lower in the areas just outside the historic district. In 1970, the average value of housing in the historic district was as high as double the average SMSA value. The area outside the historic district remained well below the SMSA.

BAH's findings were graphically summarized by the Advisory Council on Historic Preservation (ACHP) in its 1979 annual report (see Exhibit 5). ACHP referred to designation's price effect as one evidence of preservation's benefits.

The historic district price premium documented by Scribner, Rackham, and BAH is considered by these and other authors to result from numerous designation/preservation influences. For the sake of convenience, these effects may be grouped as follows:

Prestige—Landmark status accords prestige from the official recognition that a building or area has special qualities. This prestige is recognized by the real-estate market: realtors often stress this point in selling a historic property and at least some buyers are willing to pay a premium for this characteristic.

Protection—Designation adds a protective overlay to a landmarked property or area. Disruptive demolition from highway construction, urban renewal, and other government-aided projects diminishes as a threat. Landmark exteriors can be altered only if these changes are compatible from architectural and other perspectives; in some cases landmark interiors are afforded the same protection. Finally, new construction on vacant lots in the historic district is also regulated as to its scale and appearance. In short, designation increases the likelihood that the features one finds attractive in a building or an area today will be there tomorrow. Rackham describes this important, landmark-protective function as follows[10]:

> The imposition of architectural and other appropriate controls on properties in a defined district should provide a shield against adverse external

EXHIBIT 3

CHANGE IN REAL ESTATE VALUES:

ALEXANDRIA HISTORIC DISTRICT VERSUS NONLANDMARK CONTROL AREA

| Location | Current Use | Average Value Per Unit | | | | | Average 1950-1977 Annual Percentage Increase in Value |
		1950	1960	1970	1974	1977	
*Alexandria Historic District**							
100 Block Prince Street	Single Family Residence	$ 7,670	$16,270	$37,490	$76,300	$ 95,630	+43%
101 Block Prince Street	Single Family Residence	10,680	21,300	44,730	87,890	114,330	+36%
300 Block So. St. Asaph Street	Single Family Residence	11,130	20,540	50,760	98,280	131,940	+40%
Outside Historic District							
401 Block North Alfred Street	Single Family Residence	4,680	7,890	11,610	18,470	39,030	+27%
1101 Block Queen Street	Single Family Residence	3,210	6,000	11,180	16,410	22,510	+22%
901 Block Oronoco Street	Single Family Residence	2,660	6,910	12,880	15,540	60,220	+80%

Source:

Booz, Allen and Hamilton, Inc., *The Contribution of Historic Preservation to Urban Revitalization* (Washington, D.C.: Government Printing Office, 1979), study prepared for the Advisory Council on Historic Preservation.

*Note:

"Alexandria Historic District" contains properties located in the Alexandria historic area designated in 1946.

EXHIBIT 4
INDEX OF CHANGE IN REAL ESTATE VALUES:
ALEXANDRIA HISTORIC DISTRICT VERSUS WASHINGTON SMSA

Location	1950	1960	1970	1974	1977
Estimated Value Single Family Home Washington SMSA	$14,011	$17,100	$28,200	$50,300	$66,000
Alexandria Historic District* (SMSA = 100)					
100 Block Prince Street	54.7	95.1	132.9	151.7	144.9
101 Block Prince Street	76.1	124.6	158.6	174.7	173.2
300 Block So. St. Asaph Street	79.4	119.5	180.0	195.4	199.9
Outside Historic District (SMSA = 100)					
401 Block Alfred Street	33.4	46.1	41.2	36.7	59.1
1101 Block Queen Street	22.9	35.1	39.6	32.6	34.1
901 Block Oronoco Street	19.0	40.4	45.7	30.9	91.2

Source:
Booz, Allen and Hamilton, Inc., *The Contribution of Historic Preservation to Urban Revitalization* (Washington, D.C.: Government Printing Office, 1979), study prepared for the Advisory Council on Historic Preservation.

*Note:

"Alexandria Historic District" contains properties located in the Alexandria historic area designated in 1946.

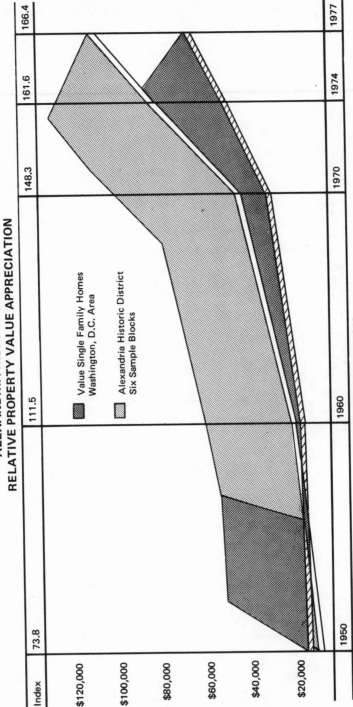

EXHIBIT 5
ALEXANDRIA HISTORIC DISTRICT
RELATIVE PROPERTY VALUE APPRECIATION

Value Single Family Homes
Washington, D.C. Area

Alexandria Historic District
Six Sample Blocks

Note: Portions of Alexandria Historic District were designated in 1946 and 1970.

Source: Advisory Council on Historic Preservation, *Report to the President and the Congress of the United States* 1979 (Washington, D.C.: Government
         Printing Office, 1979). Base data from Booz, Allen and Hamilton, Inc. (See Exhibit 4).

influences and, at the same time, spur rehabilitation efforts within, and eventually beyond, the boundaries of the district. Such controls should support existing interest in preserving and/or recovering the visible indications of the community's heritage.

Other supports—As indicated above, partially as a result of landmark's prestige and protective features, designation inculcates further interrelated positive consequences. These include fostering institutional financing, encouraging property rehabilitation, strengthening an area's retail health, tourist trade, and so on, and catalyzing formation of community organizations/activity.

Landmark Status Associated with Decreasing Property Value

For the most part this negative consequence is related to designation's alteration/demolition restrictions, although, as we shall see when we turn to the New York City studies, other landmark factors may detract from property value. Controls on property changes can impede a landmark owner's ability to modernize. As expressed by one writer[11]:

> [The landmark owner] may lose income if he is unable to bring interior space up to the standard of buildings that compete with it for tenants, and to increase its operating efficiency through periodic renovation.

More significant than the restraint to alterations are landmark restrictions concerning demolition. This relationship reflects basic property economics. A site's potential income/value is affected by the intensity of use (i.e., density) for which it may be improved: all other things being equal, the higher the intensity, the greater the potential income/value. Landmark status and attendant demolition restrictions, in turn, can curtail a site's intensity of use to its current application. This "freeze" will adversely affect property value in the case where historic status is accorded to a site whose profitability would be enhanced by demolition of the existing improvement and replacement by a higher intensity of use. Such development restriction is particularly telling in the case of the uneconomic improvement—a property that is drastically underimproved as far as its density is concerned given conventional zoning allowances and market demand for a higher intensity of use (see chapter four). An example is a small residential townhouse in the central business district. Designation of the limited improvement can drastically lower its value because it disallows replacement by more profitable use.

It is important to be aware of the difficulty of defining the practical extent of landmark alteration/demolition restrictions. As compared to other types of government land-use regulations such as zoning, designation controls are much more ambiguous—it is difficult to specify in advance what a landmark property owner may or may not do. Interior/exterior alterations are not always prohibited, only those declared inappropriate by a landmark monitoring body. Even demolition is not always precluded, as indicated in the discussion of New York City's landmark law (see chapter one). Given this ambiguity, it is very difficult to specify in advance the dollar consequences of designation. This problem was stressed by the president of the New York City Tax Commission in writing on the issues of landmark designation, property value, and property assessment[12]:

> Where extent of historic restrictions is unknown, how can [the] assessor measure effect of restrictions? Under the New York City Landmarks Law and other similar laws, actual restrictions governing designated historic properties may be unknown until application is made for a certificate to do something.... Example: Grand Central in New York City.

Despite these uncertainties, some studies have attempted to define the financial implications of designation alteration/demolition restraints. Preliminary work in this area was performed by John Costonis in his 1974 monograph, *Space Adrift*.[13] Costonis developed a formula for determining the net difference in property value of designated versus non-designated income-producing buildings—a measure he termed "Damages." For illustrative purposes, Costonis examined "Damages" on four landmarked Chicago office towers, ranging in size from 66,000 to 368,000 square feet (see Exhibit 6). All were uneconomic improvements—zoning allowances and market demand suggested redevelopment of the four structures to a density ranging from 112,000 to over 850,000 square feet. At the higher density, the buildings would be more profitable and thus would command a higher selling price (see Exhibit 6). By forestalling redevelopment, landmark designation incurred "Damages" ranging from an estimated $400,000 to over $3,500,000 per building.

Costonis developed the "Damages" concept as an input for formulating an appropriate relief mechanism in the form of an air-rights transfer program:* landmark owners suffering from "Damages" would be allowed to

---

*There is considerable legal and economic literature on TDR as a land-use preservation mechanism. See Norman Marcus and M. Groves (editor), *The New Zoning: Legal, Administrative and Economic Concepts and Tech-*

sell the development opportunity denied them to others not similarly constrained. Costonis also made the distinction that designation controls did not mean that the landmark owner would be saddled with a loss, but rather that this individual might not be able to reap the maximum profit suggested by the marketplace. In his words: "The trade-off is not between making more money and losing money; it is between a modest return...and cashing in."[14] Finally, Costonis alluded to the variable market-value impact of designation. While in some cases "Damages" would ensue, in other instances designation would[15]:

> enhance the value of a landmark property by making it a prestige address for selected tenants. In addition, tenants may prefer space in a designated building secure in the knowledge that they will not be subject to the vagaries of the redevelopment process.

More recently, Economics Research Associates (ERA) considered the implications of landmark alteration/demolition restrictions as part of their overall analysis of the economic impact of designating the St. Louis central business district (CBD).[16] ERA concluded that, while certain CBD buildings developed to their full potential would benefit or would not be affected by historic status, others, "suitable for more intense development,"[17] would be at a disadvantage. The consultants applied a side-by-side landmark versus nonlandmark financial analysis reminiscent of Costonis's "Damages" approach. Complicating ERA's financial projections were the numerous federal income-tax provisions regarding landmark demolition and rehabilitation—tax factors that did not exist in 1974 when Costonis authored *Space Adrift* (see chapter one).

In short, national reports link designation with property value-enhancing as well as detracting characteristics. Similar mixed influences are observed by the New York City evaluations.

---

niques (New York: Praeger, 1970); Jerome Rose, "A Proposal for the Separation and Marketability of Development Rights as a Technique to Preserve Open Space," *Journal of Urban Law* Vol. 51 (1974), p. 461; Jared Shlaes, "Who Pays for Transfer of Development Rights," *Planning* Vol. 40 (July 1974), p.7. George H. Nieswand, B. Budd Chavooshian, *et al*, *Transfer of Development Rights: A Demonstration* (New Brunswick, NJ: Cook College, 1976); Norman Marcus, "Villard Preserved: Or, Zoning for Landmarks in the Central Business District," *Brooklyn Law Review* Vol. 44 (1977), p.1; Norman Marcus, "The Grand Slam Grand Central Terminal Decision: A Euclid for Landmarks, Favorable Notice for TDR and a Resolution of the Regulatory/Taking Impasse," *Ecology Law Quarterly* Vol. 7 (1979), p. 731.

EXHIBIT 6

"DAMAGES" (EFFECT OF PRESERVATION RESTRICTIONS) CALCULATION FOR

FOUR SAMPLE LANDMARKED BUILDINGS

Buildings/Financial Parameters	Landmark A		Landmark B		Landmark C		Landmark D	
	Existing[1]	Potential[2]	Existing[1]	Potential[2]	Existing[1]	Potential[2]	Existing[1]	Potential[2]
Building Income								
1. Gross Building Size (sq. ft.)	295,000	625,000	368,000	854,000	65,800	111,725	300,000	807,000
2. Net Rentable Space (sq. ft.)	220,000	500,000	276,000	683,000	49,350	89,380	225,000	645,000
3. Average Rental (sq. ft.)	$ 6.50	$ 8.50	$ 6.00	$ 8.50	$ 7.00	$ 9.00	$ 7.00	$ 9.00
4. Gross Income	$1,430,000	$ 4,250,000	$1,656,000	$ 5,807,050	$350,000	$ 804,420	$1,575,000	$ 5,810,400
5. Vacancy & Credit Loss @5%	$ 71,500	$ 212,500	$ 82,800	$ 290,360	$ 17,000	$ 40,220	$ 78,750	$ 290,520
6. Effective Gross Income	$1,358,500	$ 4,037,500	$1,573,200	$ 5,516,840	$333,000	$ 764,200	$1,496,250	$ 5,519,880
7. Real Estate Taxes	$ 246,173	$ 1,009,375	$ 273,345	$ 1,379,210	$109,444	$ 191,049	$ 299,250	$ 1,379,970
8. Other Operating Expenses	$ 611,325	$ 1,211,250	$ 707,940	$ 1,655,052	$149,850	$ 229,259	$ 673,312	$ 1,655,964
9. Net Income before Recapture (NIBR)[3]	$ 501,002	$ 1,816,875	$ 591,915	$ 2,482,578	$ 73,706	$ 343,889	$ 523,687	$ 2,483,946
Building Value								
10. Overall Capitalization Rate	.10	.09	.10	.09	.10	.09	.10	.09
11. Value Estimate-Income Approach[4]	$5,010,000	$20,188,000	$5,920,000	$27,584,000	740,000	$3,821,000	$5,237,000	$27,600,000
12. Present Value of Equity[5]	$1,650,754	$4,047,996	$1,949,740	$ 5,532,171	$240,469	$ 766,217	$1,725,509	$ 5,534,329
13. Difference in Equity Values[6]		$ 2,397,242		$ 3,582,431		$ 525,748		$ 3,808,820
14. Demolition Costs		584,220		605,000		123,000		270,000
15. Damages to Landmark Owner[7]		$ 1,813,022		$ 2,977,431		$ 402,748		$ 3,538,820

Source: John Costonis, *Space Adrift: Saving Urban Landmarks through the Chicago Plan* (Urbana: University of Illinois Press, 1974).

Notes: [1] Existing property size and financial parameters.
[2] Building size and financial parameters in absence of landmark status.
[3] Equals effective gross income less the sum of real estate taxes and other operating expenses.
[4] Equals NIBR divided by indicated capitalization rate.
[5] Equals "value estimate-income approach" less outstanding mortgage and other obligations.
[6] Equals difference of "present value of equity" of landmarked versus nonlandmarked property.
[7] Equals "difference in equity values" less demolition costs.

New York City Studies

In describing some of the effects of its designation activities, the New York City Landmarks Preservation Commission notes numerous physical, social, and economic benefits, one of which is an increase in property values[18]:

> Preservation activities help revitalize, stabilize and enhance neighborhoods. One frequent result is a very tangible benefit: *increased neighborhood values* such as has been demonstrated in Historic Districts like Cobble Hill, Brooklyn Heights or Park Slope. Designation fosters neighborhood cohesion, identity, pride and concern, as well as enrichment of the aesthetic value of the area. Usually designation results in improved maintenance of the building or buildings involved and an increased sense of neighborly cooperation aimed at making the community a more pleasant one in which to live and work [emphasis added].

These attributed influences are confirmed, at least in part, by numerous empirical studies including, "A Quantitative Analysis of the Economic Impact of Historic District Designation," by Bonnie Smyth Heudorfer[19]; and, "The Economic Impact of Historic District Designation" by Raymond, Parish, Pine and Weiner, Inc. (RPPW).[20]

New York City Landmark Status Associated
with Enhanced Property Values

Bonnie Smyth Heudorfer Study: This analysis was conducted in 1975 at Pratt Institute. It compared economic/housing indicators (sales price, capital appreciation, rent levels, foreclosure activity and so on)in four designated New York City historic districts (Mount Morris Park, Riverside Drive-West 105th Street, Central Park West-76th Street and Chelsea) to four comparable adjacent areas. The latter were selected as controls in order to measure the independent effect of designation on neighborhood characteristics.

Heudorfer found that for the most part landmark status exerted little or no independent influence. To illustrate, while relatively fewer properties in historic districts were foreclosed, this discrepancy was true prior to designation and thus "may more appropriately be considered a function of the housing stock rather than designation itself."[21] Sales prices showed a similar pattern: as compared to the nondesignated control areas, properties in the historic districts sold for a premium both before and after designation, although in some instances this price spread widened after landmark status was accorded. Heudorfer thus did not find a documentable link between designation and property values. She did, however, allude to anecdotal support for a landmark-property appreciation linkage, yet even this was tentative as is evident from the following excerpt[22]:

> In my early conversations with two prominent real estate figures on the West Side, two differing attitudes emerged. A real estate broker specializing in brownstones, felt that a house on a designated block might bring up to $5,000 more than a similar house on a nondesignated block....

> Mr. - - -'s function is somewhat different. His clients include investors who aren't interested in living in the building. For the most part, he says, his purchasers neither know nor care that a building is on a landmark block other than to question how such designation might affect their alteration plans.

Raymond, Parish, Pine and Weiner (RPPW) Study: RPPW examined whether historic district designation impacted on "Economic Value"—a variable defined by this consultant to include both quantifiable factors such as property value as well as subjective influences ranging from a sense of security to expectations about the future.[23]

To examine the effect of designation, RPPW identified prototypical blocks within three historic districts (Park Slope, Mount Morris Park, and West 76th Street) and then selected comparable control study areas from adjoining, nondesignated neighborhoods. Census and other socioeconomic data trends were then examined in the historic and control locations in order to determine the possible presence of a special landmark impact.

From the side-by-side comparisons, RPPW concluded that designation did not exert a quantifiable, independent effect. In districts on the upswing such as Park Slope, designation followed rather than caused revitalization. In economically distressed historic areas, such as Mount Morris Park, designation was "insufficient to turn around the neighborhood."[24] Subjective components of "Economic Value" were, however, influenced by landmark status. As enumerated by RPPW, designation[25] is a source of pride, helps foster a sense of belonging and leads to community organization, prevents destruction of attractive brownstones, keeps out high-rise buildings, suggests to residents that the city cares about them and their problems, and provides an increased sense of security about the area's future.

RPPW's analysis is slightly ambiguous with respect to designation's effect on the property values of landmarked buildings. While the study concluded that property price was not influenced by historic status, it indicates that many of the subjective components of "Economic Value" were strengthened by designation and these attributes in turn would likely buttress the market response to landmarks. Such an interrelationship was recognized by RPPW in their summary of historic designation consequences[26]:

> Thus, the intangible or subjective benefits of historic designation appear to be real. Historic district designation has a useful role to play in drawing a community together, attracting new families, promoting stability, and creating a sense of pride. In this way, the designation indirectly serves to strengthen *both* property values and the social fabric in these portions of the city [emphasis added].

In summary, the New York City studies highlight the same beneficial effects accruing from landmark status noted in the national literature. Designation lends prestige and special recognition; its controls over demolition and renovation afford a protective mantel against harmful public/private neighborhood incursions; and in general, it is associated with property upgrading trends and forces ranging from fostering institutional financing to encouraging community organization/interest/activity. At times these influences ultimately bolster property values. This landmark-value linkage is far from universal, however, and even when believed to exist by community groups, property owners and others, is difficult to document.

New York City Landmark Status
Associated with Decreasing Property Value

As with the national studies, numerous observers have pointed to the sometimes negative property-value effect of landmark activity in New York City. While it must be stressed that this allegation is largely undocumented, designation is said to exert an adverse impact by (1) increasing facade maintenance costs; (2) adding regulatory-related expenditures; and most importantly (3) imposing alteration/demolition restrictions.

Facade Maintenance. Landmark status is said to increase facade costs by requiring retention/repair of certain difficult-to-maintain facades (i.e., terra cotta, tile, gilded exterior as well as decorative treatments, such as cornices, parapets, and ironwork) which in a nonlandmarked building might be removed and replaced by more modern and less costly to maintain finishes. As discussed in an appraisal of a New York landmark prepared by Roger M. Darby, a member of the American Institute of Real Estate Appraisers[27]:

> Another element of the Landmarks Act which would adversely affect the value of the building and of the real estate is the affirmative obligation the

owner of a designated building has to maintain and repair the building so as to preserve its external features. An example in the subject building would be required maintenance of the overhanging roof cornice. In most instances, it is more economical to remove such cornices than to attempt to maintain them. The maintenance requirements, however, would cause the property owner to incur additional expense in maintaining this aesthetic feature.

Regulatory Costs. Under New York City law, alteration/demolition of properties accorded historic status must be approved by the Landmarks Preservation Commission. Work can proceed only after an appropriate certificate has been applied for and issued (see chapter one). Landmark owners can incur additional expenses as a result of these regulatory requirements, both directly in the form of outlays for professional (i.e., architectural and legal) assistance, and indirectly from the delays attendant to such an administrative procedure. (This is in addition to other, i.e. Building Department regulatory body procedures.)

Alteration/Demolition Restrictions. Facade maintenance and regulatory expenses affect only those landmarks with the building exterior and use characteristics likely to engender these special costs, (i.e., fashionable retail stores where regular and significant storefront changes can be expected; see discussion later in this chapter). Even in these selected cases, the added outlays associated with landmark status will typically not be very significant. (The largely undocumented nature of this and the other landmark-property value relationships should again be remembered.) In contrast, landmark alteration/demolition restrictions can be much more meaningful, especially in the case of a designated uneconomic improvement. As expressed in a recent *New York Law Journal* article[28]:

> Where the highest value of the property is in its present physical form, such designation may be value adding. But usually such property is honored with designation by municipal authorities because there is a justified fear that it may be physically altered or destroyed and lost to posterity.

> Where the value depends on removal or destruction of the structure or substantial changes to it, this designation, as with any other land use regulation, which does the same, will negatively affect the value. If the most valuable use is to build an office building on the site and you are limited to retaining it as a one-family house, its value will be as the lesser valued one-family home.

Chapter three of this study examines case-study properties in New York City where landmark status possibly hindered interior renovations and subsequently these buildings' market values. It also refers to numerous designated, uneconomically improved landmarks. Examples include a townhouse on East 58th Street and a small Fifth Avenue clubhouse. Both of these structures are located in areas of New York City characterized by intensive development—the very option precluded (at least in part) by these case studies' historic status. Chapter three examines the alleged adverse property-value consequences of designation in these instances and related property-tax assessment issues.

Summary of the National and New York City Studies on Landmark Designation and Property Value

Methodological Similarities and Issues

The national and New York City studies on this subject share many similarities (see Exhibit 1). All were conducted in the middle to late 1970s—a feature reflecting this period's growing interest in historic preservation. Almost all focus on nationally known historic areas such as Georgetown in Washington, D.C., Pioneer Square in Seattle, and Park Slope in New York City. For the most part, their examination is a historical recapsulation of the changes that occurred in the landmark districts over the past decade. The only two exceptions are the ERA and Costonis studies, which do not focus at events past, but instead predict the consequences of designation by assuming different development scenarios for a selected group of proto-typical landmarked buildings.

The studies also share a similar methodological approach. While the RPPW analysis based its findings (in part) on property owner, realtor, and community group interviews, all of the others rely on macro comparisons of the historic districts' socioeconomic characteristics before and after designation. Common examples include before-and-after contrasts of neighborhood population, household income, educational attainment, crime rate, housing rehabilitation frequency, as well as property values. Implicit in this approach is the assumption that the post-landmark changes are at least partially due to designation and attendant historic preservation activities. Landmark consequences are also examined by using a control-area strategy reminiscent of the control technique employed by physical scientists. Historic district socioeconomic profiles are compared to that found in physically similar nondesignated neighborhoods. Those features distinctive to or more pronounced in the former area, such as enhanced property values, are deemed an end product of landmark status.

All of these approaches have their shortcomings. If analysis relies on local interviews, there is the difficulty of separating fact from opinion. A macro before-and-after-approach begs the question whether the post-designation changes are coincidential to rather than resulting from landmark activity. This drawback is addressed by a control-area strategy. This technique in turn, however, presents other difficulties, such as the problem of selecting truly comparable, nondesignated areas given the frequently unique features of the historic neighborhoods. With the exception of the Heudorfer and RPPW analyses, many of the studies cited in this chapter are inadequate in their control-area selections. Rackham's control to Georgetown is the District of Columbia (see Exhibit 2); Booz, Allen and Hamilton's (BAH) control to Alexandria is, at least in part, the overall Washington Standard Metropolitan Statistical Area. Are these controls in fact comparable to the above-mentioned historic districts? If they are not, then there is considerable doubt whether the observed changes in the historic areas are necessarily associated with designation.

The Inherent Difficulty of Determining the Impact of Designation

These issues are raised not to criticize the pioneering studies reviewed by this chapter. They are discussed to point to the inherent difficulties confronting any analysis attempting to define the linkage between designation and property value. If a simulation approach is attempted, such as the Costonis and ERA studies, which considered landmark property-value consequences by predicting effects on prototypical historic buildings, then the analyst is confronted with defining what is and is not permitted by historic status. Such divination is problematical for, as pointed out previously in this chapter, designation does not impose absolute restrictions on alteration/demolition, but rather disallows only "inappropriate changes"— a standard difficult to define in advance. It is partially for this reason that the Costonis and ERA investigations make many assumptions in their calculations and speak to various scenarios of impact.

This prediction difficulty is less troublesome in analyzing landmark property-value effects based on the observed historical record—the strategy followed by most of the extant studies (see Exhibit 1). Such a technique presents its own problems, however, such as the control area matching difficulties discussed previously. Even if this hurdle could be conquered, it would still be problematical to define designation's property value and other consequences based on the observed past record because the cause-and-effect relationships themselves are not clear. Most studies define designation as an independent variable influencing numerous dependent variables such as an influx of middle-class residents, increase in housing rehabilitation volume, as well as property-value appreciation. In reality, the cause-and-effect equation is much more complex because the social, economic, and housing variables discussed above both precede and follow designation and in fact sometimes influence the decision to designate an area as historic. In short, designation is not simply an independent variable affecting neighborhood change but is itself a dependent variable influenced by shifting local conditions. This interrelationship makes it quite difficult to evaluate the consequences of landmark status based on events past, especially with the rather crude methods (i.e., control neighborhood strategy) employed by the extant studies. (More sophisticated statistical tools such as regression analysis offers some potential for addressing some of these analytical problems; see chapter four for discussion of a regression technique.)

All of the above-mentioned factors make it inherently difficult to pinpoint the property value or other consequences of designation. It is therefore important to view the national and New York City studies cited by this chapter as first statements in what will be a continuing research endeavor. Bearing in mind this caveat, the existing literature suggests varied consequences of designation. *By according prestige, protective, and other supports, landmark status may bolster property values. Designation's facade maintenance, regulatory cost, and alteration/demolition restrictions can detract from value.*

While designation can affect property value, it is important to realize that in many instances its influence in this regard will be slight or even neutral. Designation's effect in New York City is illustrative. There is general consensus that many of New York's historic districts have experienced a renaissance, yet empirical investigations reveal that the act of designation alone has often exerted only a weak upward push to property value. Conversely, while it is possible to point to some instances where designation by the New York Landmarks Preservation Commission may have adversely affected the market response to a historic building (see the case studies in chapter four), these are largely exceptional situations.

In short, landmark status has the potential for both adding to or detracting from a building's selling price but in practice may not always be a significant consideration. It is difficult to predict the degree to which landmark status will affect property value in any given situation. Some insight is offered, however, by exploring the circumstances in which designation's value-enhancing and value-detracting features cited by this chapter are likely to be present or significant (see Exhibit 7).

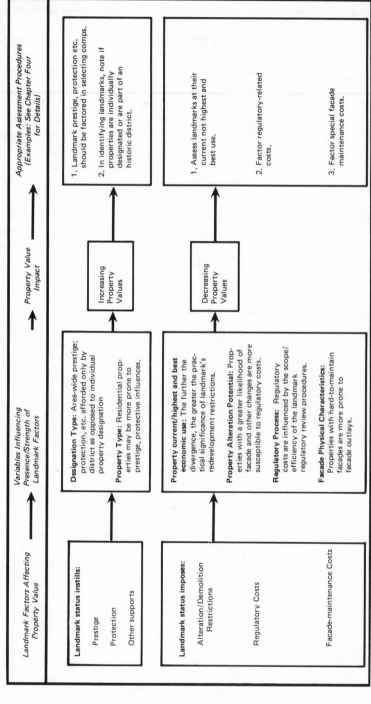

EXHIBIT 7

LANDMARK DESIGNATION, PROPERTY VALUE, AND PROPERTY ASSESSMENT:
FLOW CHART OF INTERRELATIONSHIPS

Landmark Factors Affecting Property Value → Variables Influencing Presence/Strength of Landmark Factors → Property Value Impact → Appropriate Assessment Procedures (Examples: See Chapter Four for Details)

Landmark status instills:

Prestige

Protection

Other supports

Designation Type: Area-wide prestige; protection, etc. afforded only by district as opposed to individual property designation

Property Type: Residential properties may be more prone to prestige, protective influences.

→ Increasing Property Values →

1. Landmark prestige, protection etc. should be factored in selecting comps.

2. In identifying landmarks, note if properties are individually designated or are part of an historic district.

Landmark status imposes:

Alteration/Demolition Restrictions

Regulatory Costs

Facade-maintenance Costs

Property current/highest and best economic use: The further the divergence, the greater the practical significance of landmark's redevelopment restrictions.

Property Alteration Potential: Properties with a greater likelihood of facade and other changes are more susceptible to regulatory costs.

Regulatory Process: Regulatory costs are influenced by the scope/efficiency of the landmark regulatory review procedures.

Facade Physical Characteristics: Properties with hard-to-maintain facades are more prone to facade outlays.

→ Decreasing Property Values →

1. Assess landmarks at their current not highest and best use.

2. Factor regulatory-related costs.

3. Factor special facade maintenance costs.

Variables Influencing Presence/Strength of Landmark Property Prestige, Protection, and Other Supports

Designation may bolster property values by according prestige and related benefits. The extent to which these influences are generated in turn may be affected by designation type and property type.

Designation Type. While it is difficult to generalize, prestige, protection, and other supports are more likely enhanced by district as opposed to individual property designation. Since the former acts on an areawide basis, it may achieve the spatial critical mass necessary to encourage property owner rehabilitation, financial-institution investment, community-organization activity, and other spinoffs, which ultimately may translate into enhanced property values. These reactions may or may not be present in the situation of an individual building being accorded historic status. In that case, property owners would not be protected against adverse surrounding redevelopment activity, lenders may feel more vulnerable, and organizational activity would not be kindled by a collective sense of place. Consequently, neighborhood, in contrast to individual property designation, may be more potent for bolstering historic building selling prices.

Property type. Property type (residential, commercial or industrial) may bear on whether landmark prestige, protection, and other forces translate into higher property values. While it is again very difficult to generalize, these landmark effects are more likely to be important considerations with respect to residential buildings where owner/tenants are often willing to pay a premium for special landmark recognition, assurance that desirable neighborhood features will be retained, and so on. Certain types of commercial properties may similarly benefit from designation's prestige and related supports.[29] Commercial buildings housing, or potentially containing, specialized retail, restaurant, or office uses are possible examples.* In these instances, owners/tenants, for image and ambience purposes,[30] may be willing to pay a premium for a landmarked property. In contrast, owners/tenants of second-order commercial properties and many industrial structures where utility rather than image or continuity is important

---

*It is important to be cognizant of the variability/tentativeness of these and the other generalizations made in this section. For example, owner-tenant affluence bears on the ability of these individuals to pay a premium for landmark ownership or residence. Property use—residential, commercial and so on—is also not fixed as is evidenced from the adaptive reuse of New York City industrial lofts for residential and commercial purposes.

(i.e., discount stores, warehouse or a light assembly plant) are often not willing to pay extra for a landmark imprimatur.

Variables Influencing Presence/Strength of Landmark Facade, Regulatory Cost, and Alteration/Demolition Restrictions

These landmark consequences are associated with decreasing property values. Their presence/strength, in turn, may be affected by numerous variables: facade physical characteristics; property alteration potential; landmark regulatory procedure; and property current/highest and best economic use.

Facade physical characteristics. Facade maintenance costs are a factor (and even then a minor one) only with respect to those landmarks with hard-to-maintain exteriors that, in the absence of designation, would likely be replaced. Examples include buildings with stucco, gilded finishes, or elaborate exterior ornamentation such as cornices or parapets.

Property alteration potential/landmark regulatory process. The presence/extent of landmark regulatory costs are influenced by these two variables. Regulatory expenses are more likely to be incurred with respect to properties with a greater likelihood of facade or other changes subject to regulatory review. An example is a fashionable retail establishment where significant and regular alterations for storefront and related purposes can be expected. The nature of the landmark regulatory process itself is another consideration. Regulatory costs will be higher if all landmark alterations are subject to examination and if the review procedure itself is delayed.

Property current/highest and best economic use. The relationship of these uses influences the practical significance of landmark alteration/demolition restrictions. If there is little difference between current and highest and best use, then designation's development restraints have little significance. In contrast, if there is a considerable spread, then designation's alteration/demolition restrictions can exert a severe property-value discount. Such a situation is exemplified when an uneconomic improvement is accorded historic status.

"Highest and best use" itself is subject to numerous influences. What can be built given zoning and other public land-use controls? What should a prudent investor develop, given market demand for certain types of uses and the costs of construction/rehabilitation versus the expected return from such activity?

A property's highest and best use and its relationship to the landmark's current use is one of the more, if not the most, important variables determining the extent to which designation affects a landmark's property value.

It is emphasized by all the studies considered by this chapter as well as other literature summarized in Appendix two to this study. The importance of this relationship, as well as how it may change over time, is illustrated by the following New York City example.

When New York's famous Plaza Hotel was designated in 1975, the hospitality industry was depressed. According to Frank Gilbert, then executive director of the Landmarks Preservation Commission, the owners of the Plaza were therefore considering demolishing the hotel, which they felt was an uneconomic improvement, and replacing it with a "highest and best use"—an office tower similar in size to the General Motors building that had recently been constructed across the street.[31] Designation of the Plaza prohibited its redevelopment—an impact that in 1975 the owners of the Plaza felt worked to their disadvantage. Market conditions have changed over time, and with them so has the impact of the Plaza's landmark status. First-class Manhattan hotels are today considered prime investments. The Plaza is thus close to or at its highest and best use; the current market does not support replacement of this hotel with an office tower. While the Plaza's designation may originally have had an adverse property-value effect, today the hotel's landmark status has little negative effect. Designation may even enhance the Plaza's "landmark" quality.

Conclusion

This chapter considered the association between landmark designation and property value. Based on an admittedly rudimentary literature, it appears that historic status exerts a variable effect. By according prestige, protective and other supports, designation has the potential of appreciating value. By imposing facade maintenance expenses, regulatory costs, and especially alteration/demolition restraints, historic status may lower property value. The degree to which these varying effects are exerted in any given situation in turn is influenced by numerous factors ranging from the type of designation to the relationship between a landmark's current and highest and best use (see Exhibit 7).

In considering these findings, the following caveats must be kept in mind:

1. They are based on a first-generation literature that suffers the limitations of all such efforts.

2. The chapter points to major landmark-property value relationships. It surely does not cover the full universe of the complex interactions. To illustrate, the practical extent of landmark's alteration restraints may differ depending on whether historic status is accorded to a building's interior versus exterior. Historic-district socioeconomic factors, such as owner/

tenant affluence, may also influence the nature of landmark's effects. Heudorfer, and RPPW, for example, both pointed to the fact that designation had a more forceful impact in bolstering rehabilitation and community organization activity in New York's more affluent historic neighborhoods. (Designation, in itself, can alter the district's base socioeconomic profile.) As our knowledge of designation increases, so will the refinement in specifying its consequences.

3. The relationship between landmark designation and property value is a multidimensional one. Numerous influences may converge upon the same designated building, some of which reinforce each other, others which stand in opposition. As an example, the value of a fashionable retail store may be both enhanced by landmark's prestige and reduced by restrictions to storefront alterations. In such instances, the net effect of the different vectors must be considered in determining landmark's net overall impact.

4. The landmark-property value association is a dynamic one that can change over time. Revising the zoning code to allow higher-density development can result in more landmarks becoming uneconomic improvements, thereby increasing the negative-value consequences of historic status. Down-zoning, in contrast, may temper this value detraction. Changes in the landmark regulatory review process itself also bear on the landmark-property value equation. Shifting market demand is another important consideration as was illustrated by the Plaza Hotel example.

5. The landmark-property value relationships discussed in this chapter are the basis for chapter four's assessment-policy recommendations. If the type of designation can affect the property-value consequences of historic status, then this variable should be incorporated in a landmark identification system for assessors. If designation accords prestige and other supports that affect market demand, then these factors should be noted by the assessor in his/her selection of appropriate "comps" by which to value a landmark. If designation can impede redevelopment of a landmark to its highest and best use, then historic properties should be assessed on the basis of their current use. These relationships are highlighted in Exhibit 7 and detailed in chapter four.

Notes

1. National Trust for Historic Preservation, *Economic Benefits of Preserving Old Buildings* (Washington, D.C.: Preservation Press, 1976). See also Real Estate Research Corporation, *Economics of Revitalization* (Washington, D.C.: Government Printing Office, 1981), study prepared for the Heritage Conservation and Recreation Service.

2. Advisory Council on Historic Preservation, *Report to the President of the Congress of the United States* (Washington, D.C.: Government Printing Office, 1979).

3. David Scribner, Jr., "Historic Districts as an Economic Asset to Cities," *The Real Estate Appraiser* (May-June 1976).

4. Ibid., p.11.

5. John B. Rackham, "Values of Residential Properties in Urban Historic Districts: Georgetown, Washington, D.C. and other Selected Districts," *Information: From the National Trust for Historic Preservation* (Washington, D.C.: Preservation Press, 1977).

6. Ibid.

7. Booz, Allen and Hamilton, Inc., *The Contribution of Historic Preservation to Urban Revitalization* (Washington, D.C.: Government Printing Office, 1979), study prepared for the Advisory Council on Historic Preservation.

8. Ibid.

9. Ibid.

10. Rackham, "Values of Residential Properties."

11. John Costonis, *Space Adrift: Saving Urban Landmarks through the Chicago Plan* (Urbana: University of Illinois Press, 1974).

12. Mary E. Mann, "Valuation of Historic Properties," in Eugene C. Cowan, *Historic Preservation and the Law* (Washington, D.C.: National Trust for Historic Preservation, 1978), p. viii/2.

13. Costonis, *Space Adrift*.

14. Ibid.

15. Ibid.

16. Economics Research Associates, *Economic Impact of the Multiple Resource Nomination to the National Register of Historic Places of the St. Louis Central Business District*, Report prepared for the St. Louis Community Development Agency (Boston: Economics Research Associates, 1980).

17. Ibid., p. 151.

18. Landmarks Preservation Commission. "Try to Imagine New York City without Central Park, the Brooklyn Bridge, the Jefferson Market Courthouse, the Federal Building or the brownstones in Stuyvesant Heights, Greenwich Village, Brooklyn Heights and St. Nicholas Historic Districts" (no date).

19. Bonnie Smyth Heudorfer, "A Quantitative Analysis of the Economic Impact of Historic District Designation," Masters thesis, Pratt Institute, 1975.

20. Raymond, Parish, Pine and Weiner, Inc., *The Impacts of Historic District Designation—Summary*, study conducted for the New York Landmarks Conservancy, November 16, 1977.

21. Bonnie Smyth Heudorfer, "A Quantitative Analysis."

22. Ibid.

23. Raymond, Parish, Pine and Weiner, Inc., *The Impacts of Historic District Designation*.

24. Ibid.

25. Ibid.

26. Ibid.

27. "Landmark Building Appraisal" conducted by Roger M. Darby MAI (1981). Mr. Darby requested that CUPR not identify the landmark appraised in this report.

28. M. Robert Goldstein and Michael J. Goldstein, "Valuation of Historic Property," *New York Law Journal*, December 4, 1978, p. 1.

29. Such an example is provided by the purchase of the 9-11 West 54th Street townhouses by the United States Trust Company. This financial institution bought these landmark buildings for a prestigious branch office—the first in its existence after more than a century of being headquartered in Manhattan's financial district. As discussed by Ada Louise Huxtable: "After investigating prestigious new buildings at prime avenue locations, with virtually no restrictions on price or choice the bank chose the 54th Street houses specifically for their architectural and landmark qualities. The decision was made with equal recognition of the unique ambience they would provide, the gesture to the street and the city that their use and preservation would make (see Ada Louise Huxtable, "Some Good News, and Bad for West 54th Street," *New York Times*, June 21, 1981, section 2, p. 29).

It is interesting to contrast the intentions of the United States Trust Company with that of another purchaser on West 54th Street—Mendik Realty Company. In 1979, the same year that United States Trust bought its two properties (9-11), Mendik purchased 13 and 15 West 54th Street as well as 20 and 22 West 55th Street. Whereas United States Trust was interested in rehabilitation and retaining the block's townhouse ambience, Mendik Realty bought the four townhouses allegedly to "demolish them for a new building." These differences in purchaser motives point to likely contrasting perspectives concerning the property-value implications of landmark designation. For United States Trust, designation of 9-11 West 54th Street, an act according official recognition of its office's special quality, likely is viewed as property-value enhancing. (See, for example, the advertisement celebrating the opening of the U.S. Trust's West 54th Street office in the *New York Times Magazine*, October 4, 1981, p. 19.) In contrast, from Mendik's perspective, designation of its West 54th and 55th Street townhouses is likely seen as a severe property-value impediment, interfering with its redevelopment plans.

30. See note 29.

31. Telephone interview by the author with Frank Gilbert, Esq., June 1981.

CHAPTER THREE

PROPERTY-TAX ASSESSMENT OF LANDMARK BUILDINGS: PREVAILING PRACTICE AND IMPLICATIONS

Introduction

If landmark designation affects property value, then local assessors, charged with the responsibility of valuing real property for taxation purposes, should factor in historic status. This chapter examines whether assessors in practice acknowledge designation in their calculations. A brief examination of the landmark assessment state-of-the-art at the national level is followed by detailed focus on New York City. Historic property assessment issues in New York are highlighted by consideration of six case study buildings, all landmarks, whose assessments were appealed on the basis of their historic status. The chapter is followed by two appendices: Appendix 3-A details the case-study particulars, such as when the buildings were designated, how much they were assessed for, why their owners appealed the assessments, and the resolution of these requests for adjustment. Appendix 3-B overviews the structure/administration of the New York City property tax, focusing on operative assessment practices.

Landmark-Assessment Policies at the National Level

In June through December 1980, the Center for Urban Policy Research (CUPR) contacted via telephone state and local offices involved in, or knowledgeable about, property-tax assessment and/or historic preservation. Assessors, historic-preservation officers, and professional-assessor organizations in the fifty states were asked whether and how landmark status was considered in the valuation of historic buildings for real-taxation purposes. (Further survey details are found in Appendix one of this study.)

Before discussing the CUPR survey findings, it is important to realize its limitations. Local assessment standards are often vague, change over time, and vary among individual assessors. Complicating the task of determining operative practices is the reluctance of local assessment departments to discuss their valuation procedures. In short, it is very difficult to determine how landmarks, or for that matter any other class of property, are assessed. Despite these hindrances the CUPR survey was able to obtain a "sense" if not a detailed blueprint of how designated properties are treated for assessment purposes.

National Survey Findings

Some local assessment departments factor landmark status because they are compelled to do so by law. In these cases, assessors acknowledge designation roughly according to the manner specified by local/state statutes.[1] Portland (Oregon) values landmarks at their current use as stipulated by Oregon Statute §308.740-308.790. Mobile (Alabama) keeps records of the city's historic buildings, examines whether the use/value of these properties are affected by designation, and also applies a lower assessment-to-value ratio to designated structures as required by the Alabama state constitution.[2]

The presence of a statutory provision does not guarantee that designation is acknowledged in the assessment process. This divergence is considered at length in Appendix one of this study. Numerous local assessment departments do not take landmark status into account despite statutes directing them to do so. The statutory mandate is not adhered to for reasons ranging from ambiguities in the law itself to administrative inertia.

In a few cases, assessment departments consider designation even though they are not compelled to do so by statute. To illustrate, the Newport (Rhode Island) assessor indicated to the author that he keeps careful records of historic designation because[3]:

> our job is to monitor property values, and designation can increase selling price by as much as 25 percent. The Newport market is sensitive to landmarks and so must we. Assessors do not need a special law in this regard. If designation decreased value, we would act accordingly.

In a few cases where designation is considered, the valuation approach is mechanical—landmark buildings are either always increased or always decreased in value notwithstanding the actual market effects in each case.[4]

The Society for the Preservation of New England Antiquities, for example, noted[5]:

> Localities in Massachusetts...have considerable discretion.... What constitutes true value is a subjective matter largely left to them. In Lexington, historic value is always considered an asset to a building and as such assessments are increased in all cases. In Hamilton, assessments on landmarked buildings are always lowered.

The overwhelming majority of local assessment departments do not take landmark status into account. The CUPR survey reveals that designation typically is not, as a matter of practice, factored in the valuation of properties for real-taxation purposes.* Many assessment departments are unaware that buildings are designated; even when informed of this fact (by a local historic-preservation commission or officer), they typically do not act on this information.[6] This is not to say that all local assessors ignore historic status, but rather that those who do incorporate designation's effects are a small minority. These findings are similar to those reached in prior studies.[7]

Assessment of New York City Landmarks

As a matter of practice, the New York City Landmarks Preservation Commission (LPC) forwards the block and lot numbers of all designated parcels to the city's Department of Real Property Assessment (RPA). This policy has been followed since the LPC's inception in 1965. It is difficult to determine whether and how RPA acts on this information. CUPR requested permission to interview RPA staff assessors; it was informed that longstanding RPA policy forbids this. CUPR then contacted others who might be familiar with New York City landmark assessment, including the LPC, Tax Commission of the City of New York, certiorari attorneys, and informed realtors-real estate consultants.[8] These interviews, admittedly a

---

*Similar findings were reached by Jared Shlaes in his study of Cook County, Illinois landmark assessment practices. "In conversation with staff of the Cook County Assessor's office, it appears that landmarks are not being valued consciously with regard to their landmark restrictions. The computer system utilized by the Assessor's office does not take into account the landmark designation of a property and any effect such designation may have on its assessed valuation." See Shlaes annotation in Appendix two to this study.

poor substitute for communicating directly with RPA assessors, suggest the following:

1. There are no state nor city statutes directing New York City assessors to take landmark status into account (see Appendix one for details). The New York courts have also not spoken on this issue.

2. New York City's Real Property Assessment Department (RPA) does not have an official policy concerning the assessment of landmarks as indicated in a handbook, guide, or memorandum.   •

3. RPA does not have an unofficial policy regarding the valuation of designated properties such as increasing or decreasing the assessment of all historic buildings.

4. Some New York City assessors, as a matter of practice, factor the property-value impact of designation and will correspondingly adjust the assessments of landmarks. While hard data are lacking, these individuals are especially sensitive to the encumbrance effects of historic status which can detract from property value (i.e., alteration/demolition restrictions); less attention is paid to designation's value-enhancing potential. It appears, however, that such acknowledgement of historic status is far from universal. Outside of well-known landmarks such as the Empire State or Chrysler buildings, many New York City assessors are only vaguely aware which buildings are designated. In addition, even when landmark status is known, many assessors do not always factor this variable into their calculations. In this respect, designation joins other building and market factors or property-specific income/expenses which are ignored or are only perfunctorily considered in the New York City assessment process (see Appendix 3-B).

Roughly similar assessment practices were observed by the 1975 Heudorfer study of New York City landmarks. According to Heudorfer, some New York City assessors take into account the value-detracting effect of historic status, but this was far from a universal practice. To illustrate, designation might be acknowledged only on a well-known individual landmark yet not in the case of historic districts[9]:

> It certainly appears that more consideration is given to the designation of an individual building which is located on a site that is [not] the highest nor the best use.... In such instances, the.... landmark status [is considered] an encumbrance...., thus lowering its value. Unfortunately, the doctrine does not seem to have carried over into the districts.... For the most part, the assessors were unfamiliar with the boundaries of the historic districts.

While it is difficult to assert with certainty, it appears that many New York City assessors do not, as a matter of practice, consider the many variations and effects of landmark status. In this respect, New York City joins the rest of the country, especially those jurisdictions without landmark-assessment statutory guidelines, in not factoring designation in day-to-day assessment calculations.

Implications of the Landmark-Assessment Policy

Omission of landmark status from the assessment equation implies that designated buildings sometimes will be inappropriately valued for real-taxation purposes. Where designation reduces property value and this effect is not acknowledged, then the landmark will be overassessed to the detriment of its owner. Where designation increases property value and such appreciation is not factored, then the landmark will be underassessed to the loss of the taxing jurisdiction.

It is important to realize that the absence of an assessment approach explicitly incorporating landmark status does not invariably mean that all designated buildings will always be valued unfairly for real-taxation purposes. First, as discussed in chapter two, landmark status sometimes, but not always, affects property value. When designation's effect is neutral, then by definition it does not have to enter the assessment process. Second, even if landmark status influences property value, omitting this variable from the assessment calculations may not have a practical effect if designation's impact is factored indirectly through activities/policies already part of the assessment process (i.e., valuing properties at their current and not highest and best use).

New York City is illustrative. The practical effect of many of its assessors not factoring designation is moot where LPC designation exerts a neutral or very weak influence on property value—a not uncommon occurrence as discussed in chapter two. In addition, prevailing RPA assessment policies indirectly incorporate some landmark effects. For example, RPA's reliance on area comparable sales ("comps") as an assessment standard (see Appendix 3-B) would factor possible landmark-related value appreciation in Park Slope, Brooklyn Heights, and the city's other flourishing historic districts because properties in these locations would be valued on the basis of neighborhood "comps," similarly influenced by landmark status. RPA's assessment-at-current rather than highest-and-best use standard (see Appendix 3-B) also means that landmarked uneconomic improvements that are precluded from redevelopment are not penalized in the assessment process for these buildings are valued correctly at their current utilization.

The problem of not coordinating landmark status and assessment calculations is that some, albeit not all, designated properties will be unfairly valued for real taxation purposes. Designation can be inconsequential with respect to property value. There are instances, however, where it does exert either a positive or a negative market influence—an impact suggested by both the national and the New York City studies examined in chapter two. In addition, it is unrealistic to expect that such appreciation or depreciation is always indirectly factored by serendipitous, prevailing assessment policies. New York City is again illustrative. In the absence of explicit recognition of historic status, New York City assessors could inappropriately value landmarks in numerous situations:

1. A designated uneconomic improvement is valued on the basis of a seemingly comparable underutilized yet nonlandmarked "comp." It is possible that the latter may have sold for a premium for assemblage purposes. In short, the "comp's" sale price reflects a higher value than this property's current use—a value not shared by the landmark since it cannot similarly be redeveloped. In this situation, valuing the landmark on the basis of the nondesignated comparable constitutes an overassessment.*

2. Properties in New York City's historic districts sometimes enjoy an enhanced value (see chapter two). If the neighborhood comparables used for assessing these landmarks are from the same historic area then the landmark effect will indeed be acknowledged indirectly. The problem, however, is that since this factoring is unintentional it cannot be relied upon. In the absence of New York City assessors explicitly acknowledging landmark status, there is no guarantee that properties in historic neighborhoods will be valued solely on the basis of sister designated "comps" as opposed to seemingly similar buildings located just outside the historic district's boundary. To the extent that the latter nondesignated comparables are used, assessment of the historic properties will not be sensitive to the special locational value these buildings sometimes benefit from. In this instance, the landmarks will be underassessed.

In summary, if landmark status and its attendant value implications are

---

*The fact that this landmark, as all other properties, would typically be assessed on a fractional value basis (see Appendix 3-B) does not change the fact that it would still be overassessed. To illustrate, assume designation reduces the value of a landmark from $2,000,000 to $1,500,000 and that this building is located in a jurisdiction which assesses properties at 50 percent of their true market value. An assessor valuing this landmark without factoring historic status would assign a $1,000,000 assessment ($2,000,000 x .5). While the $1,000,000 figure is below the true $1,500,000 value, the landmark in this case would still be overassessed because it should be valued at $750,000 ($1,500,000 x .5). See John Costonis, *Space Adrift* (Urbana: University of Illinois Press, 1974), Appendix IV.

not explicitly factored in the assessment equation, some, albeit not all, designated buildings will be unfairly valued for real-taxation purposes. Problems and issues of assessing landmarks are illustrated by the following New York City case studies.

New York City Case Studies

Selection of the Case-Study Properties

In the summer and fall of 1980, the Center for Urban Policy Research (CUPR) and the New York Landmarks Conservancy contacted the New York City Real Property Assessment Department, the Tax Commission of the City of New York, the New York City Landmarks Preservation Commission, and other groups knowledgeable about the city's historic buildings and their assessment.[10] These agencies/organizations were asked if they were familiar with any landmarks on which the question of designation, property value, and property assessment had been raised. Six buildings were identified where these interrelationships had been alluded to in administrative and/or judicial property-tax assessment appeals. (See Appendix 3-B for discussion of the assessment adjustment process.) Specific points raised in each case are described at length in individual case study analyses found in Appendix 3-A to this chapter. The following briefly describes the case-study properties and summarizes attendant assessment issues.

Case-Study Property Description (See Exhibit 1)

Case-study buildings are:
1. 311 East 58th Street,
2. Town Hall,
3. New York County Lawyers' Association Building (NYCLAB),
4. Hotel Chelsea,
5. Colonnade Row, and
6. Metropolitan Club.

The first, 311 East 58th Street, is a small owner-occupied townhouse (see Exhibit 2). It was built in the mid-19th century and is an example of the modest, semisuburban type houses constructed on the side streets of what was then "uptown Manhattan." The townhouse was designated in 1967.

Town Hall is a world famous concert-lecture hall. It was completed in

1923 and is famous for its historical performances and lecturers as well as the quality of its acoustics. Town Hall's interior was designated a landmark in 1978 (see Exhibits 3 and 4). It is the only interior landmark of the case studies and is one of only about 30 such interior designations in New York City.

NYCLAB is a clubhouse-type structure built in 1929. Considered a fine example of Federal eclectic architecture (see Exhibit 5), it was designated as a landmark in 1965.

Chelsea Hotel, constructed in 1883, is a pioneer Victorian Gothic structure characterized by tiers of ironwork balconies (see Exhibit 6) as well as serving as a residence for such famous writers as Mark Twain, Eugene O'Neill, and Thomas Wolfe. Chelsea Hotel was designated a landmark in 1966.

Colonnade Row is a group of four townhouses (originally there were nine) unified in appearance by a Corinthian colonnade (see Exhibit 7). Constructed in 1833, Colonnade Row, sometimes referred to as the Grange, is a "prominent example of Classic Revival residential planning."[11] The Grange was designated a landmark in 1965; in 1979 its owner donated a facade easement to the National Trust for Historic Preservation.

The Metropolitan Club is a handsome, four-story clubhouse built in 1894. Designed in a restrained neo-Italian Renaissance style by the famous architectural firm of McKim, Mead and White, the club was designated a landmark in 1979 (see Exhibits 8 and 9).

Common and Dissimilar Case-Study Characteristics

All six case studies are located in Manhattan (see Exhibit 10). The Metropolitan Club and 311 East 58th Street are in the fashionable upper East Side, Town Hall is in midtown, the others are in the downtown portion of the borough.

The six case-study properties include a range of uses. The East 58th Street townhouse is an owner-occupied residence. Colonnade Row contains both residential (apartments) and commercial (restaurant) uses. The Hotel Chelsea provides transient accommodations and longer-term studio apartments. Remaining case-study buildings are engaged for private (Metropolitan Club) or public-institutional (Town Hall, NYCLAB) purposes.

The case-study properties share other similarities. Owners of two buildings (311 East 58th Street and Town Hall) sold their landmarks' unused air rights to adjacent landholders. Two buildings enjoyed property-tax-exempt status for many years. Town Hall was about two-thirds exempt until 1978, when its ownership was transferred from a tax-exempt educational institution (New York University) to a taxable private foundation

EXHIBIT 1
SUMMARY OF THE NEW YORK CITY CASE STUDY PROPERTIES

Case Study Property	Date Constructed	Type of Property	Landmark Designation	Alleged Factor(s) Affecting Property Value	Date of Assessment Challenge (Tax Year)	Assessment Appeal Before	Initial Assessment	Initial Tax[1] Obligation (Approx.)	Final[2] Assessment	Final Tax[3] Obligation (Approx.)
311 E.58th St.	mid-19th century	Residential (Single Family)	1967	a) Landmark designation b) Sale of air rights	1973-74 1981-82	New York City Tax Commission	$85,000 $92,000	$5,900 $8,200	$73,000 $73,000	$5,000 $6,500
Town Hall	1923	Concert-Lecture Hall	1978	a) Landmark designation b) Sale of air rights	1979-80 1980-81	New York City Tax Commission	$1,000,000 $800,000	$88,000 $72,000	$600,000 $600,000	$53,000 $54,000
New York County Lawyers' Association Building	1929	Bar Association	1965	a) Landmark designation b) Property design/ conditions	1972-73 through 1979-80	New York City Tax Commission	$900,000	$59,000— $79,000	$700,000	$46,000— $61,000
Hotel Chelsea	1883	Hotel, studio apartments	1966	a) Landmark status b) Property income	1974-75 1981-82	New York City Tax Commission	$525,000 $700,000	$39,000 $63,000	$440,000 on appeal	$32,000 on appeal
Colonnade Row	1832-33	Residential (multifamily), Commercial	1965	a) Landmark status b) Property income c) Facade easement	1980-81	New York City Tax Commission	$90,000	$8,000	$72,000	$6,500
Metropolitan Club	1894	Clubhouse	1979	a) Landmark status	1980-81	New York City Tax Commission	$3,700,000	$324,000	on appeal	on appeal
					1981-82	New York Supreme Court	$4,450,000	$399,000	on appeal	on appeal

1. Equals initial assessment multiplied by the then prevailing New York City property-tax rate (see Appendix 3-A).
2. Note: assessment figures are approximate.
3. Equals final assessment multiplied by the then prevailing New York City property-tax rate (see Appendix 3-A).

EXHIBIT 2
NEW YORK CITY LANDMARK CASE STUDIES:
311 EAST 58TH STREET

EXHIBIT 3
NEW YORK CITY LANDMARK CASE STUDIES
TOWN HALL (EXTERIOR VIEW)

EXHIBIT 4
NEW YORK CITY LANDMARK CASE STUDIES:
TOWN HALL (INTERIOR VIEW)

EXHIBIT 5
NEW YORK CITY LANDMARK CASE STUDIES:
NEW YORK COUNTY LAWYERS' ASSOCIATION BUILDING

EXHIBIT 6
NEW YORK CITY LANDMARK CASE STUDIES:
HOTEL CHELSEA

EXHIBIT 7
NEW YORK CITY LANDMARK CASE STUDIES
COLONNADE ROW

EXHIBIT 8
NEW YORK CITY LANDMARK CASE STUDIES:
METROPOLITAN CLUB (EXTERIOR VIEW)

EXHIBIT 9
NEW YORK CITY LANDMARK CASE STUDIES
METROPOLITAN CLUB (INTERIOR VIEW)

EXHIBIT 10
LANDMARK CASE STUDY PROPERTIES: APPROXIMATE LOCATIONS

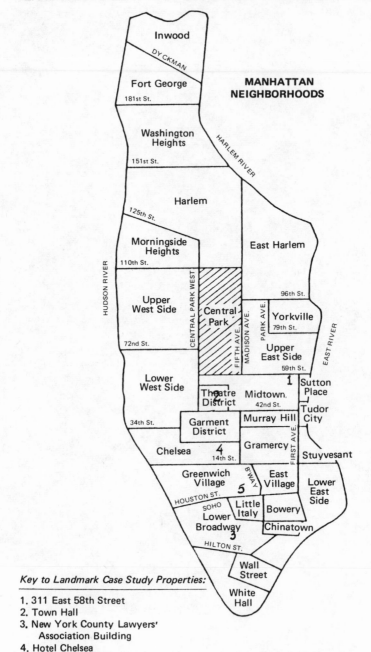

Key to Landmark Case Study Properties:

1. 311 East 58th Street
2. Town Hall
3. New York County Lawyers'
   Association Building
4. Hotel Chelsea
5. Colonnade Row
6. Metropolitan Club

(Town Hall Foundation). The New York County Lawyers' Association Building (NYCLAB) was fully tax exempt until 1978 when state and city statutes changed so as to make bar-association buildings liable to property taxation. Lifting the tax-exempt status of Town Hall and NYCLAB evoked the appeal of their assessments.

Analysis of the Case Studies

Tax-Assessment Appeals

New York City's Administrative Code gives property owners dissatisfied with their initial property-tax assessment the right to file an appeal to first an administrative level (Tax Commission of the City of New York) and then a judicial forum (State Supreme Court in the district where the property is located; see Appendix 3-B). All six case studies involve appeals before the Tax Commission. In addition, one—the Metropolitan Club— includes a further assessment challenge before the State Supreme Court presiding in New York City. In all six cases, the landmark owners charged that their buildings were overvalued by the city's Real Property Assessment Department (RPA), in part, because RPA did not factor the alleged harmful market effect of landmark designation. Specific challenges in each individual case are detailed in Appendix 3-A to this chapter; the following discussion highlights the main points of contention:

311 East 58th Street. In the late 1960s and early 1970s, the assessment of this townhouse increased by a small amount each year (i.e., from $67,000 in tax year 1970-71 to $70,000 in 1971-72). In tax year 1973-74, its valuation was raised significantly from $70,000 to $85,000. The owner of 311 East 58th Street appeared before the Tax Commission and argued that the $85,000 assessment was in error because: (a) landmark status, by prohibiting demolition, reduced the building's value because it would not be purchased for assemblage purposes; and (b) sale of the property's air rights had a similar derogatory impact on market appeal.

These arguments proved persuasive for the Tax Commission reduced the 1973-74 assessment from $85,000 to $73,000. The latter figure was retained until tax year 1981-82 when it was raised by RPA to $92,000. A second appeal was planned by the owner on similar grounds as those described above but became unnecessary when RPA, without explanation, reduced the property's assessment to $73,000.

Town Hall. For most of the 1970s, Town Hall was assessed for approximately $1,000,000, but paid taxes on only a fraction of this basis because it enjoyed a two-thirds exemption. In the late 1970s, Town Hall's tax-exempt status was lifted when its ownership was transferred from New York

University to the Town Hall Foundation. Confronted with a much higher tax obligation, the Town Hall Foundation appealed for a reduction in assessment before the Tax Commission on the following grounds: (a) landmark designation of Town Hall's interior reduced the range of the auditorium's possible entertainment uses and thus its value; (b) landmark designation also precluded the demolition of Town Hall and redevelopment to a higher intensity/value use; (c) sale of Town Hall's air rights exerted a similar adverse effect as that stated in (b). The Tax Commission ultimately reduced Town Hall's assessment to $600,000.

New York County Lawyers' Association Building (NYCLAB). A 1971 change in state and local law made NYCLAB subject to property taxation for the first time. NYCLAB was assessed for $900,000 and paid taxes on this basis from the 1972-73 until the 1980-81 tax years. In 1979, The County Lawyers' Association challenged the $900,000 assessment for the 1972-1980 period on the grounds that: (a) in its current condition, NYCLAB was unsuitable for modern offices; (b) NYCLAB's landmark designation made it problematical whether the structure could be renovated for modern office use; and (c) NYCLAB's landmark designation reduced its value because it disallowed the demolition/redevelopment of the property.

The Tax Commission lowered NYCLAB's assessment from $900,000 to $700,000 for the 1972-1980 period.

Hotel Chelsea. In tax year 1973-74, the owners of the Chelsea Hotel appealed their property's $535,000 assessment arguing that (a) the property's income did not support this valuation; (b) designation of the hotel as a landmark reduced the hotel's value because it prohibited demolition and replacement by a higher density/value use.

The Tax Commission reduced the Chelsea Hotel's assessment from $535,000 to $440,000. The latter figure was mostly retained until tax year 1981-82 when the property's valuation was increased to $700,000, an amount still being challenged as of June 1981.

Colonnade Row. The tax year 1980-81 assessment of one of the constituent buildings of Colonnade Row (434 Lafayette Street*) was appealed to the Tax Commission on the basis that (a) the property had a negative cash flow; (b) the property's landmark status precluded its redevelopment potential/value; (c) donation of a facade easement to the National Trust for Historic Preservation had a similar effect as that stated in (b). The Tax Commission reduced the property's assessment from $90,000 to $72,000.

---

*Other constituent buildings on Colonnade Row were involved in assessment adjustments; the case study in this chapter refers to one of these buildings (434 Lafayette Street).

Metropolitan Club. In the 1980-81 tax year, the New York City Real Property Assessment Department increased the assessed value of this landmark from $3,250,000 to $3,700,000. The Metropolitan Club appeared before the Tax Commission and requested a lower valuation on the grounds that the 1979 landmark designation of the clubhouse had eliminated its major market appeal—demolition and replacement with a higher-density use. This appeal was denied by the Tax Commission. The Metropolitan Club then sought judicial relief by making application to the Supreme Court of the State of New York (New York County). This request, and a subsequent appeal by the Metropolitan Club challenging its 1981-82 tax assessment of $4,500,000, have yet to be acted upon.

Case-Study Lessons

Before reviewing some of the points illustrated by the six cases, it is important to discuss the methodology and limitations of the analysis. While the Center for Urban Policy Research (CUPR) attempted to interview all the parties involved in each of the case studies it was only partially successful in this regard. New York's Real Property Assessment Department did not allow CUPR to interview the city assessors responsible for determining the value of the case study buildings. It was therefore impossible to pinpoint the basis of the city's initial assessment of the landmarks under study. CUPR was able to discuss the grounds of the tax appeals only with some of the owners of the case study buildings and/or their attorneys. The Tax Commission made its files available; however, in many instances there was little written documentation other than the form showing the resolution of the assessment challenge. Furthermore, in two of the six cases (Chelsea Hotel and the Metropolitan Club), questions of assessment have yet to be fully resolved. In short, the case studies lack certain descriptive and other details, are often unable to pinpoint the specific influence of designation on the assessment actions taken, and in a third of the buildings, are not complete as far as the final asessment decision is concerned.

The case studies also do not report all the arguments raised by the respective property owners. Their contentions are quite technical and involve legal issues not germane to our analysis of landmark effects. For example, the New York County Bar Association argued against the lifting of its tax-exempt status. Similar action was taken by the Town Hall Foundation.

Bearing in mind the above limitations, the case studies can serve as a basis for discussing a number of issues:

How Are New York City Properties Assessed
For Real-Taxation Purposes?

As indicated in other studies,[12] New York City properties are assessed at
a fraction of their true value, and this fraction varies by class of building—a
higher rate is used in nonresidential as opposed to residential situations (see
Appendix 3-B). While it is difficult to assert with certainty, assessment of
the six case-study buildings appears to reflect these patterns. They are
valued for tax purposes at a fraction of their full worth, and it appears that
this fraction is lowest with respect to 311 East 58th Street—the only owner-
occupied, single-family residence of the six properties.

The case studies also reflect the changing fortunes of the New York City
real-estate market. When it was depressed in the mid-1970s, assessments of
the case-study properties were held largely static. With the strengthening
of the real-estate market a few years later, the valuations of the case-study
buildings were sharply increased. To illustrate, the assessment of the Chelsea Hotel, kept at about $440,000 for most of the middle-to late 1970s, was
raised to $700,000 in the 1981-82 tax year. The Metropolitan Club's assess-
ment of roughly $3,300,000, similarly held nearly constant for most of the
1970s, was increased to $3,700,000 in the 1980-81 tax year and $4,500,000 a
year later.

Is Landmark Designation Factored by Assessors?

The discussion above indicates that assessment of the six-case study
buildings reflects the varied influences governing the valuation of all properties in New York City for real-taxation purposes. To what extent does the
assessment reflect the buildings' differentiating feature, namely, their
landmark status? This question cannot be definitively answered because
city assessors responsible for valuing the six landmarks could not be interviewed as to the factors they considered. In one case (Town Hall), the
president of the Tax Commission, Mary Mann, felt that RPA assessors had
directly acknowledged the impact of designation. As discussed by Ms.
Mann in a memorandum submitted to the Tax Commission[13]:

> On November 28, 1978, the property was designated a Landmark as to
> both its exterior and interior architectural features.

> ... The Landmark designation has permanently impaired both the land
> and building value. The Assessment Department has now given partial
> recognition to the situation by reducing the tentative 1980/81 assessment
> to $800,000 from the 1979 assessment of $1,000,000.

The Center for Urban Policy Research and the New York Landmarks Conservancy examined the assessments of the other case-study properties before and after they were accorded historic status. None displayed the post-designation downward reassessment alluded to by Ms. Mann in the Town Hall case. It is important to stress, however, that this does not prove that assessors ignored the effect of landmark status; for, they could have considered this variable and concluded that it exerted little or no market effect. The same reasoning applies to the Metropolitan Club's increased assessment after its designation. Landmark status might very well have been factored in this adjustment, along with other considerations. Had the Metropolitan Club not been designated, its assessment might have been increased by a much greater magnitude commensurate with the recent substantial increase in Manhattan real-estate values. In the absence of interviewing RPA assessors directly, it is impossible to determine if designation was or was not factored in the case studies.

How Does Landmark Designation Affect Property Value?

Chapter two of this study discussed that historic status could exert both positive and negative influences on a property's selling price: designation could add to value by according prestige, protection, and other supports; designation could detract from value by imposing special facade maintenance requirements, regulatory costs, and alteration/demolition restrictions. The case studies are not a neutral forum for examining the effect of designation on property value since they involve attempts by owners to have their property assessments reduced: someone benefiting from designation surely will not bring this factor to the attention of the Tax Commission. Bearing in mind the "biased" nature of the case studies, they show that the landmark owners pointed to designation's alteration/demolition restraints as adversely affecting their property's income and market appeal. In two of the cases (Town Hall, NYCLAB), the claim was made that designation detracted from value by foreclosing interior alterations which would improve their building's function/profitability. This point was secondary, however, to the major contention in all six instances that landmark status reduced property values by prohibiting demolition/redevelopment to higher density uses.

It is difficult to pinpoint the extent to which the Tax Commission of the City of New York agreed with these claims. In numerous instances, the commission appeared to accept the above-mentioned contentions. We say "appeared to accept" deliberately because the Tax Commission typically does not explain why it granted a revaluation. In only one of the six case studies (Town Hall) did Mary Mann, president of the Tax Commission, explicitly discuss the effect of landmark status[14]:

> The Landmark designation has permanently impaired both the land and building value.
>
> It seems clear that the assessment is considerably higher than the value of the property and it is respectfully urged that the Tax Commission take immediate action to reduce the assessment to its fair value as requested in the protests.

In the NYCLAB case study, the counsel to the Tax Commission wrote a legal memorandum pointing to the adverse property value impact of the NYCLAB's landmark status[15]:

> The [building's] physical layout is not meant for office space and major modifications would be required to convert it to this use.... Although the precise impact of such [landmark] designation is unclear, a reasonable assumption is that the building could not be demolished nor converted easily to commercial space. If this is so, the value of the land would likely command a lower price.

This counsel's final statement on the NYCLAB tax appeal was more neutral, however, on this issue[16]:

> No economic detriment has been attributed to the land even though it has Landmark designation. The impact of such designation is not settled in the law and therefore it has not been allowed to influence the property's valuation.

In summary, in the Town Hall and NYCLAB cases, the Tax Commission appeared to be somewhat receptive to the argument that designation could impair property values by impeding alteration/demolition of the respective landmarks. In the remaining appeals, the Tax Commission made no comment as to the effect of historic status. It is thus impossible to determine with any finality whether the designated buildings received an assessment reduction because of their designation or as a result of the other contentions advanced by their owners. Was the assessment of 311 East 58th Street lowered because of its landmark status or air-rights sale? Which factor proved decisive in the Colonnade Row reassessment—the property's operation at a financial loss, landmark designation, or the easement donation to the National Trust for Historic Preservation subsequent to designation?

The case studies illustrate another point concerning the relationship of landmark status and property value. Chapter two discussed that one of the problems of defining the impact of designation is the difficulty of predicting in advance which landmark alterations/demolition are permissible—the criterion that the changes be "appropriate" begs the question of what is appropriate. This ambiguity is evident in our analysis. Town Hall's interior designation precluded the major alterations proposed by the Hudson Guild Theatre (see Appendix 3-A) yet more moderate changes (i.e. involving a stage door and other alterations) to make the concert hall self-sustaining were permitted. It is thus problematical to define the economic consequences of Town Hall's designation. Similar difficulties were noted by William Block, currently Assistant Commissioner of the New York City Department of Finance, in discussing the NYCLAB tax appeal[17]:

> The truth of the matter is that it was uncertain which changes could or could not be made to the building. Exterior [alterations] would have to be approved; even interior alterations might be precluded if they affected the exterior, such as the windows. The situation was a grey area. No one knew the exact effect of designation.... We had to confront it though.

How Should Landmarks Be Assessed?

The six case-study buildings also can serve as examples for illustrating recommended assessment policies—a role defined in chapter four of this study. For example, chapter four refers to 311 East 58th Street to demonstrate how uneconomically improved landmarks should be valued. Other case-study buildings illustrate such concepts as the distinction between current and highest and best use, selection of appropriate comparables, definition of depreciation in landmark situations, and so on (see chapter four).

Future Landmark Assessment Issues

The case studies illustrate that the issue of landmark designation, property value, and property assessment in New York City has been raised, albeit in what is still an ad hoc approach. But as suggested by Mary Mann, president of the Tax Commission of the City of New York[18]:

> The effect of government actions on property value and the need to consider these relationships in the assessment process is a topic of growing importance. We see this in respect to such actions as tidelands and wetlands designation. Historic status is another area which will continue to confront the assessor.

We concur with Ms. Mann's prediction. The question of how New York City's landmarks are to be assessed will become more significant in the future, and require more structuring: This will be accentuated by the following developments:

Changes in Designation. Early landmarking activity in New York and many other cities often included historic buildings owned by governmental agencies or public-service institutions which were exempt from property taxation. The question of assessing such landmarks was not raised because the issue was moot to the exempt owner. In the wake of the United States Supreme Court *Grand Central* decision (see chapter one), designation is now applied to many more privately owned, taxpaying buildings. In this new era of landmark activity, the issue of designation, property value, and property assessment has very definité practical consequences and therefore will evoke more structured attention.

Changes in the Real-Estate Market. The landmark assessment issue was quiescent in New York City for many years because even when a taxpaying property was accorded landmark status, designation typically had little negative effect on property value. (Landmark owners benefiting from designation would not bring this fact to the attention of the Tax Commission.) A value-detracting influence was absent or insignificant because most land-marked properties were economically improved within the context of the real estate market conditions which prevailed. Designation's alteration/demolition restrictions were largely academic (see discussion in chapter two).

This situation is now changing. In recent years the Manhattan real-estate market has experienced a vibrancy challenging longstanding assumptions of what is an economic improvement. Existing buildings, once thought of as sufficiently profitable in their own right, are now being purchased for replacement by higher density new uses. This assemblage/redevelopment activity may not be shared by all landmarks because these buildings cannot be demolished and replaced by new uses.*

Changes in Assessment Practice. Changes in assessment procedures, in part prompted by numerous court decisions, may also stir greater interest in landmark assessment. To illustrate, New York courts have accepted the

---

*In making this prediction, potential countervailing forces must be mentioned. First is a potential downturn in the real estate market, dampening the redevelopment/assemblage pressures cited above. Such a "bust" followed the Manhattan real estate boom of a decade ago. A second and related factor is a possible New York City zoning change *reducing* maximum permissible densities in much of Manhattan. Downzoning would likewise constrain frenzied assemblage/redevelopment activity because the payoff of new construction would be reduced.

concept that rent controls should be considered in determining value for real-taxation purposes.[19] While there are differences between rent control and landmark designation, the court's acknowledgement that a government control affecting a building's profitability should enter the assessment equation perhaps may someday be followed by a similar directive with respect to designation.

The *Hellerstein*[20] decision may also prompt greater factoring of landmark status. In 1975, the New York State Court of Appeals ruled that the long-standing practice of assessing residential properties at a lower fraction of true value as compared to nonresidential buildings was unconstitutional (see Appendix 3-B to this chapter). The state legislature's response may well address not only the fractional-value issue but probably incorporate a more far reaching reform, one injecting greater objectivity and standardization into the assessment process. In this new assessment climate, more explicit attention could be paid to the many influences on property value, one of which is landmark designation.

APPENDIX 3-A

ASSESSMENT OF LANDMARK PROPERTIES: NEW YORK CITY CASE STUDIES

Introduction

This appendix details the six New York City case studies referred to in chapter three:

1. 311 East 58th Street
2. Town Hall
3. New York County Lawyers' Association Building
4. Chelsea Hotel
5. Colonnade Row
6. Metropolitan Club

Each case study is presented in a similar format. The building is first described, then a brief summary is given of when and why it was accorded landmark status. The property-assessment appeal is then detailed, including (1) synopsis of the reasons advanced by each property owner for changing the assessment; (2) outcome of assessment challenge; and (3) reasons for the amended assessment (where such evidence exists.)

311 East 58th Street

Background

Property Description

This property is a residential townhouse located on East 58th Street between First and Second Avenues in the borough of Manhattan (see Exhibit 10). It was built in mid-nineteenth century and is an example of the modest, semisuburban houses constructed in that period on the side streets of what was then "uptown" Manhattan.[21]

The two-and-a-half-story structure contains approximately 2,500 square feet of space. It is characterized by numerous fine details (see Exhibit 2). The first-floor entrance is quite handsome, consisting of double glass paneled doors with a framed over-door transom and a doorway topped by a lintel and cornice. The townhouse's windows are of the double-hung sash type with plain lintels. A molded cornice crowns the top of the building. The property's overall appearance is described by the New York City Landmarks Preservation Commission as follows[22]:

> This charming two-story and basement house with painted brick walls and stone trim has a clean scrubbed look that is refreshing to behold. Vernacular in style, it has a small wooden stoop, raised four steps above the sidewalk, and a sunken front yard, attractively landscaped, enclosed at the property line by a white picket fence.

The townhouse is owned by Charles Jones, a composer teaching at the Julliard School of Music. It was purchased by Mr. Jones in the early 1950s for his personal residence.[23] In the 1960s, Mr. Jones was offered a substantial sum of money for the property (more than ten times the purchase price) by a major real-estate developer interested in assemblage for an office building. (This bid was made before the townhouse was designated as a landmark; see below.) The offer was rejected by Mr. Jones, who wished to remain in his residence. A few years later, in 1972, Mr. Jones sold the air rights to his property (approximately 20,000 square feet of development potential) to an adjacent property owner who subsequently built an apartment house called "The Landmark" to the immediate left of 311 East 58th Street. (The property to the immediate right, at 313 East 58th Street, is a similarly landmarked building; see Exhibit 2).

Property Historic Significance/Landmark Designation

The townhouse was accorded historic status by the New York City Landmarks Preservation Commission on May 25, 1967. In the words of the Commission[24]:

> 311 East 58th Street has a special character and special historical and architectural interest and value as part of the development, heritage and cultural characteristics of New York City.

Among its important qualities, the house...is a dignified example of vernacular architecture, the modest dwelling has withstood the changes of the surrounding community, having been carefully preserved and that it is a reminder of the residential architecture of a bygone day.

The Property Assessment Appeal

Exhibit 11 indicates the assessed values of 311 East 58th Street over the past decade. For most of this time span, the assessment increased gradually, typically by a few thousand dollars a year. There were two exceptions, however. In the 1973-74 tax year, the townhouse's valuation was raised from $75,000 to $85,000; in 1981-82, its assessment was increased from $73,000 to $92,000. In both cases the valuation changes would have increased annual property-tax payments by about $1,000 to $2,000. These two reassessments were subsequently appealed and then reduced (see Exhibit 11). The basis of these challenges and their resolution are highlighted below.

EXHIBIT 11
311 EAST 58TH STREET:
REAL PROPERTY TAX ASSESSMENTS/PAYMENTS
OVER TIME

Tax Year	Initial Assessment[1]	Initial Property Tax Obligation[2]	Final Assessment[3]	Final Property Tax Obligation[4]	Difference Between Initial and Final Property Tax Obligation
1972-73	$75,000	$4,890	$70,000	$4,564	$ -326
1973-74	85,000	5,865	73,000	5,037	-828
1974-75	73,000	5,366	73,000	5,366	0
1975-76	73,000	5,979	73,000	5,979	0
1976-77	73,000	6,424	73,000	6,424	0
1977-78	73,000	6,388	73,000	6,388	0
1978-79	73,000	6,388	73,000	6,388	0
1979-80	73,000	6,388	73,000	6,388	0
1980-81	73,000	6,534	73,000	6,534	0
1981-82	92,000	8,234	73,000	6,534	-1,700

[1] Indicates assessment before tax-assessment appeal.

[2] Equals initial assessment multiplied by the official New York City tax rate for indicated year.

[3] Indicates assessment after tax-assessment appeal.

[4] Equals final assessment multiplied by the official New York City tax rate for indicated year.

Source: New York City Real Property Assessment Department. Figures are approximate.

After learning of his 1973 reassessment, Mr. Jones approached the then executive director of the New York City Landmarks Preservation Commission (LPC), Mr. Frank Gilbert, for assistance. Mr. Jones contended that the $85,000 valuation assumed an assemblage value for his property that in fact was precluded by the 1967 air-rights sale. Mr. Gilbert agreed to accompany Mr. Jones in appearing before the New York City Tax Commission "not to act as counsel, rather to express the support of his agency for equitable treatment of the designated townhouse."[25] LPC's executive director felt it was essential to secure an appropriate assessment, not only to obtain relief for one landmark owner, but also to "educate" assessors to the interaction of landmark designation, air-rights sales, and property valuation[26]:

> It will be very important for landmark and historic district commissions to gain the confidence of the local assessors so that a city's real estate tax program can reflect special landmark situations.

In May 1973, Messrs. Jones and Gilbert appeared before the Tax Commission and argued that the $85,000 assessment of 311 East 58th Street was an overvaluation because (1) the townhouse was a landmark and thus could not be demolished and redeveloped; and (2) the property's air rights had been sold, further precluding the assemblage potential of the site. On the latter point, Mr. Jones submitted the following statement[27]:

> In December of 1972 I sold the air rights above this property. This greatly limits the value of this land for purposes of resale, as the only possible structure (in the case of a replacement) would be one similar to the present two story house with basement (2,500 square feet of floor space).

> This has been done in accordance with the provisions of the Landmarks Commission and the City Planning Commission and the continuing high assessment and resulting rise in real estate taxes will make it difficult if not impossible to continue to maintain this as my residence.

On May 15, 1973, the Tax Commission offered to reduce the assessment of 311 East 58th Street from $85,000 to $73,000—a figure just slightly above the prior year's valuation (see Exhibit 11). This offer was accepted by Mr. Jones.

The $73,000 assessment was retained for the rest of the decade (see Exhibit 11). It was then raised, triggering another assessment challenge. In January 1981, Mr. Jones received notice that his property's assessment was increased to $92,000 (see Exhibit 11). Mr. Jones subsequently approached Ms. Dorothy Miner, counsel to the New York City Landmarks Preservation

Commission, and asked for assistance in appealing the higher valuation. Ms. Miner agreed to accompany Mr. Jones before the Tax Commission in much the same capacity as Mr. Gilbert a decade earlier. Such an appeal was not necessary, however, for shortly afterwards, Mr. Jones received notice that his property assessment was being returned to the prior year's $73,000 figure. No reason was given for this change.

Town Hall

Background

Property Description

Town Hall is a world-famous auditorium located at 113-123 West 43rd Street between Seventh Avenue and Broadway in Manhattan (see Exhibit 10).

Town Hall was constructed by the League for Political Education.[28] Founded in 1894 by six prominent New York suffragettes, the league had for many years sponsored frequent "town meetings" where political, economic, and other topics were discussed. These gatherings were held at various locations in New York City, including Carnegie Hall and the Berkeley-Lyceum Theatre. The league desired a permanent location for its "town meetings" and in 1919 selected the nationally prominent architectural firm of McKim, Mead and White to design an appropriate structure. Construction of Town Hall began in 1919 and was completed in 1923.

Town Hall became a popular auditorium for Theodore Roosevelt, Woodrow Wilson, Thomas Mann, Winston Churchill, and other international known speakers. From 1935 to 1956, it hosted *America's Town Meeting of the Air*, a popular radio debate show. Town Hall also served as an acoustically renowned concert hall featuring such artists as Richard Strauss, Sergei Rachmaninoff, and Mischa Elman. Many famous performers debuted there, including Elizabeth Schwarzkopf, Joan Sutherland, and Marion Anderson. Over time, Town Hall and Carnegie Hall evolved into New York City's two major concert showplaces. The former "took care of symphony orchestras and big name soloists, the latter served as a showplace for debut recitalists and for chamber music."[29]

Starting in the late 1950s, Town Hall declined in importance as an educational-cultural center. In part, this change was due to the rapid physical, economic, and cultural deterioration of the surrounding Times Square neighborhood. Lincoln Center's emergence as a major cultural facility (especially its constituent Alice Tully Hall) also posed competition to Town Hall. Town Hall's wavering fortunes induced the League for

Political Education to relinquish ownership of the facility to New York University (NYU) in 1958. NYU operated Town Hall from 1958 to 1979 as an educational, charitable, and cultural center. The university also leased a restaurant and club portion of the building to the New York University Club.

Town Hall was operated at a loss by New York University. In an attempt to recover some of its costs, in 1966, NYU sold Town Hall's air rights to the 1133 Building Corporation, owned by a large New York City real-estate company, the Durst Organization. Acquisition of these air rights enabled the Durst Organization to increase the density of an office tower (1133 Avenue of the Americas) which shortly thereafter was constructed on an adjacent lot (see Exhibit 3). Transfer of Town Hall's air rights was effectuated in the form of a lease; each year for a term of 80 years, the Durst Organization agreed to pay a $25,000 rental to New York University.[30]

The income generated from the air-rights lease was insufficient to reverse NYU's Town Hall losses. Expenses exceeded revenues by $138,000 in 1978, and over $200,000 in 1979.[31] NYU decided either to change the operation of the hall or else to transfer the property to another party. In 1978, it commenced negotiations with the Hudson Guild Theatre (HGT). HGT was willing to lease Town Hall if it could change the auditorium to a multipurpose facility for drama, concert, and dance. HGT's plan would convert Town Hall into two theaters, one downstairs, the other in the balcony area. These plans came to the attention of local Community Board no. 5, as well as other groups, and to block the conversion, they lobbied for designation of Town Hall as a landmark.[32] In November 1978, Town Hall's exterior and interior architectural features were accorded landmark status by the New York City Landmarks Preservation Commission (LPC). HGT then applied to LPC for permission to alter the Town Hall stage. After public hearings on this request were held in December 1978 and January 1979, LPC rejected the application. HGT then ceased its negotiations to lease Town Hall.

Since its efforts to change Town Hall's operation had failed, NYU decided to rid itself of the money-losing auditorium. In March 1979, it transfered ownership to a nonprofit corporation—the Town Hall Foundation—organized to "operate, support and promote educational, cultural and charitable activities."[33] While the foundation was given title to Town Hall, it would not receive the annual $25,000 air-rights lease payment from the Durst Organization. NYU did agree, however, partially to subsidize the Town Hall Foundation for a two-year period.

To stem losses, Town Hall Foundation reduced the scope of the auditorium's operation. Despite this cutback and the subsidy provided by NYU, the foundation was not able to operate on a self-sustaining basis. Its operating loss (approximately $30,000 in 1979) would have increased substantially due to the removal of Town Hall's real-estate tax-exempt status. This change, evoking the appeal of Town Hall's assessment, is examined momentarily.

Property Historic Significance/Landmark Designation

In designating Town Hall as a landmark in November 1978 (one of only approximately 30 interior landmarks in New York City), LPC discussed the auditorium's many distinctive features[34]:

> The Commission finds that among its important qualities, the Town Hall interior was designed by the prominent architectural firm of McKim, Mead and White to meet the needs of the League for Political Education for a meeting hall; that the auditorium has achieved international renown for its excellent acoustics; that for solo performances and small music groups, the auditorium has provided an unrivaled intimate and acoustically fine atmosphere; that is has become the chosen hall for countless musical debuts; and that the auditorium has been the scene of many notable speeches and lectures, including the radio program "America's Town Meeting of the Air."

Town Hall's renowned interior is gleaned from Exhibit 4, which shows the interior view from the stage.

The Property-Assessment Appeal

For most of the 1970s, Town Hall was assessed for approximately $1,000,000 (see Exhibit 12). Property taxes were paid on only one-third of this basis; for the auditorium was accorded a two-thirds tax exemption on the grounds that it was owned by an educational organization (NYU) and was used for educational purposes. (A two-thirds exemption was granted because this amount was deemed the proportional share of the value of the building operated for tax-exempt, educational objectives.) To illustrate, in the 1976-77 tax year, Town Hall was obligated to pay property taxes on an assessment base of about $370,000 ($1,115,000 total assessment x .33). Its tax bill was therefore about $32,000.

Town Hall's two-thirds tax exempt status was removed in the 1980-81 tax year, when the auditorium's ownership was transferred from New York University to the Town Hall Foundation. Another change was also made. Whereas prior to the 1980-81 tax year, the property had been assessed at roughly $1,000,000 (of which one-third was taxable), for the 1980-81 tax year, Town Hall's valuation was reduced from $1,000,000 to $800,000. This change may have been made because of the 1978 designation of Town Hall as a landmark. As discussed by the Tax Commission of the City of New York[35]:

> On November 28, 1978, the property was designated a Landmark as to both its exterior and interior architectural features....
>
> The Landmark designation has permanently impaired both the land and building value. The Assessment Department has now given partial recognition to the situation by reducing the tentative 1980/81 assessment to $800,000 from the 1979 assessment of $1,000,000.

Despite the reduction of assessment from $1,000,000 to $800,000, the lifting of Town Hall's two-thirds tax exemption meant that the Town Hall Foundation would be bearing substantially higher property taxes—about $70,000 compared to $30,000 remitted by its predecessor, NYU (see Exhibit 12). Town Hall Foundation therefore decided to appeal its assessment for both the 1979-80 tax year (when Town Hall was assessed for $1,000,000) and the 1980-81 tax year (when Town Hall was assessed for $800,000). As is often the case in assessment challenges, numerous objections were raised by the appellant. Town Hall Foundation first challenged the removal of the auditorium's tax-exempt status. It also claimed that the city's assessment constituted an over-valuation because[36]:

(1) Designation of Town Hall's interior as a landmark reduced the building's value for entertainment and cultural purposes because interior changes necessary for operating the auditorium on a profitable basis might be precluded. As an illustration, Town Hall's shallow stage made it unfit for certain types of performances, yet changing the stage might be prohibited by landmark controls.

(2) Designation of the building as a landmark "forbids its demolition[37]." Consequently a buyer would not be willing to purchase the property for assemblage purposes.

(3) Even in the absence of landmark status, Town Hall lost its assemblage value as a result of the building's air-rights sale to the Durst Organization in 1966.

In May 1980, the Tax Commission of the City of New York reduced Town Hall's assessment to $600,000—a drop of $400,000 (from the $1,000,000 assessment) in the 1979-80 tax year, and a reduction of $200,000 (from the $800,000 assessment) in the 1980-81 tax year. This reduction resulted in substantial drop in the auditorium's property taxes (see Exhibit 12). In an unusual move, the Tax Commission issued a memorandum explaining its decision. The memorandum discussed how Town Hall's air-rights sale diminished its value[38]:

EXHIBIT 12
TOWN HALL:
REAL PROPERTY TAX ASSESSMENTS/PAYMENTS
OVER TIME

Tax Year	Initial Assessment[1]	Initial Property Tax Obligation[2]	Final Assessment[3]	Final Property Tax Obligation[4]	Difference Between Initial and Final Property Tax Obligation
1971-72	$1,115,000[5]	$22,117	$1,115,000[5]	$22,117	$ 0
1972-73	1,115,000[5]	23,994	1,115,000[5]	23,994	0
1973-74	1,115,000[5]	25,392	1,115,000[5]	25,392	0
1974-75	1,115,000[5]	27,048	1,115,000[5]	27,048	0
1975-76	1,115,000[5]	30,139	1,115,000[5]	30,139	0
1976-77	1,115,000[5]	32,384	1,115,000[5]	32,384	0
1977-78	1,115,000[5]	32,200	1,115,000[5]	32,200	0
1978-79	1,050,000[5]	30,319	1,050,000[5]	30,319	0
1979-80	1,000,000	87,500	600,000	52,500	-35,000
1980-81	800,000	71,600	600,000	53,700	-17,900
1981-82	600,000	53,700	575,000	51,463	- 2,237

[1] Indicates assessment before tax-assessment appeal.

[2] Equals initial assessment multiplied by the official New York City tax rate for indicated year.

[3] Indicates assessment after tax-assessment appeal.

[4] Equals final assessment multiplied by the official New York City tax rate for indicated year.

[5] In these years Town Hall was accorded a two-thirds property-tax exempt status. For example, in 1971-72 it was taxed as if it were assessed for about $368,000 ($1,115,000 x .33). In tax years 1977-78 and 1978-79, the exemption share was partially reduced (this reduction is not shown).

Source: New York City Real Property Assessment Department. Figures are approximate.

The air rights over the property were leased by NYU in 1966 for a period of 80 years to 1133 Building Corp.... This long-term lease is, in effect, a sale of the air rights which served to substantially reduce the value of the land underlying Town Hall. However, the assessment on Town Hall was never adequately reduced to reflect this transfer of value.

The memorandum also indicated that Town Hall's landmark status had "impaired" property value[39]:

The landmark designation has permanently impaired both the land and building value.... The plain fact is that this building is an uneconomic improvement. The most pressing changes cannot be undertaken because of the landmark designation.

After noting these effects, the memorandum concluded that lowering Town Hall's assessment would be in the best interests of the city[40]:

> By designating the building as a Landmark, the city has expressed its opinion that the property is a treasure to be preserved. However, this designation has seriously undermined the economic integrity of the property. What the city has wrought, it ought now to remedy, in part, at least, by substantially reducing the assessed valuation.

> It seems clear that the assessment is considerably higher than the value of the property and it is urged that the Tax Commission take immediate action to reduce the assessment to its fair value as requested in the protests for 1979/80 and 1980/81.

New York County Lawyers' Association Building

Background

Property Description

The New York County Lawyers' Association Building (NYCLAB) is located in lower Manhattan at 14 Vesey Street (see Exhibit 10).

NYCLAB is a small clubhouse-type structure built in 1929 (see Exhibit 5). It was designed for and has been used exclusively by the New York County Lawyers' Association.

NYCLAB is four stories high. The first floor contains a large lobby, administrative offices, and court room; the second floor consists of a large auditorium; the third, a library; and the fourth, administrative offices and meeting rooms. The building is approximately 34,000 square feet in size. Only about half of this space is usable due to such features as very high (20 foot) ceilings, absence of toilet facilities on some floors, and outdated lighting and electric systems.

Property Historic Significance/Landmark Designation

NYCLAB's special historic/architectural features were summarized by the New York City Landmarks Preservation Commission as follows[41]:

> The building is an example of Federal eclectic architecture. The importance of this building consists in showing how a small clubhouse may be

both attractive and imposing. Here the handsome proportions and bas-relief ornament of the facade make a notable contribution to our urban architecture. As the building of the New York County Lawyers Association, it furnishes a home for that important organization in a structure expressly designed for it by the noted architect Cass Gilbert, who also designed the United States Supreme Court building in Washington.

NYCLAB was designated a landmark in November 1965. Designation was justified on the following grounds[42]:

> The Commission further finds that, among its important qualities, this distinguished building has set a very high standard for the planning, design and construction of a small clubhouse and that, as such, the New York County Lawyers Association Building makes a significant contribution to the architectural beauty of the City.

The Property-Assessment Appeal

For many years, religious, educational, charitable, hospital, cemetery and "moral/mental health" organizations as well as bar and medical associations in New York State were all exempt from local property taxation.[43] In 1971, a new state law was enacted (Section 420) establishing two categories—"A" and "B"—for property-tax purposes.[44] The "A" category consisted of religious, educational, charitable, hospital, cemetery and "moral/mental health" entities, which continued to be tax exempt. The "B" category included other groups, such as bar and medical associations. Section 420 gave localities the discretion of taxing or exempting the "B" groups. In 1971, New York City enacted an ordinance[45] obligating section 420 "B" organizations to pay property taxes.

This change affected the New York County Lawyers' Association Building. Prior to 1971, NYCLAB, a property used as a bar association, was exempt from property taxation. This exemption was lost in 1971, for as a bar association building, NYCLAB fell into the "B" category, which local law now opened to taxation. (The 1971 law affected others as well. To illustrate the tax exemption enjoyed by the Association of the Bar of the City of New York [ABCNY] was similarly revoked. ABCNY challenged this change, but the city's action was upheld by the Court of Appeals.[46])

For most of the 1970s, NYCLAB was assessed at about $900,000 and paid between $50,000 and $80,000 a year in property taxes (see Exhibit 13). In 1979, the New York County Lawyers' Association challenged the assessment of its headquarters for the tax years (1972-73 through 1979-1980) when the property was deemed taxable.[47] The New York County Lawyers' Association challenged the revocation of its tax exemption. It further argued that, even if its headquarters were subject to taxation, the $900,000 assessment constituted an overvaluation because[48]:

(1) In its current condition, NYCLAB was characterized by numerous structural/mechanical deficiencies which reduced its value as an office building.

(2) In the perception of the New York County Lawyers' Association, landmark status made it problematical whether it could modernize its headquarters to current office standards. Designation did not prohibit renovation. It did, however, introduce uncertainty as to which changes would be allowed. To illustrate, modernizing the NYCLAB would likely encompass lowering the building's ceilings. While this change, an interior modification, would not be subject to stringent review by the Landmarks Preservation Commission (LPC), altering the NYCLAB's ceilings might affect the building's windows (see Exhibit 5)—an exterior change subject to LPC approval.

(3) NYCLAB's landmark status also precluded its demolition and redevelopment to a more profitable use.

In October 1979, William Block, then counsel to the New York City Tax Commission, wrote a memorandum addressing the contentions raised by the New York County Lawyers' Association.[49] The memorandum argued that revocation of NYCLAB's tax-exempt status was justified and pointed to the fact that the courts had upheld similar action taken with respect to the headquarters of the Association of the Bar of the City of New York.[50] Block's memorandum supported the contention of the New York County Lawyers' Association that the $900,000 assessment constituted an overvaluation in light of the NYCLAB's obsolescence[51]:

> The building itself is old and lacks most of the facilities and amenities of a modern office building. For example, the building has a 20-foot ceiling, an old manually operated elevator, no toilet facilities on some floors and neither the lighting nor electric systems is comparable to those in more modern buildings. The physical layout is not meant for office use and major modifications would be required to convert it to this use.

Designation of NYCLAB as a landmark was also deemed to reduce the value of the property[52]:

> Although the precise market impact of such designation is unclear, a reasonable assumption is that the building could not be demolished nor converted easily to commercial space. If this is so, the value of this land is not the equivalent of the adjacent land and would most likely command a lower price.

EXHIBIT 13
NEW YORK COUNTY LAWYERS' ASSOCIATION BUILDING:
REAL PROPERTY TAX ASSESSMENTS/PAYMENTS
OVER TIME

Tax Year	Initial Assessment[1]	Initial Property Tax Obligation[2]	Final Assessment[3]	Final Property Tax Obligation[4]	Difference Between Initial and Final Property Tax Obligation
1971-72	$900,000	$ 0[5]	$900,000	$ 0[5]	$ 0
1972-73	900,000	58,680	700,000	45,640	-13,040
1973-74	900,000	62,100	700,000	48,300	-13,800
1974-75	900,000	66,150	900,000[6]	66,150	0
1975-76	900,000	73,710	700,000	57,330	-16,380
1976-77	900,000	79,200	700,000	61,600	-17,600
1977-78	900,000	78,750	700,000	61,250	-17,500
1978-79	900,000	78,750	700,000	61,250	-17,500
1979-80	900,000	78,750	700,000	61,250	-17,500
1980-81	900,000	80,550	700,000	62,650	-17,900
1981-82	700,000	62,650	700,000	62,650	0

[1] Indicates assessment before tax-assessment appeal.

[2] Equals initial assessment multiplied by the official New York City tax rate for indicated year.

[3] Indicates assessment after tax-assessment appeal.

[4] Equals final assessment multiplied by the official New York City tax rate for indicated year.

[5] Property was tax exempt in indicated year. See text.

[6] An Article 7 proceeding was not commenced for 1974-75, hence the assessment for that year remained the same.

Source: New York City Real Property Assessment Department. Figures are approximate.

Based on these findings, Block's memorandum recommended that the NYCLAB's assessment be reduced from $900,000 to $700,000 for tax years 1972-73 through 1979-1980. The proposed $700,000 valuation was justified as appropriate even without factoring designation's effects[53]:

No economic detriment has been attributed to the land even though it has Landmark designation. The impact of such designation is not settled in the law and therefore it has not been allowed to influence the proposed valuation.

In April 1980, the New York City Tax Commission followed its counsel's recommendation and lowered NYCLAB's assessment from $900,000 to $700,000.

Hotel Chelsea

Background

Property Description

Hotel Chelsea is located at 222 West 23rd Street in the Chelsea neighborhood of Manhattan (see Exhibit 10). Designed by the architectural firm of Hubert, Pirsson and Company, it opened in 1832 as a cooperative apartment house sponsored by a group of artists who wanted studio accommodations.[54] In addition to being one of the city's first cooperatives, the property also had some of the first duplexes, and one of the first penthouses in New York.[55]

The hotel has a central, towerlike section and a high, pyramidal slate roof flanked on each side by enormous brick chimneys.[56] Complementing these central features are projecting wings at each end of the building, adorned at their tops by large pointed-arch windows set in brick gables (see Exhibit 6). The most notable feature of the eleven-story building is the succession, tier upon tier, of horizontal iron balconies. These balconies, richly decorated with leaves and flowers, lend an atmosphere of charm to the high brick facade, as do the French doors opening onto them (see Exhibit 6).

Over the past century, Hotel Chelsea has been frequented by well-known artists, writers, and actors. Famous past residents include Mark Twain, Eugene O'Neill, Thomas Wolfe, Edgar Lee Masters, and Dylan Thomas.

Property Historic Significance/Landmark Designation

Hotel Chelsea was designated as a landmark in March 1966.[57] The New York City Landmarks Preservation Commission (LPC) cited the structure's historical-cultural uniqueness as well as the Chelsea's eye-appealing physical features.

The Property-Assessment Appeal

As of the early 1970s, the Hotel Chelsea was assessed for approximately $500,000 and paid about $35,000 in annual property taxes (see Exhibit 14). In 1973, the Chelsea's owner appeared before the Tax Commission of the City of New York and argued that the $500,000 assessment was not supported by the hotel's income. In addition, the owner contended that the hotel's landmark designation, prohibiting its redevelopment to a higher-intensity use, reduced the market appeal/value of the property.

In appearing before the Tax Commission, the Chelsea's owner was accompanied by Mr. Frank Gilbert, then executive director of the New York City Landmarks Preservation Commission.[58] Mr. Gilbert appealed to the Tax Commission that "within the limits of the law it would be in the city's best interests if the assessment of the hotel could be adjusted."[59] Shortly thereafter, the Tax Commission reduced the Chelsea's assessment from $535,000 to $440,000, thereby lowering the annual property-tax obligation by about $6,000 (see Exhibit 14).

The $440,000 assessment was kept for about a decade until the 1981-82 tax year,* when the Chelsea's valuation was raised to $700,000—a change increasing the annual property-tax bill from $40,000 to over $60,000 (see Exhibit 14). The $700,000 assessment is currently being challenged by the hotel's owners on the following grounds[60]: (1) the hotel's income does not support a $700,000 valuation; and (2) the Chelsea's landmark status reduces its value. As discussed by Mr. Stanley Vard, the hotel's manager[61]:

> The $700,000 assessment reflects the rising property values in the neighborhood. There is new construction and conversions of existing units going on all the time. These neighborhood changes help the Chelsea. Yet landmark status [means] that the hotel can't be demolished so it must stay in its current form.

As of June 1981, appeal of the $700,000 assessment has not yet been resolved.

Colonnade Row

Background

Property Description

Colonnade Row is a group of four townhouses located at 428 to 434 Lafayette Street in lower Manhattan (see Exhibit 10). As described by Ada Louise Huxtable in *Classic New York*[62]:

---

*There were some initial assessment increases to about $500,000 in this period, but the valuation was subsequently lowered to $440,000 (see Exhibit 14). Ms. Dorothy Miner, counsel to the New York City Landmarks Preservation Commission (LPC), was present at one such assessment adjustment. Thus, the LPC tradition of lending support to landmark property owners, practiced by Mr. Frank Gilbert in the early 1970s, was continued by Ms. Miner.

EXHIBIT 14
HOTEL CHELSEA:
REAL PROPERTY TAX ASSESSMENTS/PAYMENTS
OVER TIME

Tax Year	Initial Assessment[1]	Initial Property Tax Obligation[2]	Final Assessment[3]	Final Property Tax Obligation[4]	Difference Between Initial and Final Property Tax Obligation
1971-72	$505,000	$30,351	$505,000	$30,351	$ 0
1972-73	525,000	34,230	525,000	34,230	0
1973-74	535,000	36,915	440,000	30,360	-6,555
1974-75	525,000	38,588	440,000	32,340	-6,248
1975-76	440,000	36,036	440,000	36,036	0
1976-77	440,000	38,720	440,000	38,720	0
1977-78	500,000	43,750	440,000	38,500	-5,250
1978-79	500,000	43,750	440,000	38,500	-5,250
1979-80	440,000	38,500	440,000	38,500	0
1980-81	440,000	39,380	440,000	39,380	0
1981-82	700,000	62,650	on appeal	on appeal	on appeal

[1] Indicates assessment before tax-assessment appeal.
[2] Equals initial assessment multiplied by the official New York City tax rate for indicated year.
[3] Indicates assessment after tax-assessment appeal.
[4] Equals final assessment multiplied by the official New York City tax rate for indicated year.
Source: New York City Real Property Assessment Department. Figures are approximate.

The most splendid of New York's Greek Revival rows was one of the handsomest and most elegant groups of buildings ever to rise in the city.... Colonnade Row, originally La Grange Terrace, equals in grandeur anything of the period that London or Edinburgh have to offer. Designed by A. J. Davis and built by Seth Geer in 1836...their extreme elegance is still easily grasped. Twelve tall, slender Corinthian columns of the original twenty-seven rise two full stories on a rusticated stone base.

Colonnade Row was built to provide dignified, gracious housing. For many years it attracted well-to-do residents, such as President Franklin Roosevelt's grandfather and John Jacob Astor. Over time, the surrounding area began to deteriorate and commercial and industrial users replaced once fashionable residences. Colonnade Row was not immune to these changes; five of the original nine houses were destroyed and a portion of the ground floor area of the remaining units was converted to commercial uses.[63]

Property Historic Significance/Landmark Designation

Colonnade Row was designated a landmark in October 1965. In describing the special character of the houses, the Landmarks Preservation Commission noted that Colonnade Row[64]:

> is...a preeminent example of Classic Revival residential planning and that...the row of houses...are a beautifully executed architectural composition.

In the late 1970s, the owner of Colonnade Row donated a facade easement to the National Trust for Historic Preservation (see chapter four for discussion of historic easements). This easement restricted in perpetuity architecturally inappropriate exterior changes to the Colonnade.

The Property-Assessment Appeal

Colonnade Row consists of four properties located at 428 to 434 Lafayette Street. The tax appeal discussed below concerns one of the buildings—434 Lafayette.*

As of the middle to late 1970s, this property was assessed for approximately $90,000 and paid annual property taxes of $6,000 to $8,000. In 1980, the owner of the 434 Lafayette challenged the $90,000 valuation for the 1980-81 tax year. In an appeal to the Tax Commission of the City of New York, he argued that the city's assessment constituted an overvaluation, because[65]:

(1) the building was not profitable. For 1980, its expenses exceeded income by about $10,000. (2) Landmark status, prohibiting the demolition of 434 Lafayette Street, meant that the property was worth less than neighboring, nondesignated structures which could be redeveloped. (3) Establishment of a facade easement and the transfer of this easement to the National Trust for Historic Preservation had a similiar effect of preventing redevelopment of the landmark.

Shortly afterwards, the Tax Commission reduced the assessment of 434 Lafayette Street from $90,000 to $72,000, thereby lowering annual property taxes from about $8,000 to approximately $6,000.

---

*This case study does not report other assessment adjustments involving Colonnade Row.

Metropolitan Club

Background

Property Description

The Metropolitan Club is located at 1-11 East 60th Street in Manhattan—one of New York City's most fashionable and expensive neighborhoods (see Exhibit 10). It is a handsome four-story structure built in a neo-Italian Renaissance style (see Exhibit 8).

The Metropolitan Club was formed in February 1891 by a group of socially prominent and wealthy New Yorkers, including Cornelius Vanderbilt, William Whitney, Robert Goelet, and J. Newbold Morris.[66] A site with a 100-foot Fifth Avenue frontage was soon purchased and Stanford White, of the architectural firm of McKim, Mead and White, was hired to design an appropriate club building. Ground breaking was held in 1891; construction was completed in 1894.

The Metropolitan Club was designed in a "restrained" neo-Italian Renaissance style[67]:

> Marked by its seven-bay central facade, the Metropolitan Club is four-stories high and is symmetrically balanced.... The planar wall surfaces are handled with great restraint. A modest program of ornamentation is achieved by a combination of balconies, quoins, overhanging cornices and square-shaped attic windows. While the firm of McKim, Mead & White drew inspiration from Italian models of the 15th-17th centuries, they selected for use specific details.... Their neo-Italian Renaissance design was characterized by an emphasis on regularization, groundhugging horizontals, and a simplification of detail.

While the Metropolitan Club's exterior was purposely restrained in order to dispel charges of ostentation, its interior is quite lavish.[68] There is a monumental entrance hall sheathed in marble. In addition, many interior ceilings were painted by some of the leading artisans of the day (see Exhibit 9).

In 1912, an adjacent building was purchased as an addition and renovated to harmonize with the neo-Italian Renaissance style of the main clubhouse.

Property Historic Significance/Landmark Designation

The Metropolitan Club was designated as a landmark in September 1979 on the following grounds:[69]

The Metropolitan Club Building is characteristic of an especially American interpretation of European architecture; that among its notable features are the refined stonework and detail, the imposing cornice, and the graceful colonnade screening the courtyard; that the clubhouse led the vanguard of development north of 59th Street; that it set the style and high standard of design for the surrounding area; and that it continues to make a strong contribution to the architectural excellence of the neighborhood.

The Property-Assessment Appeal

At the start of the 1970s, the Metropolitan Club's assessment was increased by about 15 percent from $2,800,000 to $3,200,000—a change raising the annual tax bill from $168,000 to $192,000 (see Exhibit 15). Following that increase, the property's assessment was held almost constant for the rest of the decade until the 1980-81 tax year, when its valuation for real-taxation purposes was raised by a similar 15 percent from $3,250,000 to $3,700,000 (see Exhibit 15). The Metropolitan Club decided to challenge its new assessment. In 1980, it appeared before the New York City Tax Commission and claimed that the $3,700,000 valuation was an overassessment because of the landmark designation of the clubhouse[70]:

As a result of the designation, any attempt by the Club to make significant alterations to its building would undoubtedly be thwarted. Consequently, it would be extremely difficult to envision any use to which the Club's building might be put other than that of a social club. Moreover, the property could not be sold for any amount approaching its real value since any purchaser would also be prohibited by law from altering, reconstructing or demolishing any part of the Club's building without first securing approvals which are unlikely to be forthcoming. Under these circumstances, the value of the Club's property has undoubtedly diminished significantly as a result of the designation.

In June 1980, the Metropolitan Club's challenge was denied by the Tax Commission. The club then appealed to the Supreme Court of the State of New York, New York County (see Appendix 3-B for discussion of the assessment-challenge process). The Metropolitan Club's application to this court stressed the alleged harmful market impact of landmark status[71]:

The fair market value of the property has fallen substantially due to landmark designation, since neither petitioner nor any potential purchaser may now develop the Property to the highest and best use....

New York City failed to consider the substantial restrictions on the Property resulting from the landmark designation and raised the assessed valuation of the Property, irrespective of the resultant diminution in fair market value.

EXHIBIT 15
METROPOLITAN CLUB:
REAL PROPERTY TAX ASSESSMENTS/PAYMENTS
OVER TIME

Tax Year	Initial Assessment[1]	Initial Property Tax Obligation[2]	Final Assessment[3]	Final Property Tax Obligation[4]	Difference Between Initial and Final Property Tax Obligation
1970-71	$2,845,000	$168,140	$2,845,000	$168,140	$ 0
1971-72	3,200,000	192,320	3,200,000	192,320	0
—	—	—	—	—	—
1976-77	3,250,000	286,000	3,250,000	286,000	0
1977-78	3,250,000	284,375	3,250,000	284,375	0
1978-79	3,250,000	284,375	3,250,000	284,575	0
1979-80	3,250,000	284,375	3,250,000	284,375	0
1980-81	3,700,000	323,750	on appeal	on appeal	on appeal
1981-82	4,450,000	398,275	on appeal	on appeal	on appeal

[1] Indicates assessment before tax-assessment appeal.

[2] Equals initial assessment multiplied by the official New York City tax rate for indicated year.

[3] Indicates assessment after tax-assessment appeal.

[4] Equals final assessment multiplied by the official New York City tax rate for indicated year.

Source: New York City Real Property Assessment Department. Figures are approximate.

As of June 1981, the State Supreme Court had not yet ruled on the Metropolitan Club's request that its assessment for the 1980-81 tax year be reduced.

In 1981, the Metropolitan Club's valuation for tax purposes was again increased from $3,700,000 to $4,500,000 (see Exhibit 15). According to the attorneys representing the club, this new assessment will also be challenged as an overvaluation on similar grounds as those advanced in the prior appeals.[72]

APPENDIX 3-B

NEW YORK CITY PROPERTY-TAX STRUCTURE AND ADMINISTRATION

Introduction

This appendix summarizes the structure and administration of the New York City property tax. It first notes the financial significance of the levy and then turns to the New York State and City statutes governing the property tax. The appendix concludes by highlighting the property tax's operative realities, focusing on the manner in which buildings are assessed for real taxation purposes.

Significance of the Revenue

New York City's property-tax base is this community's most significant financial asset and its property tax is a local revenue mainstay.[73] In 1960, New York's property-tax base was about $30 billion and its property tax yielded about $1 billion—over 40 percent of total city revenues from all sources (see Exhibit 16). Two decades later, the city's property-tax base grew to over $80 billion and the property tax generated about $3 billion. The latter was about a quarter of the city's total revenues from all sources— a share lower than its historical contribution, reflecting the growth of intergovernmental revenues and other local taxes such as income, sales, and corporate levies. (In fiscal year 1980, New York City had total revenues from all sources of about $13 billion. Of this amount, about $3 billion was derived from the local property tax, about $3 billion from local income and

EXHIBIT 16

NEW YORK CITY PROPERTY TAX BASE, RATE, AND REVENUES

FISCAL YEARS 1960-80

Year	Assessed Taxable Value [1] (in millions)	Full or Equalized Taxable Value [2]	Assessed Value as Percent of Full Value [3]	Official Tax Rate	Effective or Equivalent Tax Rate [4]	Property Tax Collections (In Millions) [5]	Property Tax Percent of Total City Revenue From All Sources
1960	$23,549.0	$28,491.7	0.83%	$4.27	$3.53	$ 959.9	43.1%
1961	24,944.4	30,277.4	0.82	4.24	3.49	1,005.8	41.5
1962	26,094.1	33,633.6	0.78	4.23	3.28	1,041.4	40.0
1963	27,236.3	35,122.9	0.78	4.27	3.31	1,104.2	39.5
1964	28,557.5	38,366.6	0.74	4.40	3.27	1,184.3	38.2
1965	29,752.7	40,327.3	0.74	4.54	3.35	1,276.7	38.1
1966	30,901.8	42,942.3	0.72	4.64	3.34	1,363.4	36.1
1967	31,734.7	43,955.3	0.72	5.00	3.61	1,501.7	33.4
1968	32,485.9	44,903.3	0.72	5.11	3.70	1,598.1	30.2
1969	33,304.9	53,183.0	0.63	5.25	3.29	1,677.6	27.7
1970	34,292.3	56,546.1	0.61	5.54	3.36	1,830.0	27.3
1971	35,329.4	61,261.1	0.58	5.91	3.41	1,989.3	26.6
1972	36,665.0	64,677.2	0.57	6.01	3.40	2,097.8	24.7
1973	37,865.1	74,638.0	0.51	6.52	3.31	2,345.8	25.2
1974	38,529.2	79,041.2	0.49	6.90	3.36	2,487.1	24.3
1975	39,404.0	82,508.4	0.48	7.35	3.51	3,648.6	22.0
1976	39,657.9	83,030.0	0.48	8.19	3.91	2,966.6	23.4
1977	38,827.1	81,303.4	0.48	8.80	4.20	3,236.0	24.4
1978	38,611.8	86,246.2	0.45	8.75	3.92	3,230.0	23.7
1979	37,926.1	86,646.9	0.44	8.75	3.83	3,130.0	24.1
1980	38,056.0	84,385.1	0.45	8.75	3.95	3,084.0	23.7

[1] Tax-exempt veterans' property is excluded from Assessed Taxable Value, but included in Full Taxable Value. Equals Full Taxable Value multiplied by the Assessed Value as Percent of Full Value figure.
(Note figures are not exact because of rounding.)
[2] Refers to equalized or real market value.
[3] Rounded to two decimal places. Equals Assessed Taxable Value divided by Full Taxable Value.
[4] Equals Official Tax Rate multiplied by Assessed Value as Percent of Full Value (figure is not exact because of rounding).
[5] Equals Official Tax Rate multiplied by Assessed Taxable Value by Official Tax Rate (or Full Taxable Value by Effective Tax Rate) because of tax delinquency.

Source: Tom Boast and Julia Vitullo-Martin, "The Future of the Property Tax," *The Fiscal Observer* (January, 1980).

other levies, about $3 billion from federal aid, over $2 billion from state aid, and the remainder from other sources.) While New York's property tax constituted a smaller share of total city income than in past years, the property levy still dominated local revenue sources, as is dramatically evident from Exhibit 17. Clearly, the local property base/tax is a critical factor in New York's continued financial vigor.

Statutory Framework

The structure and administration of New York City's property tax is governed by (1) New York State Constitution, (2) State Real Property Tax Law, (3) New York City Charter, and (4) New York City Administrative Code.[74]

State Property-Tax Guidelines and
Administrative Structure

The state constitution regulates the amount of income that New York City may generate from the property tax. To illustrate, Article 8, section 10 of the constitution limits the amount of property-tax revenue that New York City can raise to pay for operating expenditures to 2.5 percent of a five-year average of the full value of taxable real estate. A higher property-tax share is permitted to support the city's capital outlays (Article 8, section 4).

There are also state guidelines regarding assessment for real-taxation purposes. The state constitution provides for general standards such as equal treatment of similar property owners. Specific procedures and administrative mechanisms are specified by the state's Real Property Tax Law. Section 306 stipulates that real property be assessed at its full value. Article 2 of the Real Property Tax Law provides for the creation of the State Board of Equalization and Assessment (SBEA), which supervises the administration of the real-property-tax system by local governments and determines each jurisdiction's real or equalized property-tax base. (The latter is an important variable for allocating many forms of state aid, such as educational assistance; state aid is typically granted inversely to local wealth where wealth is measured by the size of the equalized tax base.)

New York City Property-Tax Guidelines
and Administrative Structure

New York City's Charter empowers the City Council to set the tax rate on the assessed value of real estate at the level necessary to meet budgetary requirements. In recent years, the real-tax rate has been about $4.00 per $100 of assessment (see Exhibit 17). Responsibility for determining assessed value and for collecting property-tax revenues is vested with the Department of Finance. Within the Department of Finance, the Department of Real Property Assessment (RPA) administers the valuation of property. RPA has established an overall assessment office for each borough of the city, and within each such office has delineated assessment districts. Valuation of property in each district is the responsibility of an individual assessor appointed by RPA. At the current time, there are approximately 100 assessment districts and a like number of assessors.

The Administrative Code of the Department of Finance stipulates that assessors must personally visit each parcel of taxable property[75]:

> The assessors shall furnish to the finance administrator, under oath, a detailed statement of all taxable real estate showing that they have personally examined each and every house, building, lot, pier or other taxable property.

Assessors are also required to state the market value of the parcel, and separately assess land and then land and improvements combined.

Assessment Time Schedule/Appeals Process (See Exhibit 18)

The City's Administrative Code establishes a specified time period for the preparation and "setting of the assessment role." On August 1 of the preceding tax year, assessors are authorized to value real estate. Preliminary valuations are assembled and then adjusted by an equalization ratio that in recent years has ranged between 40 and 60 percent (i.e., a property valued at $100,000 is assessed at $40,000 to $60,000). Equalization ratios differ among boroughs (it is higher in Manhattan than in the outer boroughs), and classes of properties (it is highest for income-producing parcels, lowest for owner-occupied, single-family residences). The assessment process is to be completed and all properties are to have an assessed value by the end of January. Preliminary assessed values are then "opened for public inspection" until the middle of March (see Exhibit 18).

Property owners dissatisfied with their preliminary assessment may file an appeal to the Tax Commission of the City of New York. Assessment challenges are allowed on three grounds[76]:

1. *Illegality*-if a violation of statutory procedures regarding assessment has occurred.

EXHIBIT 17

NEW YORK CITY REVENUES FROM THE PROPERTY TAX
AND SIX OTHER MAJOR LOCAL TAXES.
FISCAL YEARS 1960-80 ($ IN BILLIONS)

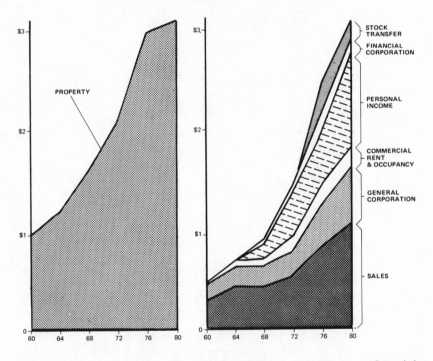

Source: Annual Report of the City Comptroller; Final Report of the Temporary Commission on City Finances, June 1977; Official Statement, June 28, 1979. Cited in Tom Boast and Julia Vitullo-Martin, "The Future of the Property Tax," The Fiscal Observer (January, 1980).

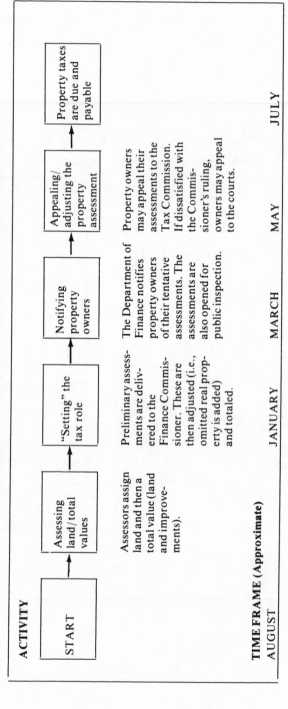

EXHIBIT 18
NEW YORK CITY PROPERTY ASSESSMENT FLOW CHART

ACTIVITY

START → Assessing land/total values → "Setting" the tax role → Notifying property owners → Appealing/adjusting the property assessment → Property taxes are due and payable

Assessors assign land and then a total value (land and improvements).

Preliminary assessments are delivered to the Finance Commissioner. These are then adjusted (i.e., omitted real property is added) and totaled.

The Department of Finance notifies property owners of their tentative assessments. The assessments are also opened for public inspection.

Property owners may appeal their assessments to the Tax Commission. If dissatisfied with the Commissioner's ruling, owners may appeal to the courts.

TIME FRAME (Approximate)
AUGUST   JANUARY   MARCH   MAY   JULY

2. *Overvaluation*-if the property is assessed at more than its full fair market value.

3. *Inequality*[77]-if a property is assessed at a higher share of full value than its counterparts in the same property class (even if these properties are assessed at less than their full value).

The Tax Commission reviews each reassessment application for adjustment and has the power to uphold or reduce the initial property valuation. The Commission's review process lasts from March to about May, depending on the number and complexity of appeals. By July 1, the assessed values are "set" and the collection of property taxes commences.

"Setting" of the tax role does not end a property owner's right of appeal, although the forum shifts from the administrative to the judicial. A property owner dissatisfied with a ruling by the Tax Commission has the right to file for an assessment adjustment before the Supreme Court in the judicial district where his/her property is located.

New York City Property Assessment: Operative Procedures

As in many other jurisdictions, New York City's assessment of real property does not fully adhere to all the procedural nuances called for by state and local law. For instance, while the Administrative Code requires that assessors "personally examine" each property, the work load assigned to each assessor (on average, about 8,000 parcels each year) does not permit this.[78] Although real property is supposed to be revalued on an annual basis, in actual practice a change in valuation (particularly in the case of owner-occupied residences) is typically triggered only by "special" circumstances, such as the property being sold or rehabilitated. A building may also be reassessed if a nearby comparable structure is sold and that sale is deemed by the assessor to be a good indicator of current market values.

The most glaring disparity between law and practice concerns the ratio of assessment to market value. According to state law, property is to be assessed at full value.[79] In practice, however, New York City (and other municipalities both in New York and other states) assesses real property at a fraction of full value where the fraction itself varies according to the type of property and its location.[80] This practice of fractional assessment was declared unconstitutional by the New York State Court of Appeals in its 1975 decision *Hellerstein* v. *Assessor, Town of Islip.*[81]

The New York State legislature is currently struggling to respond to the *Hellerstein* decision.[82] While there is consensus that full-value assessment as suggested by the Court of Appeals should be avoided because it would significantly increase the tax load of residential buildings, agreement has not yet been reached on what the replacement approach should be. It is very likely that the state law calling for full value assessment will be replaced by one legalizing fractional valuation. State Assembly Speaker Stanley Fink has introduced a bill that would institute a property classification system designating classes of real property (i.e., residential, commercial, industrial, and so on) to be assessed at varying fractions of true value.[83] In effect, this bill would legitimatize the extant assessment system.

New York City Assessment Mechanics

Neither state nor city law specifies the mechanics of valuing New York City property for taxation purposes, such as requiring that a particular appraisal methodology (i.e., income, sales, or cost) be used under certain conditions. Valuation procedures employed by New York City's assessors are difficult to determine and likely vary among the 100 individuals charged with this task. While the exact methodology cannot be specified, we can outline the overall approaches.[84]

New York City assessors typically value properties at their current use, although as indicated in this chapter, in application, assessment may also factor "higher uses" as well (i.e., when these "higher uses" are reflected in the "comp" sales prices). RPA staff use the three standard techniques—sales, income, and cost—accepted by the assessment/appraisal profession (see discussion in chapter four for explanation of each of these methodologies). All three are applied in each valuation; however, assessors emphasize varying methods in different situations: the sales approach for owner-occupied residential properties, the income method for income-producing buildings, and the cost procedure for unique or special properties such as clubs, auditoriums, and sports facilities.

RPA's application of the sales method relies on recent sales prices of roughly comparable properties ("comps") located near the building being valued. Adjustments are then typically made to this benchmark value according to the particular circumstances of the property or transaction (i.e., building condition, level of rehabilitation, location on a prestige block, owner financing, and so on).

Application of the income method requires a source of building income/expense information (see chapter four). New York City assessors do not examine the financial statements of individual buildings. Instead, they rely on data provided by RPA's Research and Equalization Divisions concerning building income/expense profiles for different classes of properties (i.e., Manhattan offices, Bronx apartment houses, and so on). The cost approach is similarly applied by referring to construction expenditure figures for different type/location buildings made available by the Research-Equalization Divisions.

RPA recognizes that its sales, income, and cost information sources described above are rough-data bases. It is currently working to provide better data inputs for the sales, income, and cost-assessment procedures and to further computerize its operation.

New York City assessors do not mechanically apply the three traditional valuation techniques. Modifications are made according to such considerations as the assessor's expertise and "feel" for what a property is really worth. Changes in procedures also occur. For instance, the sales method has increasingly been used to value prime Manhattan income-producing properties (rather than the income approach) because current sales prices are deemed a better measure of "true" worth. For example, in 1980 the Pan Am building sold for a much higher price ($400 million) than the value suggested by its then current income. The Pan Am sales price was then used as a basis for assessing other Manhattan office buildings.

Notes

1. Center for Urban Policy Research telephone interviews June through December 1980. See Appendix one of this study for details.

2. Ibid.

3. Ibid.

4. Ibid.

5. Ibid.

6. Ibid.

7. See Appendix two to this study.

8. Some of the groups and individuals contacted by the Center for Urban Policy Research and the New York Landmarks Conservancy include Mary E. Mann, Esq., president of the Tax Commission of the City of New York; William Block, Assistant Commissioner of the New York City Dept. of Finance; Eugene Morris, Esq. of Demov, Morris, Levin and Shein; Donald Schnabel of Julian J. Studley Inc.; and Roger Darby, MAI. See also acknowledgements to this study.

9. Bonnie Smyth Heudorfer, "A Quantitative Analysis of the Economic Impact of Historic Designation," Masters thesis, Pratt Institute, 1975.

10. See note 8.

11. Ada Louise Huxtable, *Classic New York* (New York: Anchor Books, 1964).

12. See Appendix 3-B to this chapter.

13. Mary Mann, president of the New York City Tax Commission, "Memorandum to Tax Commission of the City of New York, Application for Correction of Tentative Assessed Valuation," Borough of Manhattan, Block 996, Lot 21, 1980/81.

14. Ibid.

15. William K. Block, Counsel New York City Tax Commission. "Memoran-

dum—Settlement of Litigation New York County Lawyers Association," October 15, 1979.

16. Ibid.

17. CUPR interview with William K. Block, Assistant Commissioner of the New York City Department of Finance, March 1981.

18. CUPR interview with Mary Mann, president of the New York City Tax Commission, October 1980.

19. See Eugene J. Morris, "Appraisals of Realty for Taxation," in Eugene C. Cowan, ed., *Historic Preservation and the Law* (Washington, D.C.: National Trust for Historic Preservation, 1978).

20. *Hellerstein* v. *Assessor of Town of Islip* 37 N.Y. 2d 1 (1975).

21. New York City Landmarks Preservation Commission, Designation Report, May 25, 1967 LP-0503.

22. Ibid.

23. Interview by the author with Mr. Charles Jones, February 1981.

24. See note 21.

25. Interview by the author with Mr. Frank Gilbert, February, June 1981.

26. Frank B. Gilbert, "When Urban Landmarks Commissions Come to the Assessor," in International Association of Assessing Officers, ed., *Property Tax Incentives for Preservation: Use-Value Assessment and the Preservation of Farmland, Open Space, and Historic Sites* (Chicago: International Association of Assessing Officers, 1975).

27. See note 23.

28. New York City Landmarks Preservation Commission, Designation Report, November 28, 1978, LP-1012.

29. Ibid.

30. See note 13.

31. Ibid.

32. Ibid.

33. Ibid.

34. New York City Landmarks Preservation Commission, Designation Report, November 28, 1978, LP-1012.

35. Mary Mann, president of the New York City Tax Commission, "Memorandum to Tax Commission of the City of New York, Application for Correction of Tentative Assessed Valuation," Borough of Manhattan, Block 996, Lot 21, 1980/81.

36. Interview by the author with Mr. Schwartz, Esq., of Schrier, Kaufman, Schwartz and Gelles (the law firm representing Town Hall before the Tax Commission), May 1981.

37. Ibid.

38. Mary Mann, president of the New York City Tax Commission, "Memorandum to Tax Commission of the City of New York, Application for Correction of Tentative Assessed Valuation," Borough of Manhattan, Block 996, Lot 21, 1980/81.

39. Ibid.

40. Ibid.

41. New York City Landmarks Preservation Commission, Designation Report November 23, 1965 LP-0076.

42. Ibid.

43. CUPR interview with New York City Tax Commission, February 1981.

44. Ibid.

45. Ibid.

46. See Eugene J. Morris, "Appraisals of Realty for Taxation," in Eugene C.

Cowan, ed., *Historic Preservation and the Law* (Washington, D.C.: National Trust for Historic Preservation, 1978).

47. Interview by the author with Mr. Robert Goldstein, Esq. of Samuel Goldstein and Sons (the law firm representing the New York County Lawyers' Association in its appeal before the Tax Commission), June 1981.

48. Ibid.

49. William K. Block, counsel, New York City Tax Commission, "Memorandum-Settlement of Litigation New York County Lawyers' Association," October 15, 1979.

50. Ibid. See also Eugene J. Morris, "Appraisals of Realty for Taxation," in Eugene C. Cowan, ed., *Historic Preservation and the Law* (Washington, D.C.: National Trust for Historic Preservation, 1978).

51. William K. Block, "Memorandum-Settlement pf Litigation New York County Lawyers' Association."

52. Ibid.

53. Ibid.

54. New York City Landmarks Preservation Commission, Designation Report, March 1966.

55. Ibid.

56. Ibid.

57. Ibid.

58. Interview by the author with Mr. Frank Gilbert, February, June 1981.

59. Ibid.

60. CUPR interview with Mr. Stanley Vard, manager of the Chelsea Hotel.

61. Ibid.

62. Ada Louise Huxtable, *Classic New York* (New York: Anchor Books, 1964).

63. Ibid.

64. New York City Landmarks Preservation Commission, Designation Report, LP-0012, October 14, 1965.

65. Tax Commission of the City of New York, "Application for Correction of Tentative Assessed Valuation" Borough of Manhattan, Block 545, Lot 81, 1980/81.

66. New York City Landmarks Preservation Commission, Designation Report, LP-1020, September 1979.

67. Ibid.

68. Ibid.

69. Ibid.

70. Tax Commission of the City of New York, "Application for Correction of Tentative Assessed Valuation" Borough of Manhattan, Block 1375, Lot 1 1980/81.

71. Ibid. See also *In the Matter of Metropolitan Club Inc.* v. *Commissioner of Finance and the Tax Commission of the City of New York*, Supreme Court of the State of New York, Index no. 54049/80.

72. Telephone interview by the author with William Bush, Esq., of Reavis and McGrath (the law firm representing the Metropolitan Club), June 1981.

73. See Tom Boast and Julia Vitullo-Martin, "The Future of the Property Tax," *The Fiscal Observer* (January 1980).

74. Robert L. Beebe, *Real Property Tax Administration: An Historical Perspective for New York State* (Albany: State Board of Equalization and Assessment, 1979); Economic Development Council of New York City, *Reforming the Real Property Tax System in New York* (New York: The Council, 1979); Alexander M. Frame, *New York City Real Property Tax: A Review* (New York: Citizens Union Research

Foundation, March 1967); Emanuel Tobier, *Aspects of Trends in Market Values, Assessments, Effective Tax Rates and Property Tax Delinquency* (New York: Citizens Housing & Planning Council of New York, December 1975).

75. Administrative Code, New York City Department of Finance, section E17.8, a.

76. See Eugene J. Morris, "Historic Preservation and the Law-Appraisals of Realty for Taxation," in Eugene C. Cowan, ed., *Historic Preservation and the Law* (Washington, D.C.: Preservation Press, 1978).

77. The potency and coverage of the inequality contention was strengthened by the *Ed Guth Realty* and *860 Exec. Towers* decisions. See *Ed Guth Realty* v. *Gingold*, 41 A.D. 2d 479, 344 N.Y.S. 2d 270 (4th Dept. 1973) *affd.* 34 N.Y.2d 440, 358 NYS. 2d 367 (1974). *860 Exec. Towers, Inc.* v. *Board of Assessors* 53 A.D. 2d 463., 385 N.Y.S. 2d 604 (2d Dept. 1976), *affd.* 43 N.Y. 2d 769, 401, N.Y.S. 2d 1013. For an excellent discussion, see Morris, "Appraisals of Realty for Taxation."

78. This section is based on interviews with New York City's Department of Real Property Assessment and knowledgeable realtors, real-estate experts, and others. See acknowledgements to this study. See also Office of the State Comptroller, State of New York, *Assessment Practices of the Bureau of Real Property Assessment, New York City Department of Finance* (Audit Report NYC-66-26) (Albany, N.Y.: Comptroller, November 6, 1978); Office of the New York State Comptroller, Office of the Financial Deputy Comptroller for the City of New York, *Real Estate Assessment Practices in New York* (Report no. 32-81) (Albany N.Y.: Comptroller, August 8, 1980).

79. RPTL §§306.

80. See Mark A. Willis, "Reforming New York City's Property Tax: Issues and Options," *Federal Reserve Bank of New York Quarterly Review* 5, no. 2 (Summer 1980):14-16; New York State Division of Equalization and Assessment, *1976 Survey* (Albany, N.Y.: The Division, April 26, 1979); Dick Netzer et.al., *Real Property Tax Policy for New York City* (New York: New York University Graduate School of Public Administration, 1980).

81. *Hellerstein* v. *Assessor of Town of Islip*, 37 N.Y. 2d 1 (1975).

82. Kathlyn A. Gustafson, *Legislative and Administrative Response to the Hellerstein Decision-Progress Towards Full-Value Assessment* (Albany, N.Y.: New York State Division of Equalization and Assessment, November 10, 1978); New York State Assembly, Task Force on School Finance and Real Property Taxation, *The Legislative Response to the Property Tax Crisis: An Analysis of Public Policy Approaches to Classification* (Albany, N.Y.: The Assembly, September 1979).

83. Property Tax Classification Bill A. 10,000-D (1980).

84. See note 78.

CHAPTER FOUR

POLICY AND PROCEDURAL RECOMMENDATIONS FOR ASSESSING NEW YORK CITY LANDMARK PROPERTIES

Introduction

Previous chapters examined the interrelationship among landmark designation, property value, and property assessment, both nationally and in New York City. The analysis concluded that, depending on various property type/use and other characteristics, designation could increase, decrease, or not affect the price of historic buildings, and consequently landmark status should be factored by assessors in their valuing properties for real taxation purposes.

This chapter recommends specific policies and procedures for assessing landmarks in New York City. It commences with a statutory review of landmark-assessment approaches in jurisdictions throughout the United States. Summarizing the national state-of-the-art serves as a background resource for identifying possible strategies for application in this study. The chapter then recommends appropriate landmark-assessment policies for New York City and details how these revisions should be effected. Step-by-step procedures are discussed including (1) development of an appropriate data base/process so as to ensure that designation is incorporated into the assessment process; (2) specification of how the standard cost, sales, and income approaches used by assessors/appraisers should be applied in a landmark situation; and (3) consideration of appropriate supporting activities such as preparing educational materials to facili-

115

tate implementation of the proposed assessment standard. These steps are illustrated by reference to the six case-study landmarks (see chapter three). The chapter concludes with a brief discussion of how historic preservation strategies other than public designation—such as historic easements and transfer of development rights—can similarly affect property value and therefore should be factored by assessors.

An accompanying flow chart (Exhibit 1) summarizes the main steps in developing an appropriate landmark-assessment procedure. Exhibit 2 highlights the specific modifications to the cost, income, and sales valuation approaches that should be applied in the landmark case. These two exhibits provide a convenient synopsis; they are referred to and elaborated on in references throughout the chapter.

Background and Proposed Assessment Strategy

Statutory Responses by Other States

Appendix one of this study indicates that approximately half the states have enacted statutes dealing with historic-property assessment. These measures fall into two categories: assessment to reflect encumbrances and assessment at current use. Assessment to reflect encumbrances legislation typically specifies that the assessor should consider the landmark status of a property in determining its value for real-taxation purposes. South Dakota's statute §.1-19B-25 is typical. It states that the "designation and any recorded restrictions upon the property limiting its use for preservation purposes shall be considered by the assessor for appraising it for tax purposes." Almost identical language is found in Idaho (1975 Idaho Sess. Law ch 142.§.67 46515), North Carolina (N.C. Gen. Stat. §160A-399.5), and West Virginia (W. VA. Code Ann. §.8-26A-5-).

In most cases, the assessment to reflect encumbrances measures specify only that the assessor consider the presence of historic designation, thereby leaving the question of how this factor affects value to the discretion of the local assessor. There are some exceptions, however. Colorado statute §.39-1-101 prescribes that designation shall not add to value[1]: "Inclusion on the...register of historic properties shall add no value to the valuation for assessment." In contrast, Virginia statute §10-139-142 specifies that designation reduces value[2]: "Historic designation of a property shall be prima facie evidence that the value of such property for commercial, residential, or other purposes is reduced by reason of its designation." Other state statutes imply a reduction in value as a result of landmark designation. California

EXHIBIT I
FLOW CHART OF RECOMMENDED POLICIES/PROCEDURES
FOR ASSESSING LANDMARK PROPERTIES

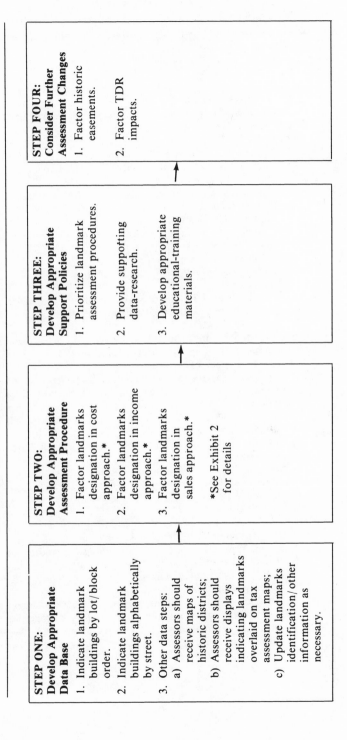

STEP ONE:
Develop Appropriate
Data Base

1. Indicate landmark buildings by lot/block order.

2. Indicate landmark buildings alphabetically by street.

3. Other data steps:
   a) Assessors should receive maps of historic districts;
   b) Assessors should receive displays indicating landmarks overlaid on tax assessment maps;
   c) Update landmarks identification/other information as necessary.

STEP TWO:
Develop Appropriate
Assessment Procedure

1. Factor landmarks designation in cost approach.*

2. Factor landmarks designation in income approach.*

3. Factor landmarks designation in sales approach.*

   *See Exhibit 2 for details

STEP THREE:
Develop Appropriate
Support Policies

1. Prioritize landmark assessment procedures.

2. Provide supporting data-research.

3. Develop appropriate educational-training materials.

STEP FOUR:
Consider Further
Assessment Changes

1. Factor historic easements.

2. Factor TDR impacts.

EXHIBIT 2
Assessment Considerations for Landmark Properties: Summary of Recommendations by Cost, Income, and Sales Valuation Procedures

I. COST APPROACH

Assess landmark properties on the basis of their land value plus improvements less depreciation.

A. Land Value
  a. The landmark site should be valued as if vacant and available.
  b. The landmark site should be valued at its current not highest and best use.
B. Improvement Value
  a. Value the landmark improvement according to its current use, not the highest and best use, even in the case where the landmark is nominally an uneconomic improvement.
  b. Calculate improvement value on a replacement, not reproduction type basis.
C. Depreciation
  a. Define and evaluate the applicable depreciation elements in the landmark case.
  b. Examine whether the ability to eliminate or "cure" depreciating characteristics is influenced by landmark status.

II. INCOME APPROACH

Capitalize net operating property income (gross property income less expenses) of the landmark building at the property's current use.

A. Landmark Property Gross Income
  a. Consider gross income at the landmark's current use; factor landmark alteration/demolition restrictions that may decrease income.
  b. Factor prestige value, protective, and other supports imbued by landmark designation that may increase property income.
B. Landmark Property Expenses
  a. Factor facade maintenance and regulatory-related expenses that can increase costs.
C. Landmark Property Capitalization Rate
  a. Determine if the components of the capitalization rate are influenced by landmark status.

III. SALES APPROACH

Assess the landmark property on the basis of appropriate comparable sales ("comps") that resemble the landmark being considered.

A. Selecting Appropriate "Comps" for Valuing the Landmark Properties
  a. The "comps" should have a similar intensity of use as the landmark.
  b. The "comps" should not have a redevelopment potential that is absent from the landmark.
  c. The "comps" should in other ways resemble the landmark property.
B. Adjusting the "Comps" in Valuing the Landmark Properties
  a. If the above conditions (III.-A.-a-c) are not met, adjustments should be made in determining the landmark property value on the basis of comparable sales.

C. The Landmark Property Sale as an Indicator of Value
   a. Where the sales price of the landmark property itself is considered as the basis for determining value, check if the sales transaction reflects actual market worth. (A higher than market price may be paid to acquire a landmark property in order to preserve it.)

Art. 13, §8 specifies that historically significant property is[3] "valued for property tax purposes only on the basis that is consistent with its restrictions and uses."

A second statutory approach is the specification that historic buildings be valued at their current rather than highest and best use. California statute §.50280-289, for example, requires that historic properties designated by the federal, state, county, or local governments be assessed for real-estate taxation purposes on the basis of their current utilization.[4] In Washington, D.C., landmarks are valued at their highest and best use and at their current use.[5] If the latter is lower than the former, then the current-use determination is the basis for the real-estate assessment (D.C. Code Encycl. §47-651-§47-654).

Recommended Assessment Policy for
New York City Landmark Properties

The range of landmark-assessment policies enacted in other jurisdictions provides a basis for discussing an appropriate response in New York City. Specifying assessment at current use, while surely an improvement, is an inadequate response. Landmark designation interfaces with property value in many ways: value may be enhanced through the conveyance of property prestige, protection, and other supports; value may be reduced by the imposition of alteration/demolition restrictions. Market attractiveness is influenced in other ways or may be independent of designation (see chapters two and three). The dynamics of this interface is not fully captured by the assessment at current use charge.

A second strategy is to direct assessors to "reflect encumbrances" in valuing landmarks. As indicated, this approach may take numerous forms. In some jurisdictions, assessors are mandated to asssume that designation decreases value; in other cases they are instructed that designation has no effect on value. Such prior specification of designation's impact is too constrictive in light of the wide range of the actual effects observed in the marketplace. Designation's specific impact must be determined by assessors on a case-by-case basis; generalizations do not suffice. It is therefore recommended that:

> the designation by the New York City Landmarks Preservation Commission of a property as a "landmark" or as being within an "historic district," which affects the property's use for preservation purposes shall be considered by the tax assessor, amongst other factors, in appraising such property for real property tax purposes.

This assessment charge is similar to that found in numerous states, including Idaho, North Carolina, and Virginia. Our landmark-property valuation recommendation thus follows the strategy taken by numerous other jurisdictions.

In proposing that New York City assessors factor landmark status, we do not specify the legal format for this charge—whether state-enabling legislation is required, if a local ordinance is necessary, if an official regulation is needed, or if the new assessment procedure can be accommodated through in-house departmental training procedures and educational programs effected by New York City's Real Property Assessment Department. While this legal issue is not considered, in the opinion of the co-chairmen of this study's advisory board (see Acknowledgments), the proposed changes in assessment do not require special statutory authorization or regulation; the New York City Real Property Assessment Department already possesses sufficient authority to provide for proper valuation procedures—for landmarks as well as other classes of property.

Develop An Appropriate Landmark-Assessment Approach

Recommending that designation "be considered" begs the question "how?" The following sections detail a four-step approach (see Exhibit 1):

Step One: Develop an appropriate data base.
Step Two: Develop appropriate assessment procedures.
Step Three: Develop appropriate support policies.
Step Four: Consider further assessment changes.

Step One: Develop An Appropriate Data Base

In order for assessors to value designated buildings, it is essential that they be able to identify which properties are landmarks. Such property identification can be effected quickly and inexpensively because the

Landmarks Preservation Commission (LPC) has a computer file already listing the block and lot numbers of all designated properties in New York City. LPC can transfer this data base to the Real Property Assessment Department (RPA).

The historic-property log can be structured in a number of possible alternative formats, all of them useful to RPA. One possibility is to display the landmarks in their numbered block and lot order for each of the five boroughs. An example, shown in Exhibit 3, lists a number of Manhattan's designated properties in block/lot sequence and also indicates their street address, name (where appropriate, i.e., Town Hall, New York County Lawyers' Association building), and landmark status (individual landmark, building in a historic district, or interior landmark).

With such a file, an assessor responsible for valuing properties in a particular area can readily identify the number and location of inclusive historic buildings by checking the latter's block/lot numbers. An assessor examining tax blocks 80 through 90 in lower Manhattan could determine, by referring to a data matrix similar to that shown in Exhibit 3, that this area includes the New York County Lawyers' Association building and other designated properties. This data log would additionally inform the assessor the category of landmarks that would be confronted on these tax blocks (i.e., individual landmark, property in a historic district, and so on)—an important notification because, as discussed in chapter two designation type may bear on the landmark-property value linkage.

Another data approach is to arrange the landmark file alphabetically by street location. Exhibit 4 illustrates how this information could be ordered. While containing similar descriptive material as that shown in Exhibit 3, it arranges the historic properties alphabetically by street address. An assessor would similarly use this file to identify the number, location, and type of landmarks to be valued in the assessment district he/she is responsible for. If this area includes Vesey Street, then Exhibit 4 indicates the presence of the landmark New York County Lawyers' Association building, an individually designated property; if it encompasses West 43rd Street, then the assessor would be responsible for valuing Town Hall, an individual landmark with interior landmark status as well.

The two information schemata discussed above are presented not as alternatives; rather they serve as illustrations of multiple possible arrangements of designation information. Given the fact that the basic landmark-property data are already computerized, it is a relatively simple matter to generate different historic building-location files if these variations are useful to the field-level assessor. Identification of historic properties would be further enhanced by the following actions:

1. The Real Property Assessment Department (RPA) should use maps of

EXHIBIT 3
EXAMPLE OF LANDMARK PROPERTY LISTING
BY BLOCK AND LOT NUMBERS

Borough	Block	Lot	Address	Name of Building	Individual Landmark	Landmark Category Property in Historic District	Interior Landmark
Manhattan	3	1	State Street and Battery Place	Battery Park Control House	X		
Manhattan	9	7	7 State Street	James Watson House	X		
Manhattan	26	1	23 Wall Street	Morgan Guaranty Trust Co.	X		
Manhattan	29	1	71 Pearl Street	Not applicable	X		
Manhattan	88	2	14 Vesey Street	New York County Lawyers Association	X		
Manhattan	497	18	72 Prince Street	Not applicable		Soho-Cast Iron District	
Manhattan	526	44	74 MacDougal Street	Not applicable		MacDougal-Sullivan District	
Manhattan	584	1	69 Morton Street	Not applicable		Greenwich Village District	
Manhattan	996	21	113-23 West 43rd Street	Town Hall	X		X

Source: New York Landmarks Preservation Commission.

EXHIBIT 4

EXAMPLE OF LANDMARK PROPERTY LISTING
ARRANGED ALPHABETICALLY BY STREET LOCATION

Borough	Street Name	Street Address (Number)	Block/Lot	Name of Building	Individual Landmark	Landmark Category Property in Historic District	Interior Landmark
Manhattan	Abingdon Square	1	624/25	Not applicable		Greenwich Village District	
Manhattan	Bank Street	1	615/36	Not applicable		Greenwich Village District	
Manhattan	Broome Street	432	483/35	Not applicable		Soho-Cast Iron District	
Manhattan	Charles Street	1	612/65	Not applicable		Greenwich Village District	
Manhattan	Charles Street	131	632/30	Charles St. House	X		
Manhattan	Hanover Street	1	27/9	India House	X		
Manhattan	Lafayette Street	428-434	545/37-40	Colonnade Row	X		
Manhattan	Vesey Street	14	88/2	New York County Lawyers' Association	X		
Manhattan	West 43rd Street	113-23	996/21	Town Hall	X		X

Source: New York Landmarks Preservation Commission.

the historic districts. These are useful for graphically showing the boundaries of the historic districts. An example for the Soho-Cast Iron District is shown in Exhibit 5.

2. The Real Property Assessment Department should consider a strategy of graphically displaying the location/type of landmarks on its assessment district maps. (Computerized mapping routines are available to facilitate such identification.) This step would give the assessor a direct, visual indication of the location, number, and type of designated properties to be valued.

3. Since there are separate RPA branch offices for each borough, and field-level assessors deal mainly with these offices, listing the number, location, and type of landmarks by borough should also be considered.

4. Each assessor should also be given copies of the very informative pamphlet *A Guide to New York City Landmarks*, published by the Landmarks Preservation Commission. The *Guide* lists and describes the historic districts and individual landmarks found in different areas of all five boroughs. District boundaries are displayed, albeit on a scale that makes it difficult to define their exact borders—hence the need for the separate district maps mentioned above. Individual landmark buildings are listed in alphabetical order (along with a brief description) for different sections of each borough. To illustrate, in the Battery to Fulton Street area of Manhattan, the Guide shows the borders of the South Street Seaport Historic District (see Exhibit 6) and then lists and describes such individual historic buildings as Citibank (55 Wall Street), Federal Hall National Memorial (28 Wall Street), and the Federal Reserve Bank (33 Liberty Street).

The data/display system envisioned above requires the joint participation of the Landmarks Preservation Commission (LPC) and the Real Property Assessment (RPA) department. It is encouraging to report that LPC and RPA have already begun to work together on preparing a suitable landmark file for assessors. LPC should also introduce RPA staff to the background, process, and significance of landmark designation in New York City. Such introduction could take the form of short lectures or summary memoranda prepared by the LPC as well as dissemination of informational booklets published by LPC. One example, *A Guide to New York City Landmarks*, has been described above. The LPC reprinting of New York City's landmark statute should also be distributed to RPA assessors. This publication is entitled *Local Laws of the City of New York Governing the Establishment, and Regulation of Landmarks, Landmark Sites, Interior Landmarks, Scenic Landmarks, and Historic Districts*. Further educational/training materials are considered later in this chapter (see Step Three).

EXHIBIT 5
SOHO - CAST IRON HISTORIC DISTRICT
MANHATTAN

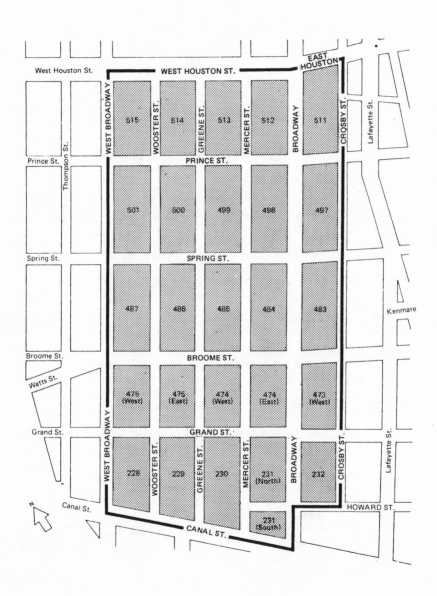

Source: New York City Landmarks Preservation Commission

EXHIBIT 6
EXAMPLE OF LANDMARK LISTING IN A GUIDE TO
NEW YORK CITY LANDMARKS

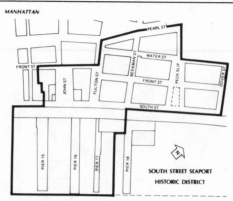

Battery to Fulton Street

SOUTH STREET SEAPORT HISTORIC DISTRICT. One of the most fascinating areas in the city, retaining much of its early 19th century atmosphere, and revitalized by the manifold cultural and restoration programs sponsored by the South Street Seaport Museum (est. 1967). Seaport activities, which evolved from a small cluster of wharves in the 18th century to one of the leading ports in the nation by the mid-19th century, are reflected in the mercantile buildings erected to serve its expanding needs in the days of packet ships, clippers and steamers. Many buildings are rare surviving examples of Georgian-Federal and Greek Revival style, formerly owned by such prominent merchants as Peter Schermerhorn, Josiah Macy and Abiel Abbot Low. (See Schermerhorn Block.)

BAKER, CARVER & MORRELL (170-176 JOHN STREET BUILDING), SOUTH STREET SEAPORT H.D. This handsome Greek Revival building of 1840, restored by the ship chandlery which occupies it, may be the last survivor of a type of commercial structure, introduced to New York from Boston in 1829 by Town & Davis, faced with granite from top to bottom, with massive piers separating the display windows.

BATTERY MARITIME BUILDING (originally MUNICIPAL FERRY PIERS), N.Y.C. DEPARTMENT OF MARINE AND AVIATION PIERS, 11 South Street. The last surviving ferry building on the East River, it served from 1909 to 1938 as the Manhattan terminal of the ferry to South Brooklyn, providing passengers with a dramatic approach to Manhattan. Designed in the Roman Classical tradition with a delightful esplanade on top of the building. Interior renovated for city offices; Coast Guard service to Governor's Island departs from here.

BATTERY PARK CONTROL HOUSE, State Street and Battery Place. One of the last remaining kiosks of the city's first subway system. Built in 1904-05, according to the plans of Heins & LaFarge, in French Beaux-Arts style.

Source: New York City Landmarks Preservation Commission, *A Guide to New York City Landmarks* (New York: Commission, n. d.), p. 2.

Step Two: Develop Appropriate Assessment Procedures

Identifying those properties which are landmarks is a first step to be followed by application of an appropriate valuation process (see Exhibit 1). Assessors must realize the diversity of impact that designation may have on property value and the consequent need of avoiding generalizations— mechanical procedures or rules of thumb will not suffice.[6] Assessment of each designated building is accomplished by applying the cost, income, and sales approaches traditionally used by assessors/appraisers with the modifications/emphases described below. Discussion is keyed to the summary of recommendations shown in Exhibit 2 (i.e., recommendation I, I.A., I.A.a., etc.) and refers to the six case-study properties to illustrate specific points. (This reference does not imply that RPA assessors did or did not follow the recommended procedures; as discussed in chapter three, it is unclear exactly how RPA valued the six case-study buildings.)

Applying The Cost-Valuation Approach To Landmark Properties

This technique examines the components of land, improvements, and depreciation: property value is equal to the sum of land value plus improvement value less depreciation. A single-family home located on a lot costing $20,000, where the construction cost of the structure is $100,000, and where the structure's depreciation is estimated at $20,000, would thus be valued at $100,000 ($20,000 + $100,000 - $20,000).

In applying the cost approach to the landmark property, the three components of land, improvement, and depreciation are factored with special attention paid to each.

Landmark-Property Land Value

> I.A.a. The landmark site should be valued as if vacant and available.

> I.A.b. The landmark site should be valued at its current, not highest and best use.

The cost-approach values land according to the assumption that the site is "vacant and available to be utilized to its highest and best use." The price that the "vacant" land would command is influenced by such factors as the property's (1) location (Central Business District, suburb, rural area, frontage on a prestige street, etc.); (2) size and other physical characteristics (total lot square footage, frontage, width, depth, and so on); (3) public/

private land use controls (zoning, subdivision regulations, easements, and covenants) affecting the permitted type and density of development; and (4) other features, such as the availability/quality of utilities and municipal services.

It is an interesting conceptual issue how the site value of a landmark should be determined. Should the basic approach of examining land as if "vacant and available" be followed if landmark designation, by impeding if not prohibiting demolition of the improvement, precludes the vacant state from being attained? In the author's opinion, the answer is yes. The separation of land from improvements and the valuation of the site as if "vacant and available" are conceptual analyses—they are not restricted only to those cases where it is likely or practical that the site will be reused. As discussed in the Society of Real Estate Appraisers' *An Introduction to Appraising Real Property*[7]:

> The Cost Approach is frequently referred to as the Summation Approach because it involves estimating the value of site and improvements independently; and then summing them to obtain the estimate of property value. It must be clear and definite, however, that the objective of value estimation in real estate appraising is the whole property, and not of its component parts. The separation is made for analytical purposes only.

While the landmark site should be valued as if "vacant and available," it should be not assessed as if available to be utilized to its "highest and best use," because designation's alteration/demolition restrictions may preclude the attainment of this state (see chapters two and three). Instead, a landmark property's land value is determined on the basis of its current use. This valuation approach is especially critical when the landmark's current use is far below its highest and best use, for, as discussed in chapter two, it is precisely in this situation that designation controls may exert a severe discount on property value. Designation of the Metropolitan Club means that the land underneath this clubhouse is not worth the amount that would be paid for a 20,000-square-foot lot (with 100 feet of Fifth Avenue frontage) located in a prime Manhattan neighborhood undergoing intense office-tower development, because landmark status disallows construction of an office building on this site. The Metropolitan Club's land value is based on its current development density, namely, a four-story clubhouse-type structure of about 50,000 square feet* located on fashionable Fifth

---

*Figure is approximate and includes clubhouse structure only, not the annex.

Avenue. Similarly, the land value of 311 East 58th Street is not determined at its nominal highest and best use (development of a roughly 20,000-square-foot residential improvement—the maximum density allowed by zoning) but rather according to its current use—a 2,500-square-foot townhouse residence—since this property's landmark status and air-rights sale impedes attainment of its highest and best use.

Landmark-Property Improvement Value

In addition to land, the cost approach also estimates improvement value. In a landmark situation an assessor should:

I.B.a.   Value the landmark improvement according to its current use, not the highest and best use, even in the case where the landmark is nominally an uneconomic improvement.

I.B.b   Calculate improvement value on a replacement, not reproduction-type basis.

This recommendation is similar to the previous one regarding the landmark's land and, as we shall see momentarily, it is based on similar reasoning. To understand the importance of always valuing the landmark improvement on the basis of current use, it is instructive to discuss briefly how improvement value normally is estimated.

The cost approach determines this component on the basis of the improvement's current use as long as the extant utilization is economically sensible—it does not have to be the most profitable exploitation (highest and best use), yet should represent a function that would be kept by a knowledgeable buyer or owner. To illustrate, a 100,000-square-foot office building located in a zone allowing a 110,000-square-foot office tower is not the highest and best use improvement, yet would likely be kept as is—the owner of such a property would not demolish the structure and replace it with a new building because the demolition/new construction costs would likely not be justified on the basis of the added 10,000 square feet of rentable office space that would then be available. In some cases, however, the current improvement so differs from the highest and best use that a knowledgeable investor would demolish the existing structure and build one dictated by market conditions. To continue the example given above, if, instead of a 100,000-square-foot office tower, there were an existing building containing 50,000 square feet, this property would more likely be replaced by a new 110,000-square-foot structure. In such an underimprovement situation as it is termed, assessor/appraisal texts stress the importance of the cost approach anticipating the market[8]: improvement value is determined according to the more profitable future function.

Landmark-property improvement is always valued on the basis of current use even in those cases where the landmark's current use is an uneconomic improvement.* The "standard procedure of assuming a hypothetical higher use in the underimprovement situation is not applicable because a historic building that is uneconomically improved today will likely remain as such because of landmark alteration/demolition restrictions. Valuing the landmark improvement on the basis of its extant use is similar to the prior recommendation of assessing landmark land at its existing, not a more intensive, utilization. The logic for both procedures is the same— the components (land and improvement) of a landmark must be valued at their actual economic basis; their use today—not according to a theoretically more profitable one that in practice is unrealizable because of landmark redevelopment restraints. The Metropolitan Club is a classic example of an underimprovement. In applying the cost approach to this property, an assessor would value the club's component land and improvements at their current use (land: 20,000-square-foot lot, located on Fifth Avenue, where a maximum improvement of about 50,000 square feet is permitted; improvement: 50,000-square-foot clubhouse structure) because the club has landmark status and therefore will likely be kept as is—it will not be demolished and replaced by an office tower. (This approach assumes that the Metropolitan Club will not be demolished. As discussed in chapter one, however, New York City's landmark statute does not absolutely prohibit the demolition of designated buildings.)

Landmark-Property Improvement Value

In addition to the intensity of the landmark improvement, assessors should consider which improvement concept is most applicable in the landmark situation: reproduction or replacement. Reproduction cost is defined as[9]:

---

*An uneconomic improvement differs from a hardship situation. In the former, the maximum profit is not realized; in the latter, there is so little return so as to threaten the property's continued maintenance/existence.

the cost of construction...of an exact duplicate or replica using the same materials, construction standards, design, layout, and quality of workmanship embodying all the deficiencies, superadequacies and obsolescence of the subject building.

Replacement outlay is the[10]:

cost of construction at current prices of a building having utility equivalent to the building being appraised but built with modern materials and according to the current standards, design and layout.... The essence of replacement cost is that it represents the same utility, whereas reproduction cost requires the same physical structure.

Which improvement notion-reproduction or replacement-is appropriate in considering a landmark? There is no definitive answer to this question. From a conceptual perspective, the former is more appealing because by stressing the special and unique qualities of each property as opposed to functional equivalents (i.e., a twelve-foot rather than an eight-foot ceiling) it seems to embody the sensitivity of preservationists to these very same features. The replacement-cost approach, however, has practical merit for the following reasons:

1. Landmark properties, almost by definition, contain materials and examples of workmanship that are rare or even nonexistent today. Consequently, it is difficult and time-consuming accurately to estimate the expenditure of reproducing the landmark. It would be problematical to determine the expense of redoing the Metropolitan Club's exterior, characterized by detail work that is rarely found in contemporary times (i.e., the marble and copper cornice has a series of detailed, classical moldings). The club's interior has marble, metal, and mural treatments that similarly are testimonials to bygone workmanship (see Exhibits 8 and 9 in chapter three). Similar one-of-a-kind crafts and materials characterize Town Hall's interior, the Corinthian Colonnade in the Grange, the facade work on the New York County Lawyers' Association building and other landmarks. Those unique building features that typically distinguish a property as historic make it inherently difficult to estimate reproduction costs.

2. An additional and more fundamental disadvantage of applying the reproduction-cost approach in a landmark case concerns its accuracy. The drawback arises from the high cost of landmark-quality reproduction. If this considerable expenditure is used for calculating the improvement value, then the overall estimate of landmark worth (land and improvements) derived by applying the cost approach will typically be in error because it will yield a figure exceeding that supported by the marketplace. It is very likely that the reproduction cost of Town Hall, New York County Lawyers'

Association, and similar historic properties (even without factoring the value added by their land component) exceeds the full price that a willing, knowledgeable buyer would pay for these buildings. In short, application of the reproduction-cost approach when considering landmarks will often violate a fundamental tenet of appraisal—that the estimate of value reflect the realities of the market. As summarized by the Society of Real Estate Appraisers[11]: "Cost is not the same as value; cost does not create value.... The value estimation is market-oriented and must reflect the market data and market behavior of purchasers."

For the reasons cited above, it is therefore recommended that the landmark improvement value be estimated on a replacement, not reproduction basis. (Valuing the landmark by considering its reproduction cost would be acceptable only in the rare case where an informed buyer would pay a premium for the property that would approach reproduction costs.) In appraising the improvement at 311 East 58th Street, an assessor should consider the current cost of constructing a 2,500-square-foot, two-and-a-half-story townhouse. Improvement value of the New York County Lawyers' Association building is the cost of replacing the extant structure with a four-story one containing approximately 30,000 square feet of office, library, conference-room space. Since the objective is to define functional replacement, not exact reproduction, it is not necessary to factor such "reproduction" type items as the lintel/cornice and scroll bracket treatments of 311 East 58th Street or the stone construction and bas relief-rail ornamentation of the New York County Lawyers' Association building.

Landmark-Property Depreciation Calculation

In addition to land and the improvement, the third component considered by the cost approach is depreciation. In assessing a landmark property the following characteristics related to depreciation should be noted:

I.C.a. Define and evaluate the applicable depreciation elements in the landmark case.

I.C.b. Examine whether the ability to eliminate or "cure" depreciating characteristics is influenced by landmark status.

Define and Evaluate Depreciation
Elements in the Landmark Case

Assessment/appraisal practice recognizes three components of depreciation: economic, physical, and functional. Economic depreciation is that loss in value experienced by a structure as a result of negative environmental forces outside the boundaries of the property. Physical depreciation is the reduction in utility relating to physical condition. Functional depreciation is impairment of functional capacity or efficiency.[12]

To illustrate, many central cities in the Northeast and Midwest have an abundance of aging and increasingly vacant factory and loft space. Economic factors impacting on this manufacturing sector, such as competition from other regions of the country or from foreign nations, are economic depreciation characteristics. Aging of the basic central-city manufacturing plant, with attendant deterioration of mechanical, plumbing, and other systems, is an example of physical depreciation. Obsolescence of this manufacturing plant in terms of space, layout, ceiling height, etc. are functionally depreciating elements.

When depreciation is considered in a landmark situation, it is first important to define what factors are applicable. Building traits that "normally" are considered value-detracting may be less of a drawback or even an attraction in an historic structure. Consumer preference as shown in the marketplace is the ultimate determinant of what is value-adding versus value-detracting and the market response is often different to landmark versus nonlandmark properties. Twelve-to fifteen-foot ceiling height, older bathroom and lighting fixtures, appealing yet difficult-to-maintain interior and exterior decorative treatments, and so on are characteristics that would typically depreciate value, yet are the very traits that may add to the attractiveness of the historic property.

While landmarks may be less vulnerable to certain commonly accepted depreciating factors (especially in residential situations), they may be more prone to other depreciating elements because of their age and design by yesterday's standards. Such traits are admittedly not caused by the act of designation; however, they are frequently associated with landmark buildings. As expressed by Richard Almy, research director of the International Association of Assessing Officers[13]:

> Owners and preservationists would be advised to examine closely depreciation estimating practices in their communities. Economic and functional obsolescence in particular are apt to apply to historic properties.

It is essential to determine in each landmark case what are the applicable depreciating characteristics. The case-study properties are illustrative for they display a variety of economic, physical, and functional depreciation. Town Hall, located in a neighborhood that has experienced steady deterioration over the past two decades, suffers from economic *cum* locational depreciation. Town Hall is also negatively affected by the economic competition posed by the construction of Lincoln Center in Manhattan and the resurgence of the Brooklyn Academy of Music. Changing concert-hall economics also puts Town Hall at a disadvantage.

Physical deterioration is evident at 311 East 58th Street. This townhouse suffers from water-damage problems as a result of roof and pointing work that has not been attended to; the property was also adversely affected by the demolition/new construction of an adjacent building. The New York County Lawyers' Association building is characterized by functional obsolescence as a result of its twenty-foot ceilings, absence of adequate bathroom facilities, and antiquated elevator, electrical, and plumbing systems. Town Hall's shallow stage (twelve feet) is another example of functional depreciation because, as a consequence, this auditorium cannot be used for plays and other performances requiring larger stage space.

Landmark Status and "Curing" Depreciation

Depreciation is not immutable; economic factors change with the varying dictates of the marketplace. To illustrate, the renewal activity planned for midtown Manhattan (construction of middle-class housing, new hotels, and office space) will likely improve the neighborhood's desirability and with this change, the location of Town Hall, now an economic drawback, may turn into an asset.

Physical and functional depreciation elements associated with a property may also be removed or "cured." Physical water damage at 311 East 58th Street can be stopped by repairing the roof and doing whatever pointing is required. Functional obsolescence can also be turned. Installation of a modern self-operating elevator and new plumbing and electrical systems in the New York County Lawyers' Association building would make it much more functional for modern office space.

Assessors/appraisers refer to the alleviation of depreciation as "curing" and test the ability to "cure" depreciation on an economic yardstick[14]:

> Physical deterioration and functional obsolescence often are considered in
> categories of curable and incurable, and it is important for the appraiser to
> understand the distinction. Nearly all deterioration can be cured if enough
> money is spent. The term curable as used in appraising, should be reserved
> for only those items of depreciation considered to be economically sound
> to cure.

A depreciating element that normally would be considered "curable" on the basis of the economics test described above may, in a landmark case, be "incurable" because the requisite change is prohibited by alteration/demolition restrictions. Expansion of the Town Hall stage, and other major interior alterations that would make this building more functional and would be justified on the basis of the dollar return of the investment, would probably be prohibited because of the auditorium's interior-landmark status (see chapter three). It is also uncertain whether alterations to the New York County Lawyers' Association building to remove certain functional depreciating elements would be permitted by the New York City Landmarks Preservation Commission (see chapter three). Assessors applying the cost approach in a landmark situation should consequently examine whether landmark status affects the ability to "cure" depreciation.

Applying the Income Valuation
Approach to Landmark Properties

The income approach determines property value by capitalizing the net generated property income. Operationally, it consists of first projecting the annual gross income and then estimating the yearly costs of property operation and maintenance. Subtracting expenses from revenues yields the annual net property income. Annual income is converted to an estimate of property value by dividing the net annual yield by an appropriate capitalization rate.

In applying the income-valuation technique to a landmark situation, special consideration should be given to the inclusive steps of determining the appropriate (1) property gross income; (2) property expenses; and (3) capitalization basis.

Landmark-Property Gross-Income Determination

Assessors examining the gross income generated by a landmark should:

II.A.a. Factor gross income at the landmark's current use; factor landmark alteration/demolition restrictions that may decrease income;

II.A.b. Factor prestige value, protective, and other supports imbued by designation that may increase income.

As discussed in chapters two and three, landmark alteration/demolition restrictions can curtail a building's intensity of use to its current application; a higher intensity, such as that afforded by demolishing a smaller structure and replacing it with a larger one, cannot be realized. Consequently, in valuing a landmark by means of the income approach, the property's gross income should be based on its current use; the assessor must thus factor landmark alteration/demolition controls that may decrease income. This valuation approach is especially critical where the landmark's current use is far below its highest and best use, for it is precisely in that situation that designation's restraining affect on building usage/income/value will be most pronounced (see chapter two).

All the case-study buildings should thus be valued at their current-income status. Income flow of 311 East 58th Street is the estimated amount for which this 2,500-square-foot townhouse could be rented, not the income that would be generated by a 20,000-square-foot structure. The Metropolitan Club's income is the estimated rent-generating capacity of the extant clubhouse, not that of the office tower that might be built on the site in the absence of landmark status. Similarly, the income flow of the New York County Lawyers' Association building is the market rent for the size and type of office space found there.

In contrast, in other instances, historic designation adds to income. Chapter two of this study cited numerous cases where tenants or owner-/users were willing to pay a premium for occupancy in a landmark because of designation's prestige, protective, and similar supports. Assessors examining a landmark's gross income should be alert to designation's supportive influences, especially in situations where these prestige and other consequences are most prone (i.e., residential or commercial uses located in a historic district; see discussion on property and designation type in chapter two). In short, both the income-detracting as well as income-enhancing features of historic status deserve scrutiny.

Landmark-Property Operating-Cost Determination

From gross property income, property expenses are subtracted to yield the net return. Property costs include those outlays directly related to building operation and maintenance, including payroll, repairs, fire/hazard insurance premiums, and management fees. Such property expenses will typically not differ for historic properties, although there are some exceptions. In valuing a landmark by means of income approach, assessors should consider special facade maintenance as well as regulatory-related expenses that may increase costs.

Designation may increase a building's facade expenses by requiring retention/repair of certain difficult to maintain exteriors (i.e., terra cotta, tile, and gilded finishes) that in a nonlandmarked building might be replaced with more modern and less costly to maintain surfaces (see chapter two). In addition, there are possible regulatory costs imposed by landmark status, namely, direct and indirect expenses to secure regulatory-body approval to alter the historic property (see chapter two; this is in addition to other regulations which New York City properties are subject to, i.e. building department specifications). While these landmark facade and regulatory features may be relatively minor as far as impact on property value is concerned, they nonetheless should be noted by the assessor, especially in those cases where they are most likely to apply—buildings with the above-mentioned special exteriors; properties with a greater likelihood of being altered and therefore subject to regulatory review (i.e., retail establishments with major storefronts); and buildings located in jurisdictions with burdensome landmark review procedures. (See discussion on facade characteristics, landmark change potential, and regulatory review process in chapter two.)

A final point concerns the type of building costs considered in the income approach. Only cash expenses for operating the property are counted—depreciation and any other purely bookkeeping deductions are therefore ignored. This specification is significant in the case of landmarks for, as indicated in chapter one, certain designated properties are eligible for special federal accelerated-depreciation provisions. Since depreciation is a bookkeeping expense item, it would not be counted in the income approach's tally of costs.

Landmark-Property Capitalization Rate

Dividing net income (gross income less expenses) by a capitalization rate yields a final estimate of property value. The capitalization rate often varies over time and across classes of investments. It is composed of four separate components[15]:

1. Real return: The return required by an investor to refrain from immediate consumption and utilize capital for investment purposes.

2. Inflation premium: The additional or incremental return that must be given to an investor to induce a deferral of consumption during a period of inflation.

3. Risk premium: The return required to compensate for investment risk.

4. Recapture premium: An element representing recapture of the original investment.

For the most part, the capitalization rate will not differ with respect to historic properties, yet there may be exceptions. Will investors, in the interest of preservation, accept a lower rate of return on a landmark? If so, the real return and inflation premium are altered and so is the capitalization rate. Risk premium may also differ in a landmark situation. The market may judge a historic property an investment of either greater risk (i.e., where extensive exterior alterations are contemplated), in which case the risk premium and consequently the capitalization rate would be higher; or lesser risk (i.e., where demand is strong for landmark buildings), in which case the risk premium and ultimately the capitalization rate will be lower. Recapture premium may also be altered: if the useful economic life of a landmark is relatively shorter (because of age, design, or other reasons), then the annual rate of return of invested capital will have to be increased, thereby raising the capitalization rate. An opposite effect will occur if the landmark's useful life is deemed relatively longer (possibly because of a favorable market reaction). Assessors should determine if the components of the capitalization rate are influenced by landmark status and, if so, should make appropriate adjustments.

Applying the Sales Approach to Landmark Properties

The sales approach involves direct comparison of the property being assessed (termed the subject property) to similar buildings (termed comparables or, for short, "comps") that have sold in the same or a similar market in order to derive a market value indication of the subject property.

Select Appropriate "Comps" for Valuing Landmark Properties

An essential step in the sales approach is to select appropriate "comps"[16]:

> Not every residential property which has recently sold on the local market is a comparable sale. Both physical characteristics and economic conditions must be investigated.

Since landmark properties may have special "physical and economic" characteristics affecting their market price, it is especially important for assessors to select appropriate "comps":

III.A.a. The "comps" should have a similar intensity of use as the landmark.

III.A.b. The "comps" should not have a redevelopment potential that is absent with the landmark.

III.A.c. The "comps" should in other ways reflect the landmark property being examined.

III.A.d. If the above conditions are not met, adjustments should be made in determining the landmark-property value on the basis of comparative sales.

Intensity of Use/Redevelopment Potential

Landmark status and attendant alteration/demolition restrictions can affect intensity of use. In estimating the value of a landmark, it is consequently important to ensure that the comparables have a parallel utilization. Chelsea Hotel should be compared to a similar type/size hospitality residence; the New York County Lawyers' Association building should be matched to a clubhouse/office structure of approximately 30,000 square feet; the appropriate "comp" for 311 East 58th Street is a townhouse of about 2,500 square feet.

In addition to the "comps" having a similar intensity of use as the landmark subject parcel, the "comps" should also not have a redevelopment potential that is absent with the subject historic building. If such equivalence is absent, the "comps" are possibly worth more than the seemingly similar landmark, for the latter's alteration/demolition restrictions impede its redevelopment possibilities. In valuing the Metropolitan Club, the properties used for "comp" purposes should be about the same size/type and should not have the potential of being demolished and replaced by an office tower because the Metropolitan Club likely cannot similarly be redeveloped. The appropriate comparable for 311 East 58th Street is a townhouse of 2,500 square feet that will remain as such, not a townhouse that an investor may have purchased for a high sum for assemblage purposes—a use not open to the subject parcel.

It is important to select appropriate "comps" in other ways as well. Landmark buildings may sometimes have prestige, protection, and other attractions that enhance value. Comparison properties should have a parallel appeal or their sales prices will have to be adjusted. (The adjustment process is considered shortly.) Other property value consequences of designation should similarly be noted in defining appropriate "comps" for designated buildings. Care in selecting correct comparables is especially critical where landmark-property value effects are most prone or severe, both in a value-enhancing sense (i.e., residential/commercial uses in historic districts), or value-detracting dimension (i.e., where the landmark's current use is far below its highest and best use; see chapter two for details).

Adjusting the "Comps" in Valuing Landmark Properties

One possible way of ensuring that "comps" indeed mirror the landmark subject parcel is to limit "comps" to landmarks only. Such an approach is most readily applied in the historic districts, especially the larger areas containing many buildings where a reasonable number of sales for comparison purposes can be obtained. The value of properties in Greenwich

Village, Park Slope, and Brooklyn Heights—the three largest historic districts—could be estimated by referring to recent sales prices of comparable structures within these same areas. Individual landmarks could also be matched with appropriate designated* sister buildings, albeit the match will often be difficult because of the frequent one-of-a-kind nature of the individual landmark. To illustrate, 311 East 58th Street could be assessed by examining sales of other close-by designated townhouses such as 312 East 53rd Street, 157-67 East 78th Street and so on.[17] In contrast, it would be very difficult to value Town Hall, the Metropolitan Club, and the New York County Lawyers' Association building on the basis of landmark "comps" because there are few buildings (landmark or not) that are similar enough to be considered for comparison purposes.[18]

There are then practical problems in limiting "comps" to other landmarks. Pragmatism dictates that historic structures be valued on the basis of comparables that include landmark as well as nonlandmark properties. Adjustments, however, must be made to reflect the special characteristics that distinguish landmarks and affect their value. These include prestige-protection and other supports as well as special facade/regulatory costs and alteration/demoliton restrictions.[19]

For example, 311 East 58th Street could be assessed by examining the sales prices of roughly comparable nonlandmark townhouses in the same Manhattan neighborhood. In such a case, the following adjustments might be made:

Differences in redevelopment potential. The non-historic "comps" potentially could be redeveloped with an improvement of 20,000 square feet. (This assumes that they are subject to the same zoning provisions that govern 311 East 58th Street.) In short, the "comps" may have been sold for a higher price than a knowledgeable buyer would offer for the subject parcel—311 East 58th Street. Consequently, in valuing the subject property on the basis of the nonlandmark sales, a downward adjustment would be made from the nominal "comp" sale prices.

Differences in prestige value. The "comps," not being landmarks, may lack a prestige value associated with the landmark 311 East 58th Street. The "comps" may therefore have been sold for a lower price than a know-

---

*The "comp" designated properties could be either individual landmarks or properties within historic districts. In most cases, the former would be the closer match because properties in historic districts are affected by spatial influences absent in the case of the individual landmark (see Chapter Two).

ledgeable buyer would offer for the more attractive subject parcel. In that case, in assessing 311 East 58th Street on the basis of nonlandmark "comps," an upward adjustment would be made from the "comp" sales figures.

Property condition/other standard adjustment items. As discussed previously, 311 East 58th Street requires roofing, pointing, and other work. These demands would have to be compared to the physical condition of the nonhistoric "comps." Other adjustments might have to be made to factor such variables as the time of sale (more current transfers are a better indicator) and sale terms (i.e., the sales price would likely be inflated in the case of the seller taking back a mortgage). All of these variables are standard factors adjusted for by assessors/appraisers in utilizing the sales approach.

The Landmark-Property Sale as an Indicator of Value

If the subject property itself has sold recently, this transaction is considered to be a very good, perhaps the best reflection of the subject's "true" worth. A recent sale of a designated property would similarly serve as an excellent indicator of its value with the following precaution kept in mind:

III.C.   When the sales price of the landmark property is considered as the basis for determining its value, check if the sales transaction reflects actual market desirability.

Historic property transfer may not be a valid indicator because in certain instances a higher than "regular" market price may have been paid to acquire a landmark in order to preserve it. In such an instance, determining value on the basis of the landmark sales price would constitute an overvaluation. Assessors should examine the landmark sales transaction to ascertain the presence of possible "special motivating conditions" influencing purchase price.

This recommendation is based on a concept that assessor/appraisal texts refer to as "motivating force."[20] In the market approach, a sale is considered a valid indication as long as it is made by a willing buyer and a willing seller "neither acting under abnormal pressure." "Abnormal pressure" includes property sales/purchases motivated by sentimental interest, assemblage purposes, estate liquidation reasons and so on. In these instances, the sales prices are likely either higher than "real" market value (i.e., in acquiring a property for sentimental interests) or lower (i.e., when the seller must liquidate for estate purposes). Since the sales prices are influenced by atypical considerations rather than overall, prevailing market conditions, they are not valid mirrors of market price.

Purchasing a landmark for a special reason such as to save it from threatened demolition may constitute a sale under "abnormal pressure." Sales price in such a situation is therefore not a good indicator of value and must be adjusted for accordingly.

Step Three: Develop Appropriate Support Policies

In addition to discussing appropriate assessment approaches for landmark properties, it is essential to consider support policies for assisting the implementation of the procedures such as (1) priority of the recommendations; (2) data needs; and (3) research needs (see Exhibit 1).

Priority of the Landmark-Valuation Recommendations

Of the many recommendations discussed previously (see Exhibit 2) some are more important than others. Assessment of designated properties on the basis of their current, not highest and best use is the most critical consideration. As seen in Exhibit 2, the stress on current use underlies approach I.B.a. in the cost approach, II.A.a. in the income approach, and III.A.a. and b. in the sales approach. This policy is emphasized because it directs itself to one of the most significant landmark-property value relationships. As discussed in chapter two, designation's alteration/demolition restrictions can severely detract from property value in the instance where the historic building's current use is far below its highest and best use because the landmark will likely not be able to attain the most profitable utilization dictated by the market. This effect is directly acknowledged by the landmark assessment-at-current-use standard so as to ensure equitable historic property assessment/taxation. Our emphasis on current use valuation parallels the statutory direction taken by many states on this issue (see Appendix one).

Other valuation procedures discussed by this chapter are much less significant, especially for certain types of properties. Factoring facade/regulatory costs is of minor or no concern, for those parcels not characterized by hard-to-maintain exteriors or where there is little likelihood of major facade changes and consequent requests for regulatory body approval (see chapter two). Consideration of the appropriate depreciation elements and capitalization rate is similarly far less critical than the assessment of landmarks at current use.

Data Needs for Valuing Landmark Properties

Exhibit 7 summarizes the necessary data for implementing each of the landmark assessment recommendations. Identification of designated properties is the most important information element. Multiple approaches for ensuring such demarcation (by listing landmarks by block/lot, alphabetically by street, and so on) were discussed earlier in this chapter. And as indicated, concrete steps to create a landmark data file have already been taken through cooperative action by the New York City Landmarks Preservation Commission (LPC) and the Real Property Assessment Department (RPA).

Additional data needs are indicated in Exhibit 7. Current property utilization—residential, commercial, industrial, and so on—is available from the property identification code already noted on the file/index card kept by RPA for each parcel in New York City. Other landmark-property characteristics such as land value, improvement/reproduction cost, and physical condition are available to assessors from the data-bank files maintained by RPA or else from field inspection, albeit RPA's current files do not pertain directly to landmark situations, and the heavy case load assigned to each assessor does not permit much individual property scrutiny.

A final data input—the "comp" sales of landmark and nonlandmark properties—can be readily generated. RPA already maintains extensive property-sales information. With the incorporation of the various landmark-property identification routines, the division of "comps" into landmark and nonlandmark categories can be effected quickly and inexpensively.

Research Needs/Opportunities for
Valuing Landmark Properties

Discussion of data demands suggests avenues of fruitful research. It would be instructive if RPA along with LPC examined the extent and cost of landmark regulatory-related expenses. Too much heresay exists on this subject; objective scrutiny is needed to ascertain the true situation as it exists today. Defining depreciation in a landmark case as well as specifying the appropriate capitalization rate also deserve further scrutiny (see Exhibit 7).

A most significant data/research opportunity is the empirical examination of the relationship between historic status and property value. As discussed, this association is a complex, dynamic one that may vary for different classes of properties, as well as over time as real-estate market conditions change (see chapters two and three). It would be possible to obtain greater

EXHIBIT 7
SUMMARY OF DATA NECESSARY FOR ASSESSING LANDMARK PROPERTIES

Landmark Valuation Recommendations[1]	DATA NEEDS					
	Landmark Status	Current Use of Landmark	Other Landmark Property Characteristics	Construction Costs	Landmark Property Sales and Other "Comps"	Research
I. Cost Approach						
A. Land Value						
a. Value as if vacant/available	X					
b. Value at current use	X	X				
B. Improvement Value						
a. Value at current use	X	X				
b. Value at replacement not reproduction cost	X			X		
C. Depreciation						
a. Define/evaluate depreciation	X		X			X
b. Examine "curability" of depreciation	X		X			
II. Income Approach						
A. Landmark Gross Income						
a. Value at current use	X	X				
b. Factor prestige value/other considerations	X					X
B. Landmark Property Expenses						
a. Factor facade/regulatory costs	X					X

EXHIBIT 7 (Continued)

SUMMARY OF DATA NECESSARY FOR ASSESSING LANDMARK PROPERTIES

Landmark Valuation Recommendations[1]	DATA NEEDS					
	Landmark Status	Current Use of Landmark	Other Landmark Property Characteristics	Construction Costs	Landmark Property Sales and Other "Comps"	Research
C. Capitalization Rate						
a. Evaluate appropriate rate	X					X
III. Sales Approach						
A. Select appropriate "comps"						
a. "Comps" similar intensity of use	X	X			X	
b. "Comps" redevelopment potential	X	X			X	
B. Adjust "Comps"	X				X	
C. Landmark Property Sale as "Comp"	X				X	

[1]See Exhibit 2
Source: See text.

insight into these interrelationships if RPA along with LPC would utilize the landmark-identification system described previously to examine the association between property selling price and historic status. Isolating the relationship of these variables can be accomplished through the techniques of regression and correlation analysis[21]—statistical tools increasingly used by assessors/appraisers[22]:

> Regression analysis (and accompanying correlation analysis) can be used to estimate the value of the subject property given its salient characteristics directly from a sample of data on comparable sales transactions....
>
> The idea is that the value of the dependent variable (sales price or value) can be estimated given the numerical value of the independent variables (property and transaction characteristics).

Analyzing the landmark consequences represents a straightforward application of regression-correlation analysis employing data available to RPA and LPC. Property value (as measured by selling price) might constitute the dependent variable. Independent variables might include economic measures (i.e., property location/size/type, etc.) as well as landmark status. Property economic characteristics are already noted in RPA files; landmark notation is available from identification routines discussed earlier. Regression analysis would determine the association of the landmark status variable with the dependent variable—property value—holding constant the influence of the economic independent variables.[23] A positive association would suggest landmark status appreciating value; a negative association would indicate a value detraction due to designation; an insignificant relationship would imply a neutral association. The strength of the relationship, if present, would be gauged by standard statistical measures.[24]

It is essential to realize that regression/correlation analysis is merely a useful tool. It does not resolve the conceptual and other difficulties pointed to in chapter two concerning the relationship between designation and property value. Regression/correlation techniques do, however, offer ordered analytical methods for directed study. To illustrate, in the above paragraph, designation was referred to as an independent variable affecting a dependent property value variable, yet chapter two raised the possibility that these relationships are reversed. Regression/correlation methods, especially applied in a time series fashion, could themselves help determine which model is better—designation as a dependent versus independent force. Time series regression/correlation would also be sensitive to changes in landmark's property value impact over time, as per modified market and other forces.

Regression/correlation analysis involving a landmark notation variable has been considered already by RPA as part of its in-house evaluation of a Computer Assisted Mass Appraisal (CAMA) strategy. CAMA would value all properties in New York City for taxation purposes on the basis of a multiple regression incorporating property value as the dependent variable and a score of independent variables, one of which is a landmark code. While CAMA's status is currently uncertain, it is very likely that the future will see RPA turn increasingly to regression property valuation. These future statistical strategies should incorporate landmark designation as a variable for examination.

Other Landmark-Property Data Research Activities

Identification of properties as landmarks opens other data research opportunities of interest to both RPA and LPC because it allows analysis of the association of historic status with the vast array of computerized property data maintained by New York City. A sampling of the information already on file includes (1) property rehabilitation status (the incidence and extent [in dollars] of improvements as recorded by building permit records); (2) property condition (number and type of housing code violations, status of the violations as far as owner corrective activity, etc.); and (3) property-tax status (extent and length of property tax arrearage). With this and other information and the ability to identify which buildings are landmarks, the opportunity is afforded to examine the dynamic association between designation and property (as well as neighborhood) characteristics over time—a relationship that is key to monitoring the stock of historic structures in New York City.

Education/Training Needs for Valuing Landmark Properties

Landmark-assessment recommendations will be carried out in practice only to the extent that assessors are educated to the need for and application of proper techniques. Education is a key consideration for one of the reasons that numerous state statutory provisions specifying how landmarks are to be valued have frequently not been adhered to by field-level assessors is that these individuals have received little or no instruction (see Appendix one).

Training New York City assessors in landmark valuation procedures could take the form of seminars, lectures, memoranda and so on delivered/prepared by RPA/LPC staff on such topics as:

1. *Introduction to historic preservation/landmark designation.* Background on national/New York City historic preservation efforts; federal/state/local designation activities, procedures and implications; type/extent of designated buildings/districts in New York City; existence/activites of local historic preservation groups, etc.

2. *Analysis of the landmark status/property value relationship.* Discussion of why there is a connection and how it may vary, including specification of: permitted/prohibited activities open to owners of designated properties and the market response to designation as revealed by illustrative case study neighborhoods/individual buildings.

3. *Landmark data available to assessors.* Summary of relevant information including materials available from LPC (such as the *Guide* and the landmarks statute discussed previously) as well as the new landmark identification systems and procedures for keeping this file current.

4. *Assessing landmark properties.* Detailed review of appropriate procedures with reference to illustrative case studies.

Consideration should also be given to modifying standard published training materials typically referred to by New York City assessors. The New York State Board of Equalization and Assessment has published three separate instructional texts for assessors on the cost, income, and sales valuation approaches. It would be worthwhile to incorporate landmark-related materials in each of these texts. *The Cost Approach to Value*[25]should discuss how historic designation affects the estimate of land value (Lesson 2); determination of an underimprovement (section 2.22); calculation of the improvement value (Lessons 3 and 4); and consideration of depreciation (Lesson 5). *The Market Value Approach to Property Appraisal*[26] should describe how designation of a property may imbue a special market attraction or detraction (chapter two and three) and indicate that landmark status should be factored along with such traditional considerations as property location, zoning, and so on (chapter four). *The Income Approach to Value*[27]could note the influence of landmark status on gross building income (Lesson 2), building expenses (Lesson three), and capitalization rates (Lesson four).

Major appraisal/assessor organizations (American Institute of Real Estate Appraisers, Society of Real Estate Appraisers [SREA], American Society of Appraisers, and the International Associaton of Assessing Officers [IAAO]) should consider similar changes in their training materials. To illustrate, it would be instructive if the SREA's basic text, *An Introduc-*

tion to Appraising Real Property,[28] would refer to landmark designation and its effects in discussing: limitations on the exercise of private property rights (chapters two and nine); dynamics of the real-estate market (chapter three); area/neighborhood analysis (chapter six); market data sources (chapter six); concepts of highest and best use (chapters four and nine); valuation of land improvements (chapters nine and eleven); elements of depreciation (chapters nine and fourteen) and the selection/adjustment of appropriate "comps" (chapter ten).

Preparing landmark-sensitive training materials, and instituting special training sessions for New York City assessors are essential steps for ensuring field application of the proposed assessment recommendations.

Step Four: Implement Other Assessment Changes

This study has focused on the interrelationship of landmark status, property value, and property assessment in New York City. Additional preservation controls and tools besides public designation, applied in New York as well as other communities, raise similar issues of property value and treatment by assessors. Prominent examples include historic easements and the transfer of development rights. While detailed consideration of these two measures goes beyond the scope of this study, we conclude by briefly considering why they should be considered in valuing historic properties for assessment-real taxation purposes.

Assessing Properties with Historic Easements

Historic easements are defined as[29]:

> less-than-fee right or interest recorded in the public lands records and almost always held in gross by a public agency, charitable trust, or corporation having as one of its purposes the conservation or preservation of environmental or historic resources.

Examples of less-than-fee historic/conservation controls include: scenic easements (protecting visual amenities); facade easements (protecting a property's exterior physical features); and interior easements (protecting interior-property characteristics).

Numerous actions were taken in the 1970s to encourage the use of easements as a preservation support measure. Efforts were expended to remove lingering legal restraints against the creation/enforcement of less-than-fee interests. (The restraints, a legacy of the nation's legal heritage, were designed to discourage easement restrictions that "might hamper the easy marketability of land that was deemed important for the convenience of industry.")[30] To this end, many states enacted legislation authorizing the acquisition, transfer, and enforcement of historic-preservation easements. To bolster the easements' legal basis further, the National Conference of Commissioners on Uniform State Laws authored a draft of a "Uniform Conservation and Historic Preservation Easement Act."[31] Historic easements also received important financial support most prominently through various Tax Reform Acts in the late 1970s that clarified the availability of federal tax benefits (for income, estate, or gift tax purposes) to property owners donating less-than-fee preservation interests.

This growing arsenal of legal/financial incentives encouraged utilization of historic easements. Numerous examples are found in New York City: easements have been transferred to the National Trust for Historic Preservation, the New York City Landmarks Preservation Commission, the New York Landmarks Conservancy, New York Landmarks Preservation Foundation, and other groups. (One of the case-study properties—the Colonnades—had a facade easement given to the National Trust for Historic Preservation.) To illustrate, the New York Landmarks Conservancy has instituted an active easements program. It evaluates offers of easements on the facades of buildings of architectural, historic, cultural, and/or aesthetic significance. If the offer of a facade is accepted, the donor (property owner) gives up the right to alter the facade without the express approval of the Conservancy. This restriction remains in perpetuity—it become part of the property deed that runs with the land as the property changes ownership.

Historic Easements, Property Value, and Property Assessment

Easements can affect property value in much the same way that landmark designation influences market response. In some instances an easement may enhance value, if, for example, it conveys a prestige or protection for which buyers will pay a premium. More frequently, a preservation easement will detract* from value[32]:

---

*This effect is the basis for the tax write-off provision provided by Section 170 (f) (3) of the Internal Revenue Code whereby property owners establishing an historic easement can treat the ensuing loss in value of their property as a charitable donation.

The factors affecting the valuation of properties...which are encumbered with preservation easements include at least these—the loss of: subdivision potential; assemblage potential; development rights; use rights; and flexibility. All of these factors are inroads into the traditional American property rights. Knowledgeable buyers, given the choice between two properties, identical in all respects except that one is encumbered with an easement will always choose the unencumbered property, unless the price is reduced commensurately.

Since historic easements can affect property value, New York City assessors should factor not only landmark status but the presence of an easement as well:

The grant by a property owner of an historic easement or other recorded restriction to a governmental body or to an approved not-for-profit corporation which affects the property's use for preservation purposes shall be considered by the tax assessor amongst other factors in appraising such property for real property tax purposes.

In calling attention to the need for acknowledging the effect of historic easements, the following points should be noted:

1. The recommendations follows the statutory action taken by numerous states specifying that assessors should analyze the impact of easements. (Such legislation is considered at length in Appendix one.) A prototypical example is Colorado Statute §38-30.5-109 stating that properties with facade or scenic easements for historic preservation are to be assessed "with due regard to the restricted uses to which the property may be placed."[33]

2. The definition of those types of historic easements which should be factored is purposely an encompassing one to include many variations of less-than-fee preservation restrictions. It includes, for example, easements donated to public as well as nonprofit groups such as the New York Landmarks Conservancy. An inclusive approach stands in contrast to relatively more restrictive easement assessment provisions adopted by some jurisdictions.[34]

3. The recommendation that New York City assessors consider the presence of easements does not address itself to the legal question whether assessors are allowed to acknowledge such controls. The basis of this issue is that historic easements are typically easements in gross,[35] rather than appurtenant,[36] and that assessors have traditionally been allowed to consider only easements appurtenant[37]. While this legal question is not considered here, a memorandum prepared for the New York Landmarks Conservancy concluded that prevailing law allowed New York City assessors to recognize historic easements in gross[38]:

New York City provides explicitly that valuation must initially be based on the sum for which the parcel would sell under ordinary circumstances.... Although the existence of divided property interests owned by different persons...normally is not recognized as affecting the assessed valuation...exception in the case of easements is universally acknowledged in New York State.... The exception clearly requires that assessment of a parcel subject to an easement take into account the reduced value resulting from the easement...[cases cited]. Although the above authorities involve easements appurtenant... at least two New York cases clarify that the rule applies equally to the less common case of easements in gross [cases cited]. It thus appears that...if the easements, whether appurtenant or in gross, reduce the value of the servient estate, then the assessment should reflect the reduction.

4. The recommendation that assessors factor historic easements does not broach data and procedural considerations. Mention should be made that the necessary information—the presence of an easement—is available from the property title/deed record because easements are officially recorded. Specific procedures for determining the easement's impact on value can be found in numerous appraisal monographs and articles.[39] This topic has been considered in the appraisal literature because appraisers have dealt with valuing historic easements for the purpose of determining the specific federal tax benefit available to owners donating such interests.[40] (The write-off or donation is equal to the reduction in property value resulting from the easement—hence the need for determining the change in value.)[41]

Transfer of Development Rights and Property Assessment

A transfer of development rights (TDR) program permits the sale of a property's authorized but unused development potential. Under a TDR strategy, an owner of an historic building containing 5,000 square feet that is located in a zone permitting a 20,000-square-foot improvement could market 15,000 square feet of development rights. By allowing the sale of the unused development potential, TDR attempts to neutralize the economic pressures confronting the underdeveloped historic property.

Numerous jurisdictions permit TDR as a historic preservation mechanism. New York City was a pioneer in this regard; in the 1960s and 1970s it adopted numerous amendments/regulations authorizing/facilitating the sale of landmark air rights to adjacent lots.[42] San Francisco and other jurisdictions adopted a similar program.[43]

A TDR strategy for historic properties has implications for property value and property assessment. One of the major impacts of designation on property value is its alteration/demolition restriction, i.e., an uneconomically improved landmark cannot be demolished and replaced with a higher intensity of use. TDR complicates this relationship. Designation would continue to prohibit redevelopment, but TDR establishes a mechanism whereby the landmark owner can sell to others what is denied him— realization of the landmark's unused development potential. The owners of Town Hall and 311 East 58th Street, two low-density structures given prevailing market and zoning conditions, both sold unused air rights to adjacent sites. (Town Hall sold its air rights prior to its designation.)

Where landmark TDR strategies are in operation, such as in New York City, assessors must examine the many ways in which landmark status affects property value and must also be alert to TDR's consequences. A landmark's right to sell unused air rights imparts to it a transferrable measure of value that is added to the bundle of rights and overall worth associated with property ownership. For example, an assessor valuing 311 East 58th Street prior to 1972 (when this building's air rights were transferred to an adjacent apartment house, called "The Landmark") should have increased the townhouse's worth by the estimated price of its unused, yet salable development rights. Upon the transfer of these air rights in 1972, the property value of 311 East 58th Street would have decreased while that of "The Landmark" site would have increased (holding constant all other factors). Similar shifts would have occurred upon the sale of Town Hall's air rights to the 1133 Avenue of the Americas Corporation (see chapter three).

In valuing TDR effects, assessors must factor numerous considerations. To whom can the air rights be sold? New York City restricts the transfer of landmark-development rights to adjacent lots. While the definition of "adjacent" has been creatively interpreted, the sale restriction to a limited number of potential buyers weakens the seller's bargaining position and thus the price he/she can command. What is the demand for development rights? New York City's changing real-estate fortunes, from depressed in the early 1970s to boom a few years later, has correspondingly affected the demand for and value of landmark air rights over the decade. More detailed consideration of TDR marketability, value, and so on, go beyond the scope of this study.[44]

Conclusion

Local historic preservation controls and programs have economic implications, one of which is impact on the value of affected buildings. Since assessors are charged with valuing properties for real-taxation purposes, they should be aware of the existence and effect of prevailing preservation measures. These economic relationships and professional obligations constitute the conceptual basis of this chapter's recommendations detailing policies and procedures for assessing New York City landmarks and briefly noting similar approaches to factoring historic easement and TDR provisions.

The recommendations should be viewed as a starting point to be refined and elaborated as we increase our knowledge of historic preservation and hone the analytical tools available to assessors. Continued analysis is essential, especially as governing influences change. Will the historic property investment credits authorized by the 1981 Economic Recovery Act affect the value of qualifying landmarks? How will the proposed Manhattan down-zoning affect the practical meaning of "underimprovement" and "highest and best use"? It is hoped that this study will assist in the ongoing analysis of historic preservation, property value, and property assessment.

Notes

1. Colo. Rev. Stat. 39-1-104 (Bradford-Robinson Supp. 1978).
2. Va. Code §§§10-139, 10-140, and 10-142 (Michie Supp. 1980).
3. Cal. Const. Art. 13- §8 (West Supp. 1980).
4. Cal. Govt. Code §50280-§50289 (West Supp. 1979) and Cal. Pub. Res. Code §5031-§5033 (West Supp. 1978).
5. D.C. Code Encycl. §47-651-§47-654 (West Supp. 1978).
6. See Jack M. Cloud, "Appraisal of Historic Homes," *The Real Estate Appraiser* (September-October 1976), p. 44; Judith Reynolds and Anthony Reynolds, "Factors Affecting Valuation of Historic Properties,"*Information: from the National Trust for Historic Preservation* (Washington, D.C.: Preservation Press, 1976).
7. William Kinnard and Byrl Boyce, *An Introduction to Appraising Real Property* (Chicago: Society of Real Estate Appraisers, 1975).
8. Ibid. See also American Institute of Real Estate Appraisers, *The Appraisal of Real Estate* (Chicago: Institute, 1981).
9. Kinnard and Boyce, *An Introduction to Appraising Real Property*, p. 13-8.
10. Ibid., p. 13-9.
11. Ibid..
12. John F. Adams, "Analysis of Factors Influencing Value," *The Appraisal Journal* (April 1969).
13. Richard R. Almy, "Considerations in Creating Property Tax Relief for Historic Preservation," in Gregory E. Andrews, ed., *Tax Incentives for Historic Preservation* (Washington, D.C.: Preservation Press, 1980), p. 128.
14. Kinnard and Boyce, *An Introduction to Appraising Real Property*. See also Jerome Knowles, Jr., "Estimating Accrued Depreciation," *The Appraisal Journal* (January 1967).
15. Alvin Arnold et al., *Modern Real Estate* (New York: Van Nostrand, 1980). See also American Institute of Real Estate Appraisers, *Readings in the Income Approach to Real Property Valuation* (Cambridge: Ballinger, 1977).
16. Kinnard and Boyce, *An Introduction to Appraising Real Property*.
17. This example assumes that sales data are available for these properties and

that an adjustment would be made for differences in property location, size, condition, and so on.

18. Even if a comparable building could be located, there may be a further limitation if there are no recent sales data for the "comp."

19. These adjustments are in addition to the "standard" modifications made in the typical application of the sales approach to factor the effect of numerous items (property type/size/condition and transaction terms) on final sale prices.

20. Kinnard and Boyce, *An Introduction to Appraising Real Property*.

21. In linear regression, the regression equation is $Y = a + \beta X + E$, where X represents the independent variable and Y represents the dependent variable. To summarize, a is the universe constant and β is the slope of the regression line. In sample data, a is referred to as a, while β is referred to as b. The constant (a or a) represents the point where the regression line (we refer to the regression line, even though in multiple regression the estimation point is really a multi-dimensional plane) crosses the Y axis (where $X = 0$) and the regression coefficient (β or b), the slope of the regression line, shows the magnitude of the change in Y for a given change in X. E is an error term showing the amount of Y's variation not explained by the independent variables. There are other common regression-correlation terms. The correlation coefficient (r) indicates the measure of association between the independent and dependent variable(s). The coefficient of determination (r^2) shows the percentage of the variation in the dependent variable explained by the independent variable(s). Beta is a standardized slope coefficient. The standard error (S_{yx}) reveals how closely the regression equation has estimated Y.

22. Kinnard and Boyce, *An Introduction to Appraising Real Property*.

23. The multiple regression involving property value, economic variables and landmark status would take the form of $Y = a + \beta_1 X_1 + \beta_2 X_2 + ... + \beta_k X_k + E$ where Y represents property value (selling price), a is the constant, $\beta_1 X_2, \beta_k X_k$ would represent the economic independent variables (i.e., property location, type, size, etc.) and the landmark status independent variable and E would represent the unexplained error. The analysis would examine the significance of the landmark status variable and the strength of association (r, r^2, Syx, etc.) between landmark status and property price. (See note 21 for explanation of terms.)

24. Ibid.

25. State Board of Equalization and Assessment (SBEA), *The Cost Approach to Value* (Albany, N.Y.: SBEA, 1978).

26. SBEA, *The Market Value Approach to Property Appraisal*, (Albany, N.Y.: SBEA, no date).

27. SBEA, *The Income Approach to Value* (Albany, N.Y.: SBEA, 1978).

28. Kinnard and Boyce, *An Introduction to Appraising Real Property*.

29. Ross D. Netherton, "Restrictive Agreements for Historic Preservation," *The Urban Lawyer* 12, no. 1 (Winter 1980): 55.

30. Ibid.

31. National Conference of Commissioners on Uniform State Laws, "Uniform Conservation and Historic Preservation Easement Act" (draft, 1980).

32. Memorandum in the reference files of the New York Landmarks Conservancy (no date).

33. Colo. Rev. Stat. 38-30.5-109 (Bradford-Robinson Supp. 1978).

34. To illustrate, in 1980 the New York State Legislature enacted a statute specifying that local assessors should note "the effect of easements or similar historical controls on the valuation of any remaining private interest in a property

for purposes of real estate taxation" (S.9791-A, A.11779, 1980). While this legislation is an important step and reflects similar efforts in other states (see Appendix one), it is restricted to less-than-fee preservation controls acquired by a local *public* body—it would not cover historic easements transferred to a private entity such as the New York Landmarks Conservancy.

35. An easement appurtenant is defined as an incorporal right that is attached to a superior right and inheres in land to which it is attached and is the nature of a covenant running with the land. An easement in gross is not appurtenant to any estate in land.

36. See note 35.

37. The basis for this distinction is that in the case of easements appurtenant the diminution of value of the property where the easement is established (servient estate) is balanced (at least in theory) by the increased value of the neighboring parcel (dominant estate) receiving the rights accorded by the servient estate. Because of this balance, the overall property-tax base is not eroded from the action of the assessor recognizing the easement appurtenant. In contrast, the overall tax base would typically be diminished with respect to easements-in-gross.

38. "Conservation Easements—Problems Relating to Their Appraisal," memorandum prepared by M.S. Gruen for the New York Landmarks Conservancy, October 21, 1974.

39. See the Annotated Bibliography (Appendix two) of this study.

40. The appraisal of easements employs what is referred to as a "before and after test," as described by one authority. "Appraising the value of preservation easements is accomplished properly by appraising the property before imposition of the easement and again after imposition of the easement. The difference between the two value estimates is the value of the easement.... The highest and best use in the before-easement case can be radically different from, or essentially the same as, the highest and best use governing the after-easement appraisals." (See Reynolds, note 41.)

41. Judith Reynolds, "Preservation Easements," *The Appraisal Journal* (July 1976), pp. 358-359.

42. See Donald H. Elliott and Norman Marcus, "From Euclid to Ramapo: New Directions on Land Development Controls," *Hofstra Law Review* 1 (1972): 72-78; David A. Richards, "Development Rights Transfers in New York-City," *Yale Law Journal* 82 (1972): 325-72.

43. John J. Costonis, *Space Adrift: Savings Urban Landmarks through the Chicago Plan* (Urbana: University of Illinois Press, 1974).

44. Ibid.

APPENDIX ONE

LANDMARK PROPERTIES AND THE PROPERTY TAX: NATIONAL STATUTORY SURVEY AND SURVEY OF PRACTICE

Introduction

Many states across the country have enacted numerous statutes dealing with different facets of the relationship between landmark properties and the property tax. This appendix summarizes the national experience. It is divided into two sections. The first is a national statutory survey, the second a national survey of practice.

The statutory survey catalogs state legislative enactments governing the assessment/property taxation of historic buildings. It categorizes the different measures and highlights key features such as the types of properties/owners qualifying for the indicated treatment, agency administering the program, and administrative procedure. The national survey of practice supplements the statutory review by examining how the landmark-property tax measures have been implemented. It is based on a telephone survey of state and local property-tax officials and historic-preservation groups. The survey of practice highlights how, to what extent, and with what effectiveness the landmark programs are utilized.

Both sections of the appendix are presented in a parallel fashion. Survey methodology is discussed first. This introduction is followed by tabular material summarizing the landmark property-tax statutes/practice for each state as well as a brief discussion of intrastate statutory/programmatic similarities and differences.

157

National Statutory Survey

Methodology

The survey commenced by examining previous studies by Shlaes, Almy, Stipe, Powers, and others analyzing state statutes governing the property assessment/taxation of landmark buildings.[1] In addition, standard legal reference-search sources were consulted such as *The Index to Legal Periodicals*.[2] The National Trust for Historic Preservation as well as state and local preservation organizations were also contacted to check if they were aware of any existing or pending state legislation on the subject. These many steps were taken in order to capitalize on the relevant literature as well as to expand/update prior analyses to derive a comprehensive and current statement of the statutory framework.

Presenting the Survey Findings

Statutes are presented in a matrix format designed to provide a reference for ready access and intrastate comparison. (See Exhibit 1 at the end of this appendix.) The matrix contains horizontal and vertical axes. The former lists states in alphabetical order; the latter contains the following information classifications:

1. *Statute/Year Authorized*: A full legal citation is given as well as the year the statute was authorized.

2. *Program Type*: For the sake of clarity and simplicity, the national statutory survey employs the classification scheme shown in Exhibit 2.[3] *Exemption/reduction* programs fully or partially reduce the property taxes of certain landmarks such as those owned by nonprofit organizations; *rehabilitation incentives* provide tax relief if the historic building is renovated; *assessment provisions* specify how in general landmarks should be valued for real taxation purposes.

3. *Eligible Property/Owners*: A brief description is given of the type of property, owner, or owner performance that must be satisfied for the indicated assessment treatment to be accorded.

4. *Historic Property Application*: A differentiation is made between *exclusive* and *inclusive* application. The former refers to those statutes which are directed exclusively to historic buildings. The latter includes measures that can assist landmarks but are not limited to such situations.

5. *Tax Provision*: This section briefly describes the specific tax treatment, where possible citing the exact language of the statute.

EXHIBIT 2
LANDMARK PROPERTIES AND THE PROPERTY TAX:
CLASSIFICATION OF STATUTORY APPROACHES

Statute Type	*Property-Tax Provision*
I. *Exemption/Reduction*	
1. Exemption	Landmark property pays no property tax.
2. Reduction	Landmark property pays a portion of nominal property taxes.
II. *Rehabilitation Incentive Programs*	
1. Rehabilitation refund	Existing prerehabilitation property taxes are *reduced* if landmark property is renovated.
2. Rehabilitation assessment	No upward reassessment of renovated landmark property.
3. Rehabilitation abatement	Partial upward reassessment of renovated landmark property.
III. *General Assessment Provisions*	
1. Assessment to reflect encumbrances	Specific charge that the assessment of landmark properties reflect their landmark status and/or the presence of an historic easement.
2. Assessment at current use	Landmark properties are to be assessed at their current use instead of highest and best use.

6. *Administrative Agency/Procedure*: The statutory specification of the agency administering the tax provision and the administrative procedure to be followed is summarized.

7. *Penalty Provision*: This section notes the penalties provided by statute in the event the landmark property owner does not fulfill prescribed requirements.

Summary of Findings

Over 30 states (including the District of Columbia and Puerto Rico) have enacted a total of approximately 60 statutes dealing with landmark properties and the property tax (Exhibit 3). States providing property-tax measures are distributed throughout the country: in the Northeast 7 states have taken legislative action, in the Midwest, 8 states, in the South, 7 states, and in the West, 11 states (see Exhibit 4).

EXHIBIT 3

LANDMARK PROPERTIES AND PROPERTY TAX PROGRAMS:
NATIONAL STATUTORY SUMMARY[1]

State	Statute[2]	Program Type[3]	Historic Property Application[3]	Eligible Properties/ Easements[3]	Eligible Owners/ Other Requirements[3]	Penalty[3]
Alabama	Const. Am. 373§217	Reduction	Exclusive	"Historic buildings and sites" (federal designation)	Not Specified	Not Specified
Alaska	§29.53.025(b)(2) (c)	Exemption/ Reduction	Exclusive	"Historic sites, buildings, monuments"	Not Specified	Not Specified
Alaska	§29.53.025(f)	Assessment/ Abatement	Inclusive	Single-family dwellings	Not Specified	Not Specified
Arizona	§42-139.01- §42-139.03	Reduction	Exclusive	"Historic properties" (federal designation)	Not Specified, access[4]	Specified
California	Const. Art.13,§8	Assessment at current use/to reflect encumbrances	Exclusive	"Historically significant property" (state designated	Specified	Not Specified
California	§50280-§50289 (Gov't. Code) & §5031-§5033 (Pub. Res. Code)	Assessment at Current Use	Exclusive	"Designated historic properties" (federal/city/ county designation)	Specified, access and maintenance[4]	Not Specified
California	§439-439.4	Assessment at Current Use	Exclusive	Local or state designation	Specified, access and maintenance	Specified
Colorado	§39-5-105(2)(a)	Rehabilitation Assessment	Inclusive	Residential structures	Not Specified	Not Specified
Colorado	§39-5-105(3)(a)	Rehabilitation Assessment	Inclusive	Commercial structures	Not Specified	Not Specified

EXHIBIT 3 (continued)
LANDMARK PROPERTIES AND PROPERTY TAX PROGRAMS: NATIONAL STATUTORY SUMMARY[1]

State	Statute[2]	Program Type[3]	Historic Property Application[3]	Eligible Properties/Easements[3]	Eligible Owners/Other Requirements[3]	Penalty[3]
Colorado	§39-1-104	Assessment to Reflect Encumbrances	Exclusive	State designation	Not Specified	Not Specified
Colorado	§38-30.5-109	Assessment to Reflect Encumbrances	Exclusive	Facade/scenic easements	Not Specified	Not Specified
Connecticut	§12-81(7) & §12-88	Exemption	Exclusive	"Designated historic properties"	Specified, non-profit charitable organizations	Not Specified
Connecticut	§7-131b	Assessment to Reflect Encumbrances	Exclusive	Easements	Not specified	Not specified
Connecticut	§12-127a	Exemption/Reduction	Exclusive	"Historically or architecturally significant"	Specified, hardship	Specified
Delaware	Tit. 9, §8103, 8104	Exemption	Inclusive	"Historic properties"	Specified, non-profit, historic	Not Specified
District of Columbia.	§47-651 - §47-654	Assessment at Current Use	Exclusive	Local designation	Specified, access and maintenance	Specified
Georgia	§85-1406-§85-1410	Assessment to Reflect Encumbrances	Exclusive	Facade/conservation easements	Not Specified	Not Specified

EXHIBIT 3 (continued)
LANDMARK PROPERTIES AND PROPERTY TAX PROGRAMS: NATIONAL STATUTORY SUMMARY[1]

State	Statute[2]	Program Type[3]	Historic Property Application[3]	Eligible Properties/ Easements[3]	Eligible Owners/ Other Requirements[3]	Penalty[3]
Hawaii	§246-34	Exemption	Exclusive	"Historical site"	Specified	Specified
Idaho	Sess. Law sch. 142, §67-4615	Assessment to Reflect Encumbrances	Exclusive	"Historic designation and easements in use"	Not Specified	Not Specified
Illinois	ch.120 §500.23-4	Rehabilitation Assessment	Inclusive	30-year old buildings with fewer than 55 units	Not Specified	Not Specified
Illinois	ch.24 §11-48.2-6	Assessed to Reflect Encumbrances	Exclusive	Easements	Not Specified	Not Specified
Indiana	§18-5-15-1	Exemption	Exclusive	"Historic properties"	Specified, non-profit	Not Specified
Kentucky	§65.430 & §65.450	Assessment to Reflect Encumbrances	Exclusive	Historic/scenic/facade easements	Not.Specified	Not Specified
Louisiana	Const. Art. VII, §18(c)	Assessment at Current Use	Exclusive	"Buildings of historic and architectural importance"	Not Specified	Not Specified
Maryland	§81-12G	Rehabilitation Refund	Exclusive	In local designated districts	Not Specified	Not Specified
Maryland	§81-9-C	Rehabilitation assessment/ Abatement	Exclusive	"Historic-architecturally significant" located in specified counties	Not Specified	Not Specified

EXHIBIT 3 (continued)
LANDMARK PROPERTIES AND PROPERTY TAX PROGRAMS: NATIONAL STATUTORY SUMMARY[1]

State	Statute[2]	Program Type[3]	Historic Property Application[3]	Eligible Properties/Easements[3]	Eligible Owners/Other Requirements[3]	Penalty[3]
Mississippi	§27-31-1(d)	Exemption	Exclusive	Not Specified	Specified, historic societies	Not Specified
Missouri	§353.110	Rehabilitation assessment/Abatement	Inclusive	Not specified	Specified, owned by Urban Redevelopment Corporation	Not Specified
Nevada	§361A.010 - §361A.280	Assessment at Current Use	Exclusive	"Land upon which historic sites are located"	Not Specified	Specified
New Jersey	§54:4-3.52-§54:4-354	Exemption	Exclusive	State designation	Specified, non-profit	Not Specified
New Mexico	§18-6-13	Rehabilitation Refund	Exclusive	State designation	Not Specified	Not Specified
New York	§1408	Exemption	Exclusive	"Designated properties"	Specified, non-profit historical societies of New York State	Not Specified
New York	S.9791-A A.11779-A	Assessment to Reflect Encumbrances	Exclusive	Easements	Not Specified	Not Specified

EXHIBIT 3 (continued)
LANDMARK PROPERTIES AND PROPERTY TAX PROGRAMS: NATIONAL STATUTORY SUMMARY[1]

State	Statute[2]	Program Type[3]	Historic Property Application[3]	Eligible Properties/ Easements[3]	Eligible Owners/ Other Requirements[3]	Penalty[3]
New York	§489	Rehabilitation Refund/Assessment	Inclusive	Residential, multifamily	Not Specified	Not Specified
New York	Ch. 8A §§205.1.0-2-8.21.0	Exemption/ Reduction	Exclusive	New York City designation statute	Tax relief in instances of financial hardship	Not Specified
North Carolina	§105-278	Reduction	Exclusive	Federal, state, local designation	Not Specified	Not Specified
North Carolina	§1979 Adv. Legis. Serv. No. 7	Assessment to Reflect Encumbrances	Exclusive	Easements	Not Specified	Specified
North Carolina	§160A-399.5(6)	Assessment to Reflect Encumbrances	Exclusive	Local designation	Not Specified	Not Specified
Ohio	§5709.18	Exemption	Exclusive	"Designated historic properties"	Specified, non-profit	Not Specified
Oregon	§358.475-§358.565	Reduction	Exclusive	National register	Specified, access and maintenance	Specified

EXHIBIT 3 (continued)
LANDMARK PROPERTIES AND PROPERTY TAX PROGRAMS: NATIONAL STATUTORY SUMMARY[1]

State	Statute[2]	Program Type[3]	Historic Property Application[3]	Eligible Properties/Easements[3]	Eligible Owners/Other Requirements[3]	Penalty[3]
Oregon	§271.710-§271.750	Assessed to Reflect Encumbrances	Exclusive	Easements	Not Specified	Not Specified
Oregon	§308.740-§308.790	Assessment at Current Use	Exclusive	Land-historic sites	Not Specified	Specified
Puerto Rico	Tit. 13 551	Rehabilitation Refund	Exclusive	San Juan or other designated district	Specified, maintenance	Specified
Rhode Island	Pub. Laws ch. 15	Rehabilitation Assessment	Inclusive	Residential dwellings	Not Specified	Not Specified
South Dakota	§1-19A-20 & §1-19A-21	Rehabilitation Refund	Exclusive	State designation	Specified, maintenance	Not Specified
South Dakota	§1-19B-25	Assessment to Reflect Encumbrances	Exclusive	Designation and easements	Not Specified	Not Specified
Tennessee	§11-15-101 - §11-15-108	Assessment to Reflect Encumbrances	Exclusive	Scenic or facade easements	Not Specified	Not Specified
Tennessee	§67-519-§67-521	Rehabilitation Assessment	Exclusive	Federal, state or local designation	Not Specified	*Specified
Texas	Amendment 4	Varies	Exclusive	Federal or state designation	Not Specified	Not Specified

EXHIBIT 3 (continued)
LANDMARK PROPERTIES AND PROPERTY TAX PROGRAMS: NATIONAL STATUTORY SUMMARY[1]

State	Statute[2]	Program Type[3]	Historic Property Application[3]	Eligible Properties/ Easements[3]	Eligible Owners/ Other Requirements[3]	Penalty[3]
Virginia	§10-139, §10-140 and §10-142	Assessment to Reflect Encumbrances	Exclusive	State designation and easements	Not Specified	Not Specified
Virginia	§58-769.4-§58-769.16	Assessment at Current Use	Exclusive	"Lands used for historical purposes"	Not Specified	Specified
Virginia	§58-12	Exemption	Exclusive	Properties owned by special historical societies	Specified, non-profit	Not Specified
Virginia	§58-760.2 & §58-760.3	Rehabilitation Assessment	Inclusive	Properties at least 25 years old	Not Specified	Not Specified
Virginia	§10-155	Assessment to Reflect Encumbrances	Exclusive	Historic, scenic and facade easements	Not Specified	Not Specified
Washington	§84.36.060	Exemption	Exclusive	Properties owned by non-profit historical societies	Specified, non-profit, historical	Not Specified
Washington	§84.34.010 - §84.34.030	Assessment at Current Use	Exclusive	Land-historic sites	Not Specified	Not Specified
West Virginia	§8-26A-4 - 8-26A-5	Assessment to Reflect Encumbrances	Exclusive	Historic, scenic or facade easements	Not Specified	Not Specified

EXHIBIT 3 (continued)
LANDMARK PROPERTIES AND PROPERTY TAX PROGRAMS: NATIONAL STATUTORY SUMMARY[1]

State	Statute[2]	Program Type[3]	Historic Property Application[3]	Eligible Properties/ Easements[3]	Eligible Owners/ Other Requirements[3]	Penalty[3]
Wisconsin	§70.11(20) & §70.11(4)	Exemption	Exclusive	Properties owned by non-profit historical societies	Specified, non-profit, historical	Not Specified
Wisconsin	§70.11(24)	Rehabilitation Abatement	Inclusive	Properties in conservation area	Not Specified	Not Specified
Totals:						
33 States	59 Statutes	59 Programs[5]	49 Exclusive 10 Inclusive	Varies	Varies, Most Not Specified	Varies, Most Not Specified

Notes:
1. This exhibit summarizes information detailed in Exhibit 1.
2. See Exhibit 1 for full citations.
3. See Exhibit 2 and text for explanation. Qualifications in quotation marks indicate statutory language.
4. Public access to and/or maintenance of landmark property; see Exhibit 1 for details.
5. 10 Exemption, 4 Reduction, 3 Exemption/Reduction, 6 Rehabilitation Refund, 3 Rehabilitation Assessment/Abatement, 8 Assessment at current use, 18 Assessment to Reflect Encumbrances and 1 Varied Program

Trends and characteristics of the property-tax provisions are discussed below following the subject headings of the survey matrix.

1. *Property-Tax Statutes: Year Authorized*

Statutes dealing with landmark properties and the property tax have been enacted quite recently—most were authorized after 1970, many between 1975 and 1980 (see Exhibit 1). This time framework reflects the fact that historic preservation in general and the treatment of landmark buildings for *ad valorem* purposes in particular have only recently come to the attention of state legislative bodies.

2. *Property Tax Statue Type/Tax Provision*

Of the roughly 60 landmark property-tax statutes, about a third grant exemptions/reductions, a quarter provide rehabilitation incentives, and the remainder are general assessment provisions (see Exhibit 3).

Property Tax Exemption/Reduction: Exemption/reduction measures grant full (exemption) or partial (reduction) property-tax relief to certain owners/types of landmark buildings. Seventeen states provide such tax treatment (ten states, exemption; four states, reduction; and three states combine exemption/reduction).* In most cases to be exempt the historic structure must be owned by a nonprofit organization. A typical statute is Ind. Code §18-5, 15-1 which provides that in the case of designated properties owned by nonprofit organizations, "all such property...shall not be liable from taxation but shall be entirely exempt therefrom."[4] There are numerous variations, however. In some cases, the statutes specify that the entity owning the landmark property satisfy the dual requirements of being an historic and a nonprofit organization.[5] There are still further variations. In some instances the landmark property is exempt only if it serves educational,[6] public,[7] or other purposes. Alaska sets financial and other requirements—it limits exemption to $10,000 of assessed value and further requires that such exemption be approved by the public at regular or special elections.[8] Connecticut and New York allow tax exemption (or reduction) only in the extreme case of landmark financial hardship where the tax relief is necessary to permit continued property operation or maintenance.[9]

---

*The counts reported here and elsewhere in this appendix refer to the distribution of the different enacted statutes—a figure which can differ slightly from the number of states adopting the different measures.

EXHIBIT 4
LANDMARK PROPERTY TAX MEASURES BY STATE AND REGION

Northeast	Number*	South	Number*	West	Number*	Central	Number*
Connecticut	3	Alabama	1	Alaska	2	Illinois	2
Delaware	1	Georgia	1	Arizona	1	Indiana	1
District of Columbia	1	Louisiana	1	California	3	Kentucky	1
Maryland	2	Mississippi	1	Colorado	4	Missouri	2
New Jersey	1	North Carolina	3	Hawaii	1	Ohio	2
New York	4	Puerto Rico	1	Idaho	1	Tennessee	1
Rhode Island	1	Virginia	5	Nevada	1	West Virginia	1
				New Mexico	3	Wisconsin	2
				Oregon	1		
				South Dakota	2		
				Washington	2		

Totals: *Northeast* 13 programs, 7 states; *South* 13 programs, 7 states; *West* 21 programs, 11 states; *Central* 12 programs, 8 states; *All Regions:* 59 programs, 33 states

*Refers to the number of landmark property tax measures adopted by each state. *Source:* See Exhibits 1 and 3.

Some states reduce the property taxes of historic buildings (see Exhibit 3). In most cases the reduction is provided by means of a classified property-tax system with landmarks designated a separate class with a lower-assessment-to-market value ratio.[10] To illustrate, Alabama's Constitutional Amendment No. 373 classifies historic buildings as Class III structures, a category assessed at 10 percent of fair-market value.[11] Without this special provision, certain types of landmarks, such as nonresidential structures or residential buildings that are not owner-occupied, would be assessed at 20 percent of fair-market value. Amendment No. 373 thus reduces the assessment and therefore the property taxes of affected historic structures by one-half.

Property Tax Rehabilitation Incentives: These programs accord favorable property-tax treatment to historic buildings undergoing renovation. The provisions range from reducing the existing property taxes (*rehabilitation refund*), to not reassessing (*rehabilitation assessment*), or only partially increasing the assessment, of the rehabilitated landmark (*rehabilitation abatement*). All of these treatments convey property-tax relief, for rehabilitating the historic property improves its value and therefore should result in an increased, rather than a decreased/frozen, property assessment/tax obligation.

About 15 states provide for various types of rehabilitation incentives (see Exhibit 3). Five permit refunds. New Mexico Statute §18-6-13, for example, provides that "local, city, county and school property taxes assessed against the property shall be reduced by the amount expended for restoration, preservation and maintenance."[12] The amount of the refund varies across jurisdictions. New York allows a credit against taxes equal to almost the full amount expended on rehabilitation.[13] In contrast, Maryland limits the refund to 10 percent of rehabilitation expenditures.[14] There are also variations in the time span over which the refund is in effect, with a range from 5 years in South Dakota and Maryland to a generous 12 years in New York.[15]

Rehabilitation refunds are quite expensive since the taxing jurisdiction is not only precluded from any gain in assessment/taxation due to rehabilitation but suffers an absolute loss in its tax base for varying periods of time. It is perhaps for this reason that rehabilitation incentive and abatement programs are more popular—they have been adopted in a total of about 10 states (see Exhibit 3). These statutes typically allow a 5- to 10-year period during which the rehabilitated historic building either will not be revalued or else is reassessed by only a fraction of the true value added by the renovation. Some states combine rehabilitation assessment/abatement provisions. Maryland provides a two-year period after renovation of a landmark when there is no increase in assessed value.[16] Afterwards, the following schedule is maintained: in year three, the upward reassessment is limited to 20 percent of the improvement; in year four, 40 percent; in year five, 60 percent; in year six, full upward reassessment is permitted. Other combinations are also found. New York, for example, combines a rehabilitation assessment and refund.[17]

General Assessment Provisions: These provisions, adopted by over 25 states, specify that landmarks be assessed at their "true" value (see Exhibit 3). They include assessment to reflect encumbrances (18 states) and assessment at current use provisions (8 states). As both strategies were discussed in chapter four, they are only summarized here.

Assessment to reflect encumbrances typically requires that the assessor consider either landmark status or the presence of a historic easement, or both, in determining value for real-taxation purposes. In most cases, these measures call only for the assessor to consider the presence of designation/easements and leaves the question of how these factors affect value to the assessor's discretion.[18] Some jurisdictions, however, specify the impact of designation/easements, stipulating that their presence always affects property value in a certain manner.[19]

Another assessment provision is that landmarks be valued at their current rather than highest and best use. To illustrate, historic buildings in the District of Columbia are assessed at their highest and best use and their current use.[20] If the latter is lower than the former then the current use value is the basis for assessment.

3. *Property-Tax Statutes: Eligible Properties/Owners*

Property-tax provisions are often restricted to designated historic structures of a certain size/type/location owned by specified organizations/individuals. Historic designation is almost a universal requirement although the type of specified designation may vary (see Exhibit 3). Some states require inclusion in the Federal Register.[21] Most, however, extend benefits if the property is designated as a landmark by the federal or state or local government.[22] In some cases, designation may not be required. Tennessee's rehabilitation assessment can be applied to nondesignated structures that are at least 175 years old or in cases where such action is recommended by the Local Historic Review Board.[23]

In addition to designation, there are further property requirements such as stipulations governing building size, type and/or location. Illinois' rehabilitation assessment is targeted to large multifamily structures.[24] California's assessment-at-current-use measure, in contrast, is applied only to smaller properties, those with a maximum of three dwelling units.[25] Colorado differentiates rehabilitation assessment provisions for residential and non-residential properties.[26] Maryland's rehabilitation assessment/ abatement can be applied only in Allegany, Frederick, and Baltimore counties.[27] Tennessee's rehabilitation assessment is limited to counties of 200,000 or greater population.[28]

There are also numerous property-owner requirements. In some cases only certain owners are eligible, i.e., non-profit, historic organizations, and so on. In other instances, owners must perform certain actions such as providing appropriate maintenance and allowing some public access. Owners taking advantage of South Dakota's rehabilitation refund must attach a restrictive covenant running with the land that states that the property will be operated in an "appropriate manner."[29] California's assessment-at-current-use statute[30] requires that the landmark owner enter into a 20-year renewable contract guaranteeing that (1) necessary preservation/maintenance chores will be satisfied; and (2) "reasonable" public access will be allowed.[31]

4. Property-Tax Statutes: Landmark-Property Application

Property-tax exemption/reduction and assessment to reflect encumbrances/assessment at current use are almost universally exclusive to landmark properties, that is, they apply only to such structures (see Exhibit 3). This characteristic stems from the fact that these measures are directed to concerns or situations unique to landmarks. Rehabilitation incentives, in contrast, have a much broader application. Consequently, it is not surprising that most of the rehabilitation incentive programs are inclusive to landmarks—they apply to both historic and nonhistoric structures (see Exhibit 3).

5-6. Property-Tax Statutes: Administrative Agency/Procedure

Program implementation typically entails a joint effort involving the (1) tax assessor (local or county depending on jurisdiction); (2) historic preservation officer/group; and (3) landmark owner. The owner applies for the tax benefit (especially in the case of exemption/reduction and rehabilitation incentives) and agrees in writing to any prescribed requirements. The historic-preservation agency certifies that designation, building, and other specifications are satisfied and performs other duties such as checking that the planned rehabilitation is historically appropriate. Multiple tasks are performed by the tax assessor, such as acting as a coordinator (receiving the owner's application, forwarding the application to the historic preservation organization, etc.), and valuing the landmark as specified by statute.

7. Property-Tax Statutes: Penalty Provisions

Penalty provisions indicate the consequences in the event the property owner does not satisfy the prescribed requirements for receiving the landmark-property-tax treatment. In some cases when this occurs, the tax benefits simply lapse. In California, a property no longer eligible for assessment at current use is assessed accordingly—at highest and best use.[32] Some jurisdictions, however, recapture accrued past benefits and many impose further penalties (see Exhibit 5). Oregon provides that if an owner breaches an agreement made to qualify for property-tax reduction, then all past tax savings are recaptured and an additional penalty of 15 percent is imposed.[33] Similar recapture clauses are found in Arizona, Nevada, and Virginia.[34]

Conclusion

The national statutory survey summarized both common and distinctive features of the statutes dealing with landmark properties and the property tax. Further state-by-state details are contained in Exhibit 1. The merits of the different general assessment statutory provisions—the category most relevant to this study—and their applicability to New York·City were discussed in chapter four.

National Survey of Practice

Objective and Methodology

This section extends analysis of statutes dealing with landmark properties and the property tax to summary examination of their *implementation*. Scrutiny of practice is important because the property tax is frequently administered in a manner that does not fully adhere to all nominal state statutory requirements. The national survey was therefore effected to determine the current (1980) operational reality of programs dealing with the property taxation of historic buildings. It reports on the status of property-tax reduction, rehabilitation incentive, and general assessment provisions, as of the June through December 1980 survey period. (Limited resources did not permit review of the implementation of tax-exemption programs.)

The survey was conducted by contacting via telephone state and local

EXHIBIT 5
LANDMARK PROPERTY TAX STATUTES: PENALTY PROVISIONS[1] BY STATE

State/Statute[2]	Program Type[3]	Penalty Provisions	
		Recapture of Past Benefits	Interest Penalty
Arizona §42-139.01- §42-139.03	Reduction	Lesser of half of reduction in taxes or half of property's fair market value.	15 percent of recaptured taxes if owner does not give notice.
California §439-439.4 (Rev. & Tax Code)	Assessment at current use	Difference between full cash value and preferential value is discounted and taxed.	None
Connecticut §12-127a	Exemption/ Reduction	All abated taxes must be paid.	None
District of Columbia §47-651- §47-654	Assessment at current use	All abated taxes must be paid.	Interest is due. The rate is not specified.
Hawaii §246-34	Exemption	All abated taxes must be paid.	5 percent per year of abated taxes.
Nevada §361A.010- §361A.280	Assessment at current use	Difference between taxes due on full value and preferential value is due for each year preferential value was in effect for up to 7 years.	6 percent of deferred taxes per year plus 20 percent of deferred taxes for each year owner fails to give notice.
North Carolina §105-278	Reduction	Taxes abated for 3 years prior to disqualification must be paid.	Interest is due. The rate is not specified.

EXHIBIT 5 (cont'd)

LANDMARK PROPERTY TAX STATUTES: PENALTY PROVISIONS[1] BY STATE

State/Statute[2]	Program Type[3]	Penalty Provisions Recapture of Past Benefits	Interest Penalty
North Carolina 1979 Adv. Legis. Serv. No. 7	Assessment to reflect encumbrances	Money damages may be awarded for breach of obligations.	
Oregon §358.475-§358.565	Reduction	All abated taxes must be paid.	15 percent on abated taxes if owner is at fault.
Oregon §308.740-§308.790	Assessment at current use	Land is reassessed to reflect higher value.	None
Tennessee §67-519-§67-521	Rehabilitation assessment	All abated taxes must be paid.	None
Virginia §58-769.4-§58-769.16	Assessment at current use	Difference between taxes due on assessment at highest use and at current use for prior five years is due.	6 percent per year of recaptured taxes, plus 100 percent of recaptured taxes if owner fails to give notice.
Puerto Rico tit. 13 §551	Rehabilitation refund	All abated taxes must be paid.	6 percent per year of abated taxes.

1. Penalties are incurred when the property or owner no longer meets eligibility criteria or becomes disqualified for landmark property tax incentives.
2. See Exhibit 1 for full citation.
3. See text and Exhibit 1 for details.

agencies/individuals concerned with or knowledgeable about property taxation or historic preservation. These included (1) state/local treasury or revenue departments; (2) state/local agencies involved in property tax assessment/equalization; and (3) state/local historic-preservation organizations. (See Exhibit 6 for a partial listing of those interviewed.)

Different state/local groups were contacted in an interactive fashion. State treasury/property-tax departments were called first and they usually recommended that the state historic preservation agency/officer be interviewed. Local assessors in a sampling of large cities in each state were also contacted (i.e., in California, Los Angeles and San Francisco were chosen). The survey was conducted in the above described "network" fashion because centralized statistics on the landmark taxation programs were typically unavailable at either the state or even local level[35] and consequently numerous individuals had to be called to obtain an "educated guess" of program implementation.

National Survey of Practice: Findings

The survey of practice reveals no discernible differences in program implementation by such state and local variables as population size, location, or property-tax system (i.e., assessment by local versus county officials, assessor training/accreditation and so on). The survey also indicates that the landmark-property-tax programs, when they are implemented, are almost invariably used with other (nonproperty-tax) supports. Exhibit 6 illustrates the "packaging" of aids. In many instances the property-tax provisions are employed with (1) federal income-tax incentives authorized by the 1976 and 1978 Tax Acts; and/or (2) rehabilitation loan programs funded by the federal, state, or local governments. Combining incentives is prompted by financial necessity. As discussed by the Richmond Historic Landmarks Commission[36]:

> Rehabilitation can be accomplished only when a bundle of incentives are available. In addition, technical assistance is often necessary along with a lot of hand holding.

The most interesting finding of the survey of practice concerns the usage of the landmark-property-tax provisions. In a few instances there is extensive utilization. Alabama's reduction program, effected through the instrumentality of a classified property tax, is one example. In just a few years, property reduction has been applied to many landmarks in Mobile and other Alabama cities. Oregon and a few other jurisdictions also report relatively active programs (see Exhibit 6).

EXHIBIT 6
LANDMARK PROPERTIES AND THE PROPERTY TAX:
NATIONAL SURVEY OF PRACTICE

State/Locality[1]	Agencies Contacted[1]	Program Utilization[2]	Comments[3]
Alabama	State Department of Taxation	No statewide data are available.	Reduction program is "well received."
Birmingham	Birmingham (Jefferson County) Assessor Birmingham Historic Society	Reduction program applied to 40 properties.	"Program just begun but becoming effective, used in conjunction with rehab program."
Montgomery	Montgomery (Montgomery County) Appraiser	Reduction program applied to over 300 properties.	"Law has been of incredible benefit in revitalizing large numbers of properties . . . has attracted people back to city."
Mobile	Mobile (County) Tax Assessor Mobile Historic Commission	Reduction program applied to about 100-200 properties to date (out of a maximum total of about 1000).	"Very effective" . . . private individuals are researching history of their properties and applying for historic designation; program challenged in federal court but ruled constitutional.
Alaska	State Office of History and Archaeology	Exemption/reduction program not operative.	Fairbanks and Anchorage are conducting historic preservation studies which include examination of property tax incentives.
	State Department of Natural Resources	Information not available on rehabilitation assessment/abatement program.	
Arizona	State Historic Preservation Office	Reduction program used on 10-15 properties, mainly in Tuscon	"Could be more effective but need to educate public and assessors."

EXHIBIT 6 (continued)
LANDMARK PROPERTIES AND THE PROPERTY TAX: NATIONAL SURVEY OF PRACTICE

State/Locality[1]	Agencies Contacted[1]	Program Utilization[2]	Comments[3]
Arizona (cont'd)			"Difference in assessment for historic property (8% of full value versus 10%) not sufficient inducement." (The difference used to be 8% versus 15%.)
			Resistance because of feared deterioration in the municipality's fiscal health.
			"For program to be more effective, need greater inducement (see above) and education program for staff and assessors."
California	State Department of Taxation	No statewide data on assessment at current use/assessment to reflect encumbrances programs.	"Proposition 13 has made everything chaotic."
Los Angeles	Los Angeles Office of Historic Preservation	"Los Angeles has no program."	"Assessors need mandate and instruction from state."
San Diego	San Diego Historic Site Board	"Limited utilization."	"Owner resistance because properties must be open to public .... Not all historic properties have been surveyed and brought to attention of tax assessor."
San Francisco	San Francisco Tax Assessor	"Some utilization."	"Used in conjunction with local historic preservation ordinance which delays demolition of historic properties."

EXHIBIT 6(continued)

LANDMARK PROPERTIES AND THE PROPERTY TAX:

NATIONAL SURVEY OF PRACTICE

State/Locality[1]	Agencies Contacted[1]	Program Utilization[2]	Comments[3]
Colorado	State Historic Society	No statewide data available on assessment to reflect encumbrances/rehabilitation assessment programs.	
Denver	Denver Landmarks Preservation Committee	Some utilization of rehabilitation assessment, however assessment to reflect encumbrances program has yet to be used.	Recommends rehabilitation refund program.
Connecticut	State Office of Policy and Management	Exemption/reduction program not used.	"State reimbursement of tax revenue lost to municipalities has never been funded."
District of Columbia	D.C. Tax Assessor	Assessment at current use program applied on 7-8 properties.	"Program has little practical value because there is little difference between highest and best and current use of most historic properties."
Georgia	State Department of Property Taxation	Little or no utilization of assessment to reflect encumbrances program.	Lengthy application procedure discourages utilization.
Savannah	Tax Assessor	Assessment to reflect encumbrances program used once.	Chief Tax Assessor currently researching relationship of historic preservation and the property tax. All property in Savannah will be reassessed in 1981 and historic properties in the city will be valued as per state statute.

EXHIBIT 6(continued)
LANDMARK PROPERTIES AND THE PROPERTY TAX: NATIONAL SURVEY OF PRACTICE

State/Locality[1]	Agencies Contacted[1]	Program Utilization[2]	Comments[3]
Atlanta	Atlanta (Fulton County) Tax Assessor	Assessment to reflect encumbrances program not used.	
Hawaii	Office of the State Director for Historic Sites	Exemption program has seen little utilization.	Current proposal to provide property tax incentives to landmark buildings.
Idaho	State Division of Property Tax	Assessment to reflect encumbrances program not used.	"Historic properties treated like all others with reference to tax purposes."
Illinois	State Department of Revenue	No statewide information available on rehabilitation assessment or other programs.	
Kentucky	State Department of Revenue	While exact data are lacking, little or no utilization of assessment to reflect encumbrances program.	
Louisiana	State Department of Revenue and Taxation	Statewide data on assessment at current use program not available.	
Baton Rouge	Baton Rouge Parish Tax Assessor	Assessment at current use program not utilized.	"Not aware of any special provision, taxed same as others."
New Orleans	Vieux Carre Historic District of New Orleans	Limited utilization of assessment at current use program.	"Property taxes in Louisiana are low to begin with."
Maryland	State Department of Taxation

Maryland Historic Trust | No statewide data available on rehabilitation assessment, abatement or refund programs. | Used in conjunction with 1976 income tax act. |

EXHIBIT 6(continued)
LANDMARK PROPERTIES AND THE PROPERTY TAX:
NATIONAL SURVEY OF PRACTICE

State/Locality[1]	Agencies Contacted[1]	Program Utilization[2]	Comments[3]
Baltimore	City Assessor Housing & Commercial Development Agency	Some utilization of rehabilitation incentive programs.	"Special arrangements are made for property tax relief. Rehabilitation incentive used in conjunction with city loan programs."
Missouri	State Tax Commission	No statewide data on utilization of rehabilitation assessment/abatement program.	
Kansas City	City Landmarks Commission	Some usage of rehabilitation incentive for historic properties.	Rehabilitation incentive cannot be used by individuals, just redevelopment corporations.
St. Louis	City Tax Assessor	Historic preservation has been fostered by rehabilitation incentive.	Legislation has been introduced at both the state and local levels to provide tax incentives to individuals restoring historic properties.
Nevada	State Dept. of Taxation State Dept. of Assessment Standards	No statewide data available on assessment at current use program.	"Very limited usage."
New Mexico	State Property Tax Office State Historic Preservation Office	Rehabilitation refund program used on approximately 40 historic properties; potential in excess of 1,000.	"Program is effective; not used more extensively because of stringent owner requirements (i.e. property be kept open to public for 12 days each year and owner must publish [at own expense] description of property). Lack of publicity impedes program."

EXHIBIT 6(continued)
LANDMARK PROPERTIES AND THE PROPERTY TAX: NATIONAL SURVEY OF PRACTICE

State/Locality[1]	Agencies Contacted[1]	Program Utilization[2]	Comments[3]
New York State	State Parks & Recreation Dept.	"Too early to evaluate operation of assessment to reflect encumbrances program (enacted in 1980)."	
	State Board of Equalization and Assessment	Extensive utilization of rehabilitation refund/assessment/abatement program in New York City (J.51) and Buffalo (235-A).	
North Carolina	State Department of Revenue	No statewide data on reduction or encumbrances program.	"Tax relief should be tied to need of property owner."
Raleigh	Raleigh (County) Tax Assessor	Reduction program applied to 50 properties.	"Program effective, used in conjunction with 1976 federal tax act."
Charlotte	County Tax Assessor	Reduction program applied to 100 properties.	"It's doing its job ... A fine law ... proud to have it."
Wilmington	New Hanover County Tax Assessor	Program not operative because of city council's opposition.	"Council opposes program because of the loss to city's tax base."
Oregon	State Historic Preservation Office	Reduction, assessment at current use, and assessment to reflect encumbrances programs applied to 350-400 properties.	"Programs successful though grumbling from owners of non-historic properties. Used in conjunction with 1976 federal income tax law.
Portland	Portland Tax Assessor	Reduction program applied to about 25 properties; assessment at current use also applied.	"Effective, though some owner complaints about application procedure."

EXHIBIT 6 (continued)
LANDMARK PROPERTIES AND THE PROPERTY TAX: NATIONAL SURVEY OF PRACTICE

State/Locality[1]	Agencies Contacted[1]	Program Utilization[2]	Comments[3]
Salem	Salem Tax Assessor	Reduction program applied to 28 properties.	"Program is effective, used in conjunction with federal (1976) income tax law."
Rhode Island	Rhode Island Preservation Committee	No statewide data on rehabilitation assessment program.	Rehabilitation assessment used in conjunction with federal (1976) income tax law."
South Dakota	State Department of Revenue	Rehabilitation refund program applied to 80 properties; program enacted in 1978, is expected to increase in volume (potential of 2,500 properties).	"Program is well received, used in conjunction with federal (1976) income tax law."
Tennessee	State Board of Equilization	Both assessment to reflect encumbrances and rehabilitation assessment program are "barely used."	"State Attorney General questioned constitutionality of rehabilitation assessment program. Public and assessors not aware of program. No guidelines from state."
Texas	Texas State Historical Commission	Program has been adopted in approximately 5 communities including Austin, Galveston and San Antonio.	"Proud of program and stress the importance of the program's flexibility — the details of the property tax benefit are determined by local communities."
Virginia	Virginia Landmarks Commission	Rehabilitation assessment program applied to about 100 properties in Richmond, Roanoke, Chesapeake, Norfolk, and Fairfax Counties; program volume is expected to increase; statewide data not available on	

EXHIBIT 6(continued)

LANDMARK PROPERTIES AND THE PROPERTY TAX:
NATIONAL SURVEY OF PRACTICE

State/Locality[1]	Agencies Contacted[1]	Program Utilization[2]	Comments[3]
Virginia (cont'd)			
Alexandria	Alexandria Tax Assessor	assessment to reflect encumbrances program. Assessment to reflect encumbrances is applied but not rehabilitation assessment program.	City Council felt there was no need for rehabilitation assessment program because historic properties have already been renovated without this incentive.
Washington	State Department of Revenue	"Minimum implementation of assessment at current use and assessment to reflect encumbrances programs."	"Most assessors not aware of programs."
	State Property Tax Office		
West Virginia	State Department of Taxation	Assessment to reflect encumbrances program not implemented.	
	West Virginia Historic Preservation Commission		
Wisconsin	State Department of Revenue	Insignificant utilization of rehabilitation abatement program.	

EXHIBIT 6(continued)
LANDMARK PROPERTIES AND THE PROPERTY TAX: NATIONAL SURVEY OF PRACTICE

State/Locality[1]	Agencies Contacted[1]	Program Utilization[2]	Comments[3]

Notes: 1. See text; a sampling of large cities were contacted in most states. The exhibit does not list the responses of all agencies contacted.

2. See Exhibit 1 for listing of landmark property tax programs by state; does not include utilization of property tax exemption programs.

3. This survey is based on telephone interviews conducted (by James J. Nemeth of the CUPR staff) between June and December, 1980 with the following individuals/organizations (partial listing):

Alabama: James K. Green, Alabama Department of Taxation; Jefferson County Assessor's Office; Ms. Becky Robbins, Office of Director of Economic Development, Jefferson County; Tommy Miller, Chief Appraiser, Montgomery County; William Malone, Tax Assessor, County of Mobile. **Alaska:** Bob Mitchell, Historic Preservation Architect, Office of History and Archaeology. **Arizona:** James Ayers, Arizona State Historic Preservation Officer. **Arkansas:** Larry Yancey, Esq., Tax Attorney for Historic Properties in State of Arkansas, firm of House, Holmes, and Jewell. **California:** Alan J. Dutra, Principal Property Appraiser, Assessment Standards Division, State Board of Equalization; Lee Gilmore, Assessment Standards Division, State Board of Equalization; Don Davis, Real Property Division, Los Angeles County Assessor's Office; David Bell, San Bernardino County Assessor's Office; Howard Whitcomb, Orange County, Manager of Assessments; San Francisco City/County Tax Assessor's Office; Ron Buckley, San Diego Historic Site Board; Mr. Truesdale, Supervisor of Tax Collections, San Diego County. **Colorado:** Ms. Barbara Handy and Jim Hartman, Colorado State Historic Society; David Wicks, Denver Landmarks Preservation Commission. **Connecticut:** Ms. Mary Winn, Office of Policy and Management; John McDermott, Tax Assessor, Hartford; Edward Clifford, City Assessor, New Haven. **Delaware:** Dover County Receiver of Taxes; M. E. Merriam, City Assessor, Wilmington. **District of Columbia:** James Coffee, D.C. Assessor's Office. **Florida:** Louis Roach, Tax Assessor, State Department of Revenue; Dade County Tax Assessor's Office. **Georgia:** J. Philip Napoletan, Property-Tax Appraiser, Department of Revenue, State of Georgia; James Hopper, Fulton County Tax Assessor; Ben A. Karnosky, Acting Chief Tax Assessor, Chatham County; James Meades, Chief Appraiser, Richmond County. **Hawaii:** Ralston Nagata, State of Hawaii, Director for Historical Sites. **Idaho:** State Director of Property Tax. **Illinois:** Louis Canterbury, Illinois Department of Revenue. **Indiana:** State Board of Tax Commissioners. **Iowa:** Ed Henderson, State Department of Taxation. **Kansas:** State Historical Society, Preservation Office. **Kentucky:** State Department of Revenue, Property Evaluation Division. **Louisiana:** Roy Sellars, Department of Revenue and Taxation, State of Louisiana; Baton Rouge City/Parish Tax Assessor's Office; Vieux Carre Historic District of New Orleans. **Maine:** Fred Wilson, Department of Revenue, Property Tax Division; Fred Lucchi, Tax Assessor, City of Portland. **Maryland:** Mr. Frumper, Maryland Department of Taxation; Jack Finglass, Maryland Historical Trust; Mr. William Reilley, City of Baltimore. , Assessor of Real Property. **Massachusetts:** Joseph Orphant, Massachusetts Historic Commission; Mr. Daniel Lohnes, Society for the Preservation of New England Antiquities; Massachusetts Historic Society; State Property Tax Bureau. **Michigan:** Dennis Hall, Department of Natural Resources; Ms. Martha Bigelow, Historic Preservationist; William Knapp, Tax Assessor, City of Detroit. **Minnesota:** Minnesota Historical Society. **Mississippi:** Alan Bissell, State Tax Division; Todd Williams, Assistant Assessor, Natchez. **Missouri:** Philip Baker, State Tax Commission; Ms. Jane Flynn, Administrator, Landmarks Commission, Kansas City; Stanley Miller, Manager of Real-Estate appraisal, St. Louis. **Montana:** Marcella Sherfy, Montana Historical Society. **Nebraska:** Barry Hasty, Tax Bureau. **Nevada:** Rich Clemenson, Department of Taxation, Department of Assessment Standards. **New Hampshire:** Lloyd Price, State Tax Assessor; John Prentiss, Planning Board, Manchester. **New Jersey:** Terry Karschner, Office of Historic Preservation; Al Bills, State Bureau of Taxation; Victor Hartsfield, Assessor, East Orange; Joseph Frisina, Tax Assessor, Newark; Trenton Tax Assessor's Office; New Brunswick Tax Assessor's Office; Joseph Spaturo, Assessor, West Orange. **New Mexico:** Aug Narbutas, Deputy Director, State Property Tax; Tom Merlind, State Historic Preservation Office. **New York:** Tom Murphy, City of Buffalo; Town of Oyster Bay; Robert Cullen, Tax Assessor, Poughkeepsie; David Rowe, Landmarks Association of Central New York; Austin O'Brien, State of New York, Department of Parks and Recreation. **North Carolina:** Mr. Holbrook, Department of Revenue, Property Tax Commission Office; Mr. Mayes, Mecklenberg County Tax Assessor; New Hanover County Tax

EXHIBIT 6(continued)
LANDMARK PROPERTIES AND THE PROPERTY TAX: NATIONAL SURVEY OF PRACTICE

State/Locality[1]	Agencies Contacted[1]	Program Utilization[2]	Comments[3]
	Assessor; Wake County Tax Assessor. **North Dakota:** Barry Nashings, State Tax Department. **Ohio:** Ms. Carol Mahaffey, Department of Tax Equalization; Mr. Matthew Chambers, county attorney, Cuyahoga County; Tax Assessor, Franklin County (Columbus). **Oklahoma:** Malvina Sternam, Oklahoma Historical Society. **Oregon:** Leroy Hood, Division of Assessment and Appraisal, State of Oregon; David Powers, Deputy, Historic Preservation Office; Jess Decair, Marion County Tax Assessor (Salem); Tax Assessor, Multnomah County (Portland). **Pennsylvania:** Bob Statton, Department of Revenue, Office of Property Tax; Richard Tyler, Philadelphia Historical Commission. **Rhode Island:** Kevin Monroe, Rhode Island Preservation Committee; Providence Tax Assessor; Mr. Weiss, Newport City Tax Assessor. **South Carolina:** Mr. Pitts, Director, State Department of Revenue, Property Division; Mr. Colson, Director, Preservation Society of Charleston. **South Dakota:** Paul Putz, Historic Preservation Center, University of South Dakota; Duke Goodell, director of Equalization, Sioux Fall (Minnehana County). **Tennessee:** Mr. Ballentine, State Board of Equalization, Property Assessments Division; Jerry Shelton, Executive Secretary, State Board of Equalization; Steve Nichol, Property Assessor, Nashville/Davidson County. **Texas:** Ms. Annas Ried, Texas State Historical Commission; Joseph Opperman, Director of Grants-in-Aid, Texas State Historical Commission; Joseph Williams, Texas State Historical Commission; Ms. Betty Baker, Austin Planning Department; Tax Assessor, Houston; Margo Garcia, tax assessor, San Antonio. **Utah:** Alan Jiles, Department of Revenue, Division of Land Appraisal. **Vermont:** Charlene Lanthrop, State Division of Property Valuation; Jane Lindway, State Historic Preservation Division. **Virginia:** Brian Mitchell, Historic Landmarks Commission; John Osten, Deputy Assessor, Office of Real Estate Assessment, Alexandria; Tax Assessor, City of Richmond. **Washington:** Daniel Meyers, State Property Tax Office, Exempt Property Section; Al Martin, Kings County Tax Assessor's Office. **West Virginia:** Clarence Moran, West Virginia Historic Preservation Commission; Mr. Hoffman, State Department of Taxation. **Wisconsin:** Pam Hennessy, Department of Revenue, Property Tax Office. **Wyoming:** Jim Orr, State Tax Division.		

These are the exceptions, however. The survey of practice reveals that in most cases the landmark-property-tax provisions—tax reduction, rehabilitation incentive, and general assessment—have only infrequently been applied. Connecticut's reduction measure has never been used; the District of Columbia's assessment at current use measure has been utilized seven or eight times; and Arizona's property-tax-reduction program has been activated on only ten to fifteen buildings. (See Exhibit 6 for further examples.) California's assessment at current use has also experienced minimal usage as evident from the following responses to a questionnaire administered by the California State Board of Equalization to the state's 58 county assessors.[37] While almost all (55 out of 58) assessors reported the presence of eligible landmarks qualifying for the program in their counties, a negligible number (2 of 58) indicated that the landmark assessment provision was actually utilized.[38]

This finding of limited program application parallels the observations of Shlaes, Levy, Stipe, Powers, and other early studies on this subject.[39] As summarized by Powers[40]:

> The ineffectiveness in the District of Columbia of a statute providing for assessment of historic property on the basis of actual use, rather than the most economically advantageous highest and best use, demonstrates the limited utility that an otherwise useful technique may have in the special circumstances of a city like Washington.... According to District of Columbia officials, only two out of approximately 350 potentially eligible structures have taken advantage of the tax relief offered by the statute.

While it is difficult to pinpoint the exact reasons for the frequent low level of landmark property-tax program utilization, the following factors can be identified:

1. *The programs are new.* Many of the measures have been enacted quite recently and as such have not had the necessary lead time to be implemented on any large scale. In Texas, Amendment 4 to the state constitution, adopted in 1978, authorized localities to accord preferred property taxation of historic buildings. While Amendment 4 treatment has not yet applied on a large scale, the Texas State Historic Commission reports that more extensive implementation is only a matter of time— Amendment 4 has been received enthusiastically by Austin, Galveston, and San Antonio and additional Texas communities have voiced interest in establishing programs of their own.[41] Other recently enacted provisions such as South Dakota's rehabilitation refund (1978) and New York's assessment to reflect encumbrances (1980) will also likely experience more extensive future use as localities become aware of and respond to the new assessment mandate.

2. *Legal questions.* The survey of practice reveals numerous instances where the landmark-property-tax provisions confronted legal challenges, typically on the grounds that by providing special treatment of landmark properties they violated the mandate that all properties be treated equally for tax purposes. Tennessee's Attorney General questioned the constitutionality of the state's rehabilitation assessment.[42] California's assessment at current use also experienced an initially hostile legal reception, requiring an amendment to the state's constitution. As described by Shlaes[43]:

> The California law, passed in 1972 and popularly known as the Mills Act, has had a fitful history.... The only contract executed under this law involved the La Jolla Women's Club in San Diego and resulted in a forty percent tax reduction for the property. Shortly thereafter, however, the Mills Act was found to be in violation of the state constitutional provisions requiring uniformity of taxation. Consequently, a constitutional amendment was passed in 1976 to remedy this legal impediment to implementation of the Mills Act.

Court challenges in California and other jurisdictions initially put the landmark-property-tax provisions in a legal limbo which delayed their field-level usage.

3. *Opposition to the measures by local assessors/legislative bodies.* In numerous instances, implementation has been impeded because of resistance by local assessors and/or legislative bodies on the grounds that the landmark measures erode the overall tax base, and are unfair to non-designated-property owners. Numerous Arizona assessors "resisted" the state's reduction program on the grounds that it "deteriorated local fiscal health."[44] Wilmington's (North Carolina) city council delayed implementation of a reduction measure because of "the loss to local tax base."[45] California's assessment at current use was viewed warily by local assessors, especially in the climate of Proposition 13 where the local property-tax base in general was under assault. In some instances, local fears concerning erosion to the tax base went so far as to induce legislative resistance to historic preservation/designation activities that would trigger the special landmark-assessment provisions. Numerous North Carolina communities delayed establishing local historic preservation commissions because preferred landmark taxation was contingent on the existence/actions of these local bodies.[46] Powers reports similarly induced resistance in Oregon[47]:

> The statute has generated some resistance to the creation of new National Register historic districts. According to the statute, all properties in National Register historic districts are eligible to have their assessments frozen for the 15-year period stipulated. The fear, apparently unjustified, is that additional Register districts could seriously erode the tax base of

small communities. The fear is present in towns like Jacksonville, where almost the entire town is or is proposed to be included in a National Register historic district.

Another point of contention is that the landmark-property-tax measures add an additional obligation to the already overburdened local assessor[48] and in some cases to the local legislature itself if the latter must take such requisite actions as designating historic districts, approving contract provisions, etc.[49] Finally, some assessors/legislators oppose the landmark-property programs on the philosophical ground that using the tax system to aid historic preservation is an undesirable "backdoor approach." These individuals prefer a more direct financial strategy, such as offering loans or grants, where costs/benefits can more readily be scrutinized on a regular basis.

4. *Inadequate instruction to or education of assessors.* Implementation of the landmark-property-tax provisions requires that local assessors be alerted to the existence of these measures and trained in their application. Instruction is critical because most assessors are not aware of the implications of historic designation and possible effects on property value. The national survey of practice reveals that these steps have largely not been taken—assessors charged with administering the landmark programs have received little or no notification, instruction and/or education.[50] Numerous California assessors complained that they were given insufficient legal/administrative clarification of the state's complicated assessment at current use/assessment to reflect encumbrances measures.[51] In Los Angeles, for example, the landmark-tax programs were not implemented because of "ambiguities in the law and that the County Board of Supervisors did not provide a legal medium by which the 20-year contract could be finalized."[52] Tennessee's assessment to reflect encumbrances and rehabilitation assessment programs were similarly "barely"[53] used in part because local assessors did not "receive adequate guidelines."[54]

5. *Stringent property-owner requirements.* Owners of landmarks qualifying for preferred property-tax treatment have themselves often not applied because in their judgment the tax benefits are not worth the access, maintenance, and other requirements that must be satisfied. New Mexico's rehabilitation refund has been spurned by many nominally eligible owners because the refund is available only if significant public access (for twelve days annually) is allowed—a stipulation that, in the opinion of the state's Historic Preservation Office, "scares just about everyone."[55] California's assessment-at-current-use provision similarly has often not been activated because property owners are wary about signing a 20-year contract keeping their buildings open to the public for a set period each year.

Significant penalty provisions for not satisfying the statutory access, maintenance, and other requirements add to owner reluctance to apply for the landmark-tax relief. As discussed by Shlaes[56]:

> If a property is disqualified under North Carolina law the penalty incurred is a loss of the deferral privilege and a five-year recapture of back unpaid taxes plus a severe interest penalty.... According to the North Carolina Office of Historic Preservation numerous problems have developed with the North Carolina legislation which include...a hesitancy on the part of some owners to apply...for fear of the penalty provision.

6. *Other inhibiting factors.* In some cases the landmark-property-tax programs have not been used because they simply do not apply. Washington, D.C.'s assessment at current use measure is illustrative. This program has been utilized only a handful of times because the statute is limited to individually designated buildings only—the more numerous landmarks in historic districts do not qualify. In addition, many of the capital's landmarks do not benefit from an assessment at current as opposed to highest and best use mandate because these structures (i.e., designated residential townhouses) are already at their highest use.[57]

Other factors inhibiting utilization of the tax measures include: landmark owners are not aware of the programs and therefore do not apply[58]; owners/assessors/historic groups have little inducement to press for implementation in jurisdictions with relatively insignificant property taxation[59]; and that assessors are hesitant to act in cases where there are ambiguities in the landmark statutes themselves.[60]

The six restraints discussed above suggest numerous strategies for facilitating implementation of landmark-property-tax programs.

1. The legal basis of the measures should be carefully researched.
2. The need for the provisions should be aired so as to mitigate charges that the programs are unnecessary or worse are inequitable.
3. Emphasis must be placed on training assessors in the implementation of the landmark provisions.
4. Owner requirements should not be unreasonable nor should an excessive penalty for noncompliance be imposed.
5. Consideration should be given to the practical application of the programs, including review of which landmarks will and should qualify.

These considerations have been incorporated in chapter four's landmark-assessment recommendations for New York City.

Summary

The national survey of practice is a preliminary effort to obtain a sense of the field-level usage and emphasis of programs dealing with landmark properties and the property tax. Together with the national statutory survey, it provides a glimpse of what is happening today, and suggests avenues of improvement for the future.

Notes

1. Shlaes & Co., *Property Tax Incentives for Landmark Preservation: Draft Program for Use in Chicago and Cook County, Illinois* (prepared for Commission on Chicago Historical and Architectural Landmarks, August, 1977); Gregory E. Andrews, ed., *Tax Incentives for Historic Preservation* (Washington, D.C.: the Preservation Press, 1980); Richard R. Almy, "Property Taxation and the Preservation of Historic Properties," *Research and Information Series* (Chicago: International Association of Assessing Officers, August 1977); Lonnie A. Powers, "Tax Incentives for Historic Preservation: A Survey, Case Studies and Analysis: *The Urban Lawyer,* 12, no. 3 (1980): 105; Lisa A. Koch, "State and Federal Tax Incentives for Historic Preservation," *University of Cincinnati Law Review* 46 (1977): 833; "Use of Tax Incentives for Historic Preservation," *Connecticut Law Review* 8 (1976): 334; and "State Preservation Laws," *Wake Forest Law Review* 12 (1976): 121. See also "The Theory of Property Tax and Land Use Restrictions," *Wisconsin Law Review* (1974), p. 751; Russell L. Brenneman, "Techniques for Controlling the Surroundings of Historic Sites," *Law and Contemporary Problems* 31 (1971): 416; and "Landmark Preservation Laws: Compensation for Temporary Taking," *University of Chicago Law Review* 35 (1968): 362. See Appendix two of this study for annotation of many of the above references.

2. *The Index to Legal Periodicals* (New York: Wilson, 1981).

3. See Appendix two in this study for annotation of prior efforts to categorize the landmark-property tax programs.

4. Ind. Code §18-5, 15-1 (Bobbs-Merrill Supp. 1979).

5. Wash. Rev. Code. Ann. §84.36.060 (West Supp. 1980); Wisc. Stat. Ann. §§70.11 (20) & 70.11(4) (West Supp. 1979).

6. N.M. Stat. Ann. §18-6-13 (1978); Ohio Rev. Code Ann. §5709.18 (Anderson Supp. 1978).

7. Ohio Rev. Code Ann. §5709.18 (Anderson Supp. 1978).

8. Alaska Stat. § 29.53.025(b) (2) (c) (Michie Supp. 1979).

9. Conn. Gen. Stat. Ann. §12-127a (West Supp. 1980); New York City ch. 8A §§205.1.0-2-8.21.0.

10. 1901 Ala. Const. Amendment No. 373 §217 (1978).

11. Ibid.

12. N.M. Stat. Ann. §18-6-13 (1978).

13. N.Y. Real Property Tax Law §489 (as amended by L. of 1977, ch. 850).

14. Md. Ann. Code. §81-12G (Michie Supp. 1979).

15. Md. Ann. Code §81-9-c (Michie Supp. 1979); S.D. Compiled Laws Ann. §1-19A-20-§1-19A-21 (Alan Smith Supp. 1978); N.Y. Real Property Tax Law §489 (as amended by L. of 1977, ch. 850).

16. Md. Ann. Code §81-9-c (Michie Supp. 1979).

17. N.Y. Real Property Tax Law §489 (as amended by L. of 1977, ch. 850).

18. Conn. Gen. Stat. Ann. §7-131b (West Supp. 1980); 1975 Idaho Sess. Laws ch. 142 §67-4615; NY S.9791§A, A.11779-A (May 12, 1980); N.C. Gen. Stat. §160A-399.5(6) (Michie 1979).

19. Colo. Rev. Stat. §39-1-104 (Bradford-Robinson Supp. 1978); Va. Code §§§10-139,10-140, and 10-142 (Michie Supp. 1980).

20. D.C. Code Encycl. §47-651-§47-654 (West Supp. 1978).

21. 1901 Ala. Const. Amendment No. 373 §217 (1978; Ariz. Rev. Stat. Ann. §42-139.01-§42-139.03 (West Supp. 1979); Or. Rev. Stat. §358.475-§358.565 (1977).

22. Cal. Govt. Code §50280-§50289 (West Supp. 1979) and Cal. Pub. Res. Code §5031-§5033 (West Supp. 1979).

23. Tenn. Code Ann. §67-519-§67-521 (Cum. Supp. 1978).

24. Ill. Ann. Stat. ch. 120 §500.23-4 (West Supp. 1979).

25. Cal. Govt. Code §50280-§50289 (West Supp. 1979) and Cal. Pub. Res. Code §5031-§5033 (West Supp. 1979).

26. Colo. Rev. Stat. §39-5-105(3)(a) (Bradford-Robinson Supp. 1978); Colo. Rev. Stat. §39-5-105(2)(a) (Bradford-Robinson Supp. 1978).

27. Md. Ann. Code §81-9-c (Michie Supp. 1979).

28. Tenn. Code Ann. §67-519-§67-521 (Cum. Supp. 1978).

29. S.D. Compiled Laws Ann. §1-19-20-§1-19A-21 (Alan Smith Supp. 1978); S.D. Compiled Laws Ann. §1-19B-25.

30. Cal. Govt. Code §50280-§50289 (West Supp. 1979) and Cal. Pub. Res. Code §5031-§5033 (West Supp. 1979).

31. Ibid.

32. Cal. Rev. & Tax Code §439-§439.4 (West Supp. 1979).

33. Or. Rev. Stat. §358.475-§358.565 (1977); Or. Rev. Stat. §271.710-§271.50 (1977); Or. Rev. Stat. § 308.740-§308.790 (1977).

34. Ariz. Rev. Stat. Ann. §42-139.01-§42-139.03 (West Supp. 1979); Nev. Rev. Stat. §361A.280 (1977); Va. Code §58-769.4-§58.769.16.(Michie Supp. 1980).

35. The absence of state and local monitoring is not surprising; states have historically maintained a distant approach toward the "local" property tax, and most localities have neither the will nor the resources to document property-tax assessment procedures.

36. Telephone interview conducted by the Rutgers University Center for Urban Policy Research, September 1980.

37. California State Board of Equalization, Assessment Standards Division, *Report on Assessment of Historical Property Enforceably Restricted* (Sacramento, California, December 31, 1980).

38. Ibid.

39. See note 1 in this Appendix and the Annotated Bibliography (Appendix two). See also Lonnie A. Powers, "State Historic/Preservation Tax Statutes: Three Case Studies" in Andrews, *Tax Incentives for Historic Preservation*, p. 108; Robert E. Stipe, "State and Local Incentives for Historic Preservation," in Andrews, *Tax Incentives for Historic Preservation*, p. 91.

40. Powers, "State Historic Preservation Tax Statutes."

41. Telephone interview conducted by the Rutgers University Center for Urban Policy Research, July 1980.

42. See Exhibit 6.

43. Shlaes, *Property Tax Incentives for Landmark Preservation*, p. 8.

44. See Exhibit 6.

45. Ibid.

46. Ibid.

47. Powers, "State Historic Preservation Tax Statutes," p. 110.

48. As expressed by Stipe, "State and Local Incentives for Historic Preservation" (see footnote 39); "However, when one examines the details of administration and procedure involved in the implementation of these programs, it becomes apparent that they are not self-executing, nor are they necessarily inexpensive. In fact, it has been argued that they add an element of audit to local and state property tax administration to the extent that preservation projects must be approved and inspected as they proceed, and periodically inspected and monitored for compliance on completion. These hidden costs may be said to strengthen the traditional argument that the purpose of taxation is to raise revenues for the running of the government and that public policy and democratic ideals are better served by approaching preservation (or any other) problem through the front door of loan and grant rather than through the back door of hidden tax preferences."

49. As expressed by the California State Board of Equalization (see footnote 37): "The intent of this legislation is to assist in the preservation of qualified historical property for the public good. Due to several interrelated reasons, the impact of the legislation has been insignificant. From contacts with local officials, the following reasons appear to be principally responsible for the lack of participation in this program:

1. The complex requirements imposed by the legislation upon the local government entities who must create historical property zones and develop contract provisions for each respective property submitting applications.

2. The restrictive nature of the contract provisions upon the owner of the qualified historical property which includes the following: (a) continuing 20-year contract term; (b) the right of public access to the property under contract; (c) requirements as to the renovation and maintenance of the qualified historical property in conformance with the rules and regulations of the Department of Parks and Recreation.

3. The enactment of Proposition XIIIA and the related reduction of the property tax burden to real estate."

50. See Exhibit 6.

51. Ibid.

52. Ibid.

53. Ibid.

54. Ibid.

55. Ibid.

56. Shlaes, *Property Tax Incentives for Landmark Preservation*.

57. See Powers, "State Historic Preservation Tax Statutes."

58. See Exhibit 6.

59. Ibid.

60. Ibid.

EXHIBIT 1
LANDMARK PROPERTIES AND THE PROPERTY TAX: NATIONAL STATUTORY SURVEY

PROGRAM DESCRIPTION (See last page of exhibit for explanation)	ALABAMA	ALASKA	ALASKA
Statute:	1901 ALA. Const. Amendment No. 373 §217 (1978)	ALASKA STAT. §29.53.025 (b) (2) (c) (Michie Supp. 1979)	ALASKA STAT. §29.53.025 (f) (Michie Supp 1979)
Year Authorized:	1978	1972	1972
Program Type:	Reduction	Exemption/Reduction	Rehabilitation assessment/ abatement for four-year period.
Eligible Properties/ Owners:	Historic buildings and sites listed on the National Register or in a National Historic District.	Historic sites, buildings, monuments.	All real property; single-family dwellings.
Application:	Exclusive	Exclusive	Inclusive
Tax Provision:	All Class III property, including all historic buildings and sites, is assessed at 10 percent of fair market value.[1]	Exemption may not exceed $10,000 of assessed value for any one residence.	Increase in property value due to rehabilitation is not counted for four years. Improvements must enhance exterior appearance or aesthetic quality.
Administrative Agency:	County tax assessor	Municipalities. The exemption must be adopted by local ordinance and ratified by popular vote at regular/special election.	Local tax assessor
Procedure:	Not specified	Not specified	Not specified
Penalty Provision:	Not specified	Not specified	Not specified

1. Amendment No. 373 designated three classes of properties for *ad valorem* purposes. Class I includes all property of utilities used in the business of such utilities and is assessed at 30 percent of fair market value. Class III includes "all agricultural, forest and single-family owner occupied residential property, and historic buildings and sites." It is assessed at 10 percent of fair market value. Class III includes "all property not otherwise classified" and is assessed at 20 percent of fair market value. Without Amendment No. 373, historical properties which are: (a) nonresidential or (b) residential but are not owner-occupied would be classified as Class II for *ad valorem* taxation purposes. In short, this constitutional provision reduces taxes of affected historic structures (see (a) and (b) above) by one-half.

EXHIBIT 1
LANDMARK PROPERTIES AND THE PROPERTY TAX: NATIONAL STATUTORY SURVEY

PROGRAM DESCRIPTION (See last page of exhibit for explanation)	ARIZONA	CALIFORNIA	CALIFORNIA
Statute:	ARIZ. REV. STAT. ANN. §42-139.01 - §42-139.03 (West Supp. 1979)	CAL. CONST. art. 13, §8 (West Supp. 1980)	CAL. GOVT. CODE §50280-§50289 (West Supp. 1979) and CAL. PUB. RES. CODE §5031 - §5033 (West Supp. 1979)
Year Authorized:	1977	1974	1972
Program Type:	Reduction	Assessment at current use/assessment to reflect encumbrances.	Assessment at current use.
Eligible Properties/ Owners:	Historic properties listed on the National Register. Properties must be open to the public at least 12 days per year.	Historically significant property designated by the state legislature.	Designated historic properties, listed in either the National Register, or in a city or county register. Property owners must enter into 20-year renewable contracts with their city or county governments providing that the historic buildings will be preserved and maintained; that the property's use may be restricted; and that reasonable public access to the property will be permitted.
Historic Property Application: *Tax Provision:*	Exclusive Arizona has a classified property tax system. Historic residential properties are assessed at *eight* percent of full cash value; without a special provision, these properties would be assessed at *fifteen* percent of full cash value. (This has subsequently been changed to 10 percent of full cash value).	Exclusive Property will be "valued for property tax purposes only on a basis that is consistent with its restrictions and uses."	Exclusive Property assessment is based on current use.
Administrative Agency:	County tax assessor, state Historic Preservation Officer.	Not specified	Local tax assessor
Procedure:	Owner applies to county assessor; application cannot be disqualified solely because of the potential loss of revenue that may result from granting the application.	Not specified	Not specified
Penalty Provision:	If property is disqualified, owner is subject to tax penalty of either half the reduction in taxes of or half the property's fair market value, whichever is less.	Not specified	Not specified

EXHIBIT 1

LANDMARK PROPERTIES AND THE PROPERTY TAX: NATIONAL STATUTORY SURVEY

PROGRAM DESCRIPTION (See last page of exhibit for explanation)	CALIFORNIA[1]	COLORADO	COLORADO
Statute:	CAL. REV. & TAX CODE §439–§439.4 (West. Supp. 1979)	COLO. REV. STAT. §39-5-105(2) (a) (Bradford-Robinson Supp. 1978)	COLO. REV. STAT. §39-5-105 (3) (a) (Bradford-Robinson Supp. 1978).
Year Authorized:	1977	1975	1975
Program Type:	Assessment at current use.	Rehabilitation assessment (5 years)	Rehabilitation assessment (5 years).
Eligible Properties/Owners:	Locally or state designated historic property subject to owner's 20-year contract with the local government to maintain the building and to provide some public access.	Residential structure of three units or less and more than 30 years old.	Commercial building or structure which is part of a development or redevelopment project area, and is more than 30 years old.
Historic Property Application:	Exclusive	Inclusive	Inclusive
Tax Provision:	Current use assessment is based on capitalization method even for owner-occupied single-family dwellings.	Rehabilitation or modernization shall not be taken into account in determining the assessment of the structue for the five tax years immediately following completion of the work.	Renovation or rehabilitation completed after Jan. 1, 1976 shall not be taken into account in determining the valuation for assessment of improvements for the first 5 taxable years after completion. If the property changes ownership, other than by assent, or inheritance, during the first 5 taxable years, the provision does not apply.
Administrative Agency:	County tax assessor, Board of Capitalization	Local tax assessor	Local tax assessor
Procedure:	Not specified	Not specified	Not specified
Penalty Provision:	If the property is no longer eligible for tax treatment under an historic preservation contract (see above), the property's full cash value is determined and the property value is taxed accordingly.	Not specified	Not specified

1. CAL. REV. & TAX CODE §229 (West Supp. 1978) provides a five-year rehabilitation assessment program for improvements up to $15,000. This program is inclusive to historic properties.

EXHIBIT 1
LANDMARK PROPERTIES AND THE PROPERTY TAX: NATIONAL STATUTORY SURVEY

PROGRAM DESCRIPTION (See last page of exhibit for explanation)	COLORADO	COLORADO	CONNECTICUT
Statute:	COLO. REV. STAT. §39-1-104 (Bradford-Robinson Supp. 1978)	COLO. REV. STAT. §38-30.5-109 (Bradford-Robinson Supp. 1978)	CONN. GEN. STAT. ANN. §12-81(7) and §12-88 (West Supp. 1980)
Year Authorized:	1975	1976	1949
Program Type:	Assessment to reflect encumbrances (designation)	Assessment to reflect encumbrances (easements)	Exemption
Eligible Properties/Owners:	Properties included on state register of historic properties.	Properties with: facade and scenic easements for historic preservation and designated of historic significance.	Designated historic properties owned by non-profit, charitable institutions.
Historic Property Application:	Exclusive	Exclusive	Exclusive
Tax Provision:	"Inclusion on the state register of historic properties . . . shall add no value to the valuation for assessment."	Subject properties are assessed "with due regard to the restricted uses to which the property may be devoted."	Subject properties exempt from real property taxation.
Administrative Agency:	Not specified	Local tax assessor	Not specified
Procedure:	Not specified	Not specified	Not specified
Penalty Provision:	Not specified	Not specified	Not specified

EXHIBIT 1

LANDMARK PROPERTIES AND THE PROPERTY TAX: NATIONAL STATUTORY SURVEY

PROGRAM DESCRIPTION (See last page of exhibit for explanation)	CONNECTICUT	CONNECTICUT[1]	DELAWARE
Statute:	CONN. GEN. STAT. ANN. §7-131b (West Supp. 1980)	CONN. GEN. STAT. ANN. §12-127a (West Supp. 1980)	DEL. CODE ANN. tit. 9, §§ 8103, 8104 (Michie Supp. 1978)
Year Authorized:	1963	1969	1915 (§8130); 1852 (§8104) (amended later)
Program Type:	Assessment to reflect encumbrances (easements)	Exemption/Reduction	Exemption
Eligible Properties/Owners:	Lands with easements promoting historic preservation	Historically or architecturally significant structures if "the current level of taxation is a material factor which threatens the continued existence of the structure." The determination of historical significance is to be made by the municipality or by a local private preservation or architectural group selected by the municipality.	Historic properties owned by non-profit historical societies.
Historic Property Application:	Exclusive	Exclusive	Inclusive
Tax Provision:	Owners of such lands are entitled to revaluation to reflect the existence of such encumbrances.	Authorizes municipalities to abate, in whole or in part, real property taxes.	Subject properties are exempt from local property taxes.
Administrative Agency:	Local tax assessor	Local tax assessor; local preservation group (see above)	Not specified
Procedure:	Owner must file a written application to the Assessor or Board of Assessors of the municipality.	On application by owner	Not specified
Penalty Provision:	Not specified	All abated taxes must be repaid by the owner if the structure subsequently is demolished or remodeled and thereby loses its significance.	Not specified

1. Conn. Gen. Stat. Ann. §12-65 b-e (West Supp. 1978) provides various property tax rehabilitation incentives. This program is inclusive to historic properties.

EXHIBIT 1
LANDMARK PROPERTIES AND THE PROPERTY TAX: NATIONAL STATUTORY SURVEY

PROGRAM DESCRIPTION (See last page of exhibit for explanation)	DISTRICT OF COLUMBIA[1]	GEORGIA	HAWAII
Statute:	D.C. Code Encycl. §47-651-§47-654 (West Supp. 1978).	GA. Code Ann. §85-1406-§85-1410 (Harrison Supp. 1979).	Haw. Rev. Stat §246-34 (1979)
Year Authorized:	1974	1976	1965
Program Type:	Assessment at current use	Assessment to reflect encumbrances (easements)	Exemption
Eligible Properties/Owners	Properties designated as historic landmarks by the Joint Committee on Landmarks of the National Capital. The owner must sign a 20-year covenant guaranteeing the property's maintenance and preservation, and other conditions as the Council finds to be necessary to encourage preservation of historic buildings.	Properties with facade or conservation easements granted to government agencies or certain non-profit agencies. Properties must have architectural/historic significance or be located within an officially designated historic district.	Urban land which may be used by the public as historical site.
Historic Property Application: *Tax Provision:*	Exclusive Assessment at current use if that value is lower than fair market value.	Exclusive Recording of easement constitutes "notice to the board of tax assessors . . . and shall entitle the owner to a revaluation of the encumbered real property."	Exclusive Property tax exemption if the Tax Director determines that the dedicated land has a benefit to the public equal to the value of the real property taxes (measured by the cost of improvements, the continuing maintenance thereof, and other factors pertinent for the director).
Administrative Agency:	Joint Committee on Landmarks of the National Capital, local assessor.	County Board of Tax Assessors	State Tax Director
Procedure:	Not specified	See above	Owner must petition the Director of Taxation stating the exact area of the land to be dedicated. Approval is for a renewable period of 10 years.
Penalty Provision:	Failure to abide by the covenant causes the recovery of back taxes, with interest, which would have been due and payable in the absence of the program.	Not specified	Failure of the owner to observe the restrictions on use shall cancel the special tax exemption privilege retroactive to the date of the original dedication. The difference in taxes shall be payable together with interest of 5 percent a year.

1. D.C. Code Encycl. §47-651 (West Supp. 1977) provides that the District of Columbia Council can adopt a five-year rehabilitation assessment program. This program would be exclusive to historic properties. The District Tax Assessor's Office reports that this provision has been tabled by the Council.

EXHIBIT 1
LANDMARK PROPERTIES AND THE PROPERTY TAX: NATIONAL STATUTORY SURVEY

PROGRAM DESCRIPTION (See last page of exhibit for explanation)	IDAHO	ILLINOIS
Statute:	1975 Idaho Sess. Laws ch. 142 §67-4615	ILL. ANN. STAT. ch 120 §500.23-4 (West Supp. 1979)
Year Authorized:	1975	Effective July 1, 1980
Program Type:	Assessment to reflect encumbrances (designation and easements)	Rehabilitation assessment (4 years)
Eligible Properties/Owners:	Properties with historic designation and restrictions in use (i.e. conveyance of easements).	Buildings of less than 55 dwelling units which are at least 30 years old and used primarily for residential purposes (single-family units and properties).
Historic Property Application:	Exclusive	Inclusive
Tax Provision:	"The designation and any recorded restrictions upon the property limiting its use for preservation purposes shall be considered by the tax assessor in appraising it for tax purposes."	Exemption pursuant to Article IX, Section 6 of 1970 Constitution of maximum of $15,000 in actual value of improvements per dwelling unit, and shall last four years from date improvements completed.
Administrative Agency:	County tax assessor - Local Historic Preservation Commission	Local assessor, board of assessors or supervisor of assessments
Procedure:	Local Historic Preservation Commission gives notice of designation to the county tax assessor.	Owner of the property makes a verified application to assessor with documentation.
Penalty Provision:	Not specified	Not specified

EXHIBIT 1
LANDMARK PROPERTIES AND THE PROPERTY TAX: NATIONAL STATUTORY SURVEY

PROGRAM DESCRIPTION (See last page of exhibit for explanation)	ILLINOIS	INDIANA[1]	KENTUCKY
Statute:	ILL. ANN. STAT. ch. 24 §11-48.2-6 (Smith Hurd Supp. 1980)	IND. CODE §18-5 15-1 (Bobbs-Merrill Supp. 1979)	KY. REV. STAT. §65.420 §65.450 (Banis Baldwin Supp. 1979)
Year Authorized:	1961	1911	1972
Program Type:	Assessment to reflect encumbrances (easements)	Exemption	Assessment to reflect encumbrances (easements)
Eligible Properties/Owners:	Historic properties with encumbrances or restrictions placed upon them.	Designated historic properties owned by non-profit organizations.	Properties with historic, scenic or facade easements conveyed to public bodies or authorized historic preservation organizations.
Historic Property Application:	Exclusive	Exclusive	Exclusive
Tax Provision:	"Any depreciation occasioned by such encumbrances or restrictions shall be deducted in the valuation of such property."	"All such property so acquired and preserved shall not be liable to taxation but the same shall be entirely exempt therefrom."	Assessment reflects "any change in the market value of the property" due to easements.
Administrative Agency:	Local tax assessor	Not specified	Local tax assessor
Procedure:	Not specified	Not specified	Not specified
Penalty Provision:	Not specified	Not specified	Not specified

1. IND. CODE ANN. E6-1. 1-12-22 (Burns Supp. 1977) provides various property tax rehabilitation incentive programs. These programs are inclusive to historic properties.

EXHIBIT 1
LANDMARK PROPERTIES AND THE PROPERTY TAX: NATIONAL STATUTORY SURVEY

PROGRAM DESCRIPTION (See last page of exhibit for explanation)	LOUISIANA	MARYLAND	MARYLAND[1]
Statute:	LA. CONST. art VII §18(c)	MD. ANN. CODE §81-12G (Michie Supp. 1979)	MD. ANN. CODE §81-9-c (Michie Supp. 1979)
Year Authorized:	1974	1965	1975
Program Type:	Assessment at current use	Rehabilitation refund	Rehabilitation assessment (for 2 years), rehabilitation abatement (for years 3 to 5)
Eligible Properties/Owners:	Buildings of historic or architectural importance.	Properties in locally designated historic districts.	Rehabilitation of historically and architecturally significant structures located in Allegany and Frederick Counties and the City of Baltimore.
Historic Property Application:	Exclusive	Exclusive	Exclusive
Tax Provision:	Subject properties are assessed at "10 percent of use-value rather than fair market value." The value is determined in accordance with criteria established by law and applied uniformly throughout the state.	Up to 10 percent of an owner's expenses for restoration and preservation is credited against property taxes. Tax credit is allowed once but may be spread over five years.	Tax credit against property tax lasts five years on an increasing proportion of increase in assessed valuation attributable to improvements.[2]
Administrative Agency:	Assessor in parish or district	County or municipality	-Allegany County (§9C(b)) -Frederick County (§9C(j)) -Baltimore City (§9C(a))
Procedure:	Not specified	County may establish application procedures.	Local tax assessor
Penalty Provision:	Not specified	Not specified	Not specified

1. Michigan and Minnesota provide property tax rehabilitation incentive programs which are inclusive to historic properties. See Mich. Comp. Laws Ann. §§ 125.1651 and Minn. H.F. 1803, Ch. 620.
2. For the first two years after rehabilitation there is no increase in the property's assessed value. In year three, the upward reassessment is limited to 20 percent of the improvement, in year four, 40 percent, and year five, 60 percent. In year six, full upward reassessment is permitted.

EXHIBIT 1
LANDMARK PROPERTIES AND THE PROPERTY TAX: NATIONAL STATUTORY SURVEY

PROGRAM DESCRIPTION (See last page of exhibit for explanation)	MISSISSIPPI[1]	MISSOURI[2]	NEVADA
Statute:	MISS. CODE. ANN. §27-31-1(d) (Lawyers Coop. Supp. 1979)	MO. ANN. STAT.§353.110 (Vernon)	NEV. REV. STAT §361A.010-§361A.280 (1977)
Year Authorized:	1940	1945	1975
Program Type:	Exemption	Rehabilitation assessment/abatement	Assessment at current use.
Eligible Properties/Owners:	Properties of historic societies.	Property owned by an urban redevelopment corporation within an approved project area.	Land upon which designated historic sites are located.
Historic Property Application:	Exclusive	Inclusive	Exclusive
Tax Provision:	"Exemption from taxation"	The real property tax owed by an urban redevelopment corporation is measured by the assessed valuation of the land, exclusive of improvements in the year preceding acquisition. The property tax may be frozen at this level for ten years from the date of acquisition. For the next fifteen years taxes on land and improvements are assessed at one-half of full value.	Subject property is assessed at 35 percent of its full cash value.
Administrative Agency:	Not specified	The Board of Aldermen shall approve or disapprove a development proposal after review by the Mayor and appropriate public agencies.	County assessor
Procedure:	Not specified	See above.	Owner applies to county assessor. Public hearings by governing bodies of city and/or county government, are conducted to weigh costs in lost revenue versus historic benefits.
Penalty Provision:	Not specified	Not specified	When land is converted to a higher use, the owner pays the difference between the taxes payable at the 35 percent assessment and full value assessment plus penalties.

1. Miss. Code Ann. §21-33-91 provides a property tax rehabilitation incentive program which is inclusive to historic properties.
2. Montana provides a property tax rehabilitation incentive program which is inclusive to historic properties. See Mont. Rev. Codes Ann. §84-7513.1 (Supp. 1977).

EXHIBIT 1
LANDMARK PROPERTIES AND THE PROPERTY TAX: NATIONAL STATUTORY SURVEY

PROGRAM DESCRIPTION (See last page of exhibit for explanation)	NEW JERSEY[1]	NEW MEXICO	NEW YORK
Statute:	N.J. STAT. ANN §54:4-3.52-§54:4-3.54. (West Supp. 1980)	N.M. STAT. ANN. §18-6-13 (1978)	N.Y. NOT-FOR-PROFIT-CORP. LAW §1408 (McKinney 1977)
Year Authorized:	1962	1969	1969
Program Type:	Exemption	Rehabilitation refund	Exemption
Eligible Properties/Owners:	Historic buildings listed in the state register and owned by non-profit corporations.	Historic buildings listed in the state register of historic places and available for educational purposes.	Designated historic properties owned by incorporated historical societies of N.Y. state.
Historic Property Application:	Exclusive	Exclusive	Exclusive
Tax Provision:	Subject buildings are "exempt from taxation."	"Local city, county and school property taxes assessed against the property . . . shall be reduced by the amount expended for restoration, preservation and maintenance each year." Expenses incurred in one year may be carried forward for tax purposes for up to ten years.	Historic properties are exempt from taxation.
Administrative Agency:	Local tax assessor; State Department of Environmental Protection (DEP) Division of Taxation.	Local tax assessor and state review board. Continued allowance of the credit requires approval by state review board of all restoration, preservation and maintenance plans.	Not specified
Procedure:	Initial application filed with the Director of the State Division of Taxation. State DEP certifies historic status.	Not specified	Not specified
Penalty Provision:	Not specified	Not specified	Not specified

1. New Jersey offers various property tax rehabilitation incentive programs which are inclusive to historic properties. See N.J. Stat. Ann. §54: 4-3.75 and §34.4-3.95.

EXHIBIT 1
LANDMARK PROPERTIES AND THE PROPERTY TAX: NATIONAL STATUTORY SURVEY

PROGRAM DESCRIPTION (See last page of exhibit for explanation)	NEW YORK	NEW YORK[1]	NORTH CAROLINA
Statute:	S.9791-A, A. 11779-A (May 12, 1980)	N.Y. REAL PROPERTY TAX LAW §489 (as amended by L. of 1977, ch. 850).	N.C. GEN. STAT. §105-278 (Michie 1979)
Year Authorized:	1980	1977	1977
Program Type:	Assessment to reflect encumbrances (easements).	Rehabilitation refund/rehabilitation assessment (12-20 yrs.)	Refund
Eligible Properties/Owners:	"Historic and/or cultural place or property where the city, town, village or county legislative body has acquired fee or any lesser interest, development right, easement, covenant or other contractual right."	Multiple residential dwellings, non-residential structures converted to multiple residential dwellings.	Designated properties, under federal, state or local ordinance.
Historic Property Application:	Exclusive	Inclusive	Exclusive
Tax Provision:	"After acquisition of any such interest . . . the effect of the acquisition on the valuation placed on any remaining private interest in such property for purposes of real estate taxation shall be taken into account.	*Rehab assessment:* For twelve years to extent of any increase in assessed valuation resulting from rehabilitation of improvements to a property including alterations and improvements to exterior walls. *Rehab refund:* Up to 8-1/3 percent of the cost of improvements each year for not less than nine, nor more than twelve years. (90 percent of certified construction costs may be allocated).	Historic properties taxed uniformly as a class at 50 percent of their value as opposed to 100 percent of value.
Administrative Agency:	Local tax assessor	In New York City, Dept. of Housing Preservation and Development (HPD).[2]	Tax supervisor of the County
Procedure:	Not specified	Applicants must submit evidence of construction costs to HPD within 48 months of the commencement of construction. Construction must be completed within 36 months of the starting date. If all provisions are met, benefits are "as-of-right"	Annual application of the owner is required.
Penalty Provision:	Not specified	Not specified	Not specified

1. The application of New York City is described for illustrative purposes.
2. This exhibit does not indicate New York City's tax exemption/reduction provision in the case of financial hardship contained in its landmarks law (New York City ch. RA §§205.1.0-2.8.21.0)

EXHIBIT 1

LANDMARK PROPERTIES AND THE PROPERTY TAX: NATIONAL STATUTORY SURVEY

PROGRAM DESCRIPTION (See last page of exhibit for explanation)	NORTH CAROLINA	NORTH CAROLINA[1]	OHIO
Statute:	1979 N.C. ADV. LEGIS. SERV., N0. 7.	N.C. GEN. STAT. §160A-399.5(6) (Michie 1979).	OHIO REV. CODE ANN. §5709.18 (Anderson Supp. 1978)
Year Authorized:	1979	1971	1976
Program Type:	Assessment to reflect encumbrances (easement).	Assessment to reflect encumbrances on property (designation).	Exemption.
Eligible Properties/Owners:	Historically significant sites.	Properties designated historic under local ordinance.	Designated historic buildings owned by non-profit, charitable institutions and dedicated to public uses.
Historic Property Application:	Exclusive	Exclusive	Exclusive
Tax Provision:	"For purposes of taxation, land and improvement subject to a conservation or preservation agreement shall be assessed on the basis of the true value of the land and improvement less any reduction in value caused by the agreement."	"The designation and any accorded restrictions upon the property limiting its use for preservation purposes shall be considered by the tax supervisor in appraising it for tax purposes."	Subject properties are "exempt from taxation."
Administrative Agency:	County tax assessor	County tax assessor	Not specified
Procedure:	Preservation and conservation agreements filed with Register of Deeds in county where site is located.	The local historic properties commission notifies county assessor.	Not specified
Penalty Provision:	"Where appropriate, damages or other monetary relief may be awarded for breach of any obligations."	Not specified	Not specified

1. North Dakota provides a property tax rehabilitation program which is inclusive to historic properties. See N.D. Cent. Code §§57-02.2-02 to 03 (Supp. 1975).

EXHIBIT 1

LANDMARK PROPERTIES AND THE PROPERTY TAX: NATIONAL STATUTORY SURVEY

PROGRAM DESCRIPTION (See last page of exhibit for explanation)	OREGON	OREGON	OREGON[1,2]
Statute:	OR. REV. STAT. §358.475 - §358.565	OR. REV. STAT. §271.710 - §271.50	OR. REV. STAT. §308.740 - §308.790
Year Authorized:	(1977) 1975	(1977) 1967	(1977) 1971
Program Type:	Reduction. (No applications for special assessment may be made after December 31, 1985.)	Assessment to reflect encumbrances (easements).	Assessment at current use.
Eligible Properties/Owners:	Properties listed in the national register and open to the public at least once a year. In addition, eligible property owners must agree to maintain their properties according to standards established by the State Historic Preservation Officer.	Properties with historic facade or other easement conveyed to public bodies or authorized non-profit historic preservation organizations.	Open space land whose maintenance in its present condition and use will preserve historic sites.
Historic Property Application: *Tax Provision:*	Exclusive. An assessment freeze for 15 consecutive years at the true cash value of the property at the time of initial application.	Exclusive. Applicable property is "assessed on the basis of the true cash value of the property less any reduction in value caused by the ... easements."	Exclusive. The assessor must "assume the highest and best use of the land to be the current use."
Administrative Agency:	County assessor, State Historic Preservation Officer, State Advisory Committee on Historic Preservation.	Local tax assessor, other government bodies.	County assessor, State Dept. of Revenue.
Procedure:	Owner applies to county assessor on state-approved form. State reviews application and notifies county assessor.	Hearing is conducted on easement acquisition; afterwards local tax assessor is notified.	Owner applies to county assessor.
Penalty Provision:	Loss of the special assessment triggers the recapture of all tax savings plus a penalty of 15 percent of those savings if the owner is at fault.	Not specified.	If change in use, land is reassessed to reflect the higher value.

1. Oregon provides property tax rehabilitation incentive programs which are inclusive to historic properties. See OR. REV. STAT. §§308.690-§308.700.
2. Pennsylvania provides numerous property tax rehabilitation incentive programs which are inclusive to historic properties. See PA. STAT. ANN. tit. 72 § 4714 (Purdon Supp. 1977), S.B. 64, Act No. 1977-42, and S. 305 Act 1977-76.

EXHIBIT 1
LANDMARK PROPERTIES AND THE PROPERTY TAX: NATIONAL STATUTORY SURVEY

PROGRAM DESCRIPTION (See last page of exhibit for explanation)	PUERTO RICO	RHODE ISLAND[2]
Statute:	P.R. LAWS ANN. tit. 13 §551 (Equity 1962) 1955	1966 R.I. Pub. Laws ch. 15
Year Authorized:		1966 - As enacted, the statute applied to alterations and improvements commenced between June 1, 1966 and June 1, 1968. It has been extended several times. The Rhode Island Historical Preservation Commission reports that it is still in effect.
Program Type: Historic Property Application:	Rehabilitation refund (5-10 years)	Rehabilitation assessment for five years.
Eligible Properties/Owners:	Exclusive Improved or restored properties in San Juan historic district or any other designated historic zone.	Inclusive Any dwelling used exclusively for residential purposes. Program applies only in City of Providence.[2]
Tax Provision:	Exemption from all property tax for up to 10 years for total restoration, or up to 5 years for partial restoration.[1]	No upward reassessment due to rehabilitation for five years.
Administrative Agency:	Local tax assessor; Institute of Puerto Rico Culture, Secretary of the Treasury, Puerto Rico Planning Board.	Tax assessor, City of Providence. The assessor certifies that alteration costs are reasonable.
Procedure:	Person doing restoration requests exemption from the Secretary of the Treasury. Application must also be approved by Puerto Rico Planning Board and Institute of Puerto Rico Culture.	Not specified
Penalty Provision:	Status may be revoked if property is not restored, not maintained in good condition, or not used according to zoning regulations. Upon revocation, property owner pays back taxes plus 6 percent interest.	Not specified

1. There is an additional income tax exemption. Gross income from rehabilitated buildings in the San Juan Historic zone is exempt from income taxation.
2. A 1978 statute allows city councils to adjust taxes on realty to encourage rehabilitation: see H 7580 ch. 132.

EXHIBIT 1

LANDMARK PROPERTIES AND THE PROPERTY TAX: NATIONAL STATUTORY SURVEY

PROGRAM DESCRIPTION (See last page of exhibit for explanation)	SOUTH DAKOTA	SOUTH DAKOTA
Statute:	S.D. COMPILED LAWS ANN. §1-19A-20-§1-19A-21 (Alan Smith Supp. 1978)	S.D. COMPILED LAWS ANN. §1-19B-25
Year Authorized:	1978	1974
Program Type:	Rehabilitation refund (five years)	Assessment to reflect encumbrances (designation and easements)
Historic Property Application:	Exclusive	Exclusive
Eligible Properties/Owners:	Properties listed in the state register of historic places. Properties must have been either: (1) assisted through a Federal Preservation Grant-In-Aid; (2) substantially restored or rehabilitated with a state historic preservation loan, or (3) privately restored or rehabilitated and approved by the State Board of Cultural Preservation. Another requirement is that the property owner must attach a restrictive covenant running with the land that states that the property will be maintained in an appropriate manner.	Historic designated properties and properties with historic easements.
Tax Provision:	Rehabilitated property pays no property taxes. The moratorium begins in the year that approval of the completed work is granted and extends for a period of 5 years.	"The designation and any recorded restrictions upon the property limiting its use for preservation purposes shall be considered by the tax assessor for appraising it for tax purposes."
Administrative Agency:	Local tax assessor, State Board of Cultural Preservation	Local Historic Preservation Commission, local tax assessor
Procedure:	Not Specified	Not Specified
Penalty Provision:	Not Specified	Not Specified

EXHIBIT 1

LANDMARK PROPERTIES AND THE PROPERTY TAX: NATIONAL STATUTORY SURVEY

PROGRAM DESCRIPTION (See last page of exhibit for explanation)	TENNESSEE	TENNESSEE
Statute:	TENN. CODE ANN. §11-15-101-§11-15-108	TENN. CODE ANN. §67-519-§67-521 (Cum. Supp. 1978)
Year Authorized:	1973	1976
Program Type:	Assessment to reflect encumbrances (easements)	Rehabilitation assessment (10 to 15 years)
Eligible Properties/Owners:	Properties or land with historic, scenic or facade easements conveyed to public bodies or authorized historic preservation organizations.	The property must be designated historic by the local, state or federal governement and be located in a county of 200,000 or more population. Non-designated properties may also be eligible on the basis of age (i.e. all properties 175 years or older are qualified), or upon recommendation by the Local Historical Review Board.
Historic Property Application:	Exclusive	Exclusive
Tax Provision:	The "subject property is assessed on the basis of true cash value of the property . . . less such reduction from the granting of the . . . easements."	Exemption for value of improvements or restoration. The exemption lasts 10 years for partial or exterior restorations and improvements and 15 years for total restorations.
Administrative Agency:	Local tax assessor	The Local Historic Properties Review Board, local tax assessor, State Historical Commission and State Preservation Officer.
Procedure:	Not specified	Owner application
Penalty Provision:	Not specified	If any structure receiving an exemption is demolished or significantly altered, as determined by the Local Historic Properties Review Board, the owner will be liable for the difference between the tax paid and tax which would have been due on the improved value.

EXHIBIT 1

LANDMARK PROPERTIES AND THE PROPERTY TAX: NATIONAL STATUTORY SURVEY

PROGRAM DESCRIPTION (See last page of exhibit for explanation)	TEXAS	VIRGINIA
Statute:	Amendment 4 to Texas State Constitution	VA. Code §58-12 (Michie Supp. 1980)
Year Authorized:	1978	1971
Program Type:	Localities have the discretion to allow special property tax treatment of historic properties. This may include exemption, reduction, and rehabilitation refund, assessment or abatement.	Exemption
Eligible Properties/Owners:	Properties on the National Register or state landmarks.	Properties of specified non-profit histori- cal societies such as Historic Richmond Foundation and Virginia Historical Society.
Historic Property Application:	Exclusive	Exclusive
Tax Provision:	See above. Austin, for example, has adopted a reduction program; Galveston, a rehabilitation incentive program.	Properties are exempt from state and local taxation.
Administrative Agency:	Local tax assessor	Local tax assessor
Procedure:	Determined by local community	Owner application
Penalty Provision:	Not specified	Not specified

EXHIBIT 1
LANDMARK PROPERTIES AND THE PROPERTY TAX: NATIONAL STATUTORY SURVEY

PROGRAM DESCRIPTION (See last page of exhibit for explanation)	VIRGINIA	VIRGINIA	VIRGINIA
Statute:	VA. CODE §10-155	VA. CODE §§10-139, 10-140, & 10-142 (Michie Supp. 1980).	VA. CODE §58-769.4 - §58-769.16 (Michie Supp. 1980)
Year Authorized:	1978	1966	1971
Program Type:	Assessment to reflect encumbrances (easements)	Assessment to reflect encumbrances (easements and designation)	Assessment at current use
Eligible Properties/Owners:	Historic, scenic, or facade easements conveyed to specified public bodies such as county or municipality.	Properties designated by Virginia Historic Landmarks Commission.	Lands used for historical purposes.
Historic Property Application: *Tax Provision:*	Exclusive "Assessments made on the property for taxation shall reflect any change in the market value of the property which may result from the less than fee interest held by the public body."	Exclusive Historic designation of a property "shall be *prima facie* evidence that the value of such property for commercial, residential or other purposes is reduced by reason of its designation."	Exclusive Qualifying lands assessed on actual use.
Administrative Agency:	Local tax assessor; authorized public bodies (see above)	Local tax assessor; Virginia Historic Landmarks Commission	Any city, county or town
Procedure:	Owner application	Virginia Historic Landmarks Commission	Owner application to local tax assessor on forms prepared by State Tax Commission.
Penalty Provision:	Not specified	Not specified	Upon change of property from historical use, tax exemption is removed. In addition, owner must pay on the basis of highest and best use valuation for past five years plus penalty of 6 percent interest. If the owner fails to give notice, a penalty of 100 percent of recaptured taxes is also due.

EXHIBIT 1
LANDMARK PROPERTIES AND THE PROPERTY TAX: NATIONAL STATUTORY SURVEY

PROGRAM DESCRIPTION (See last page of exhibit for explanation)	VIRGINIA	WASHINGTON	WASHINGTON[1]
Statute:	VA. CODE §§58-760.2 & 58.760.3 (Michie Supp. 1978)	WASH. REV. CODE. ANN. §84.36.060 (West Supp. 1980)	WASH. REV. CODE. ANN. §84.34.010-§84.34-030 (West. Supp. 1980)
Year Authorized:	1978	1973	1970
Program Type:	Rehabilitation assessment.	Exemption	Assessment at current use.
Eligible Properties/Owners:	Rehabilitated residential, commercial or industrial structures 25 years or older. To qualify, the rehabilitation must be significant, defined as increasing the assessed value of residential structures by 40 percent, and commercial/industrial structures by 60 percent.	Properties of non-profit historical societies operated solely for historical purposes and receiving funding from U.S. or any state or any political subdivision or general public.	"Land, the preservation of which in its present use would . . . preserve historic sites."
Historic Property Application:	Inclusive	Exclusive	Exclusive
Tax Provision:	No upward reassessment due to rehabilitation for up to 10 years	See above	Applicable lands are valued according to their "current use classification."
Administrative Agency:	Local tax assessor, governing body of any city, county, or town	County assessor	County assessor
Procedure:	Owner application to governing body	Not specified	Owner applies to county assessor or county legislative authority on forms provided by State Department of Revenue.
Penalty Provision:	Not specified	Not specified	Not specified

1. WASH. REV. CODE ANN. 84.36.700 provides a property tax rehabilitation incentive program which is inclusive to historic properties.

EXHIBIT 1
LANDMARK PROPERTIES AND THE PROPERTY TAX: NATIONAL STATUTORY SURVEY

PROGRAM DESCRIPTION (See last page of exhibit for explanation)	WEST VIRGINIA	WISCONSIN	WISCONSIN
Statute:	W. VA. CODE ANN. §§8-26A-4 & 8-26A-5 (West Supp. 1980)	WISC. STAT. ANN §§70.11 (20) & 70.11(4) (West Supp. 1979)	WISC. STAT. ANN. §70.11 (24) (West Supp. 1978)
Year Authorized:	1973	1949	1949
Program Type:	Assessment to reflect encumbrances (easements)	Exemption	Rehabilitation abatement (for 5-year period)
Eligible Properties/Owners:	Properties with historic, scenic or facade easements (restrictions) conveyed to public bodies or authorized historic preservation organizations.	Properties owned by non-profit historical societies.	Properties in conservation area.
Historic Property Application: Tax Provision:	Exclusive "The county assessor shall take such factors (see above) into consideration in assessing the properties."	Exclusive See above.	Inclusive Five-year partial taxation on improvements.
Administration Agency:	Municipal or county historic landmarks commission; county assessor.	Local tax assessor/tax commissioner.	Local tax assessor/tax commissioner.
Procedure:	Easement agreement is made between historic commission and owner in writing and recorded in office of county clerk. Historic commission then notifies county assessor of historic designation.	Owner application	Applications are made by the property owner to assessor or tax commissioner in city, town, or village.
Penalty Provision:	Not specified	Not specified	Not specified

EXHIBIT NOTES

Statute/Year Authorized: The exhibit indicates the full legal citation as well as the year the statute was authorized.

Program Type: There are seven categories of property tax programs relating to landmark properties.

   1. Exemption   Landmark property pays no property tax.

   2. Reduction   Landmark property pays a portion of nominal property taxes.

   3. Rehabilitation refund   Existing (pre-rehabilitational) property taxes are reduced if landmark property is renovated.

   4. Rehabilitation assessment   No upward reassessment of renovated landmark property.

   5. Rehabilitation abatement   Partial upward reassessment of renovated landmark property.

   6. Assessment to reflect encumbrances   Specific charge that the assessment of landmark properties reflect their landmark status and/or the presence of a preservation/facade easement.

   7. Assessment at current use   Landmark properties are to be assessed at their current use instead of highest and best use.

Eligible Properties/Owners: The property characteristics and the type of owner or owner performance which must be satisfied for the indicated property tax treatment to be accorded.

Historic Property Application: The exhibit differentiates between *exclusive* and *inclusive* historic property application. The former refers to those statutes which are directed exclusively to landmark properties. The latter refers to those statutes which can assist landmark properties but are not limited to such situations.

Tax Provision: This section briefly describes the specific tax treatment, where possible citing the exact language of the statute.

Administrative/Agency Procedure: The statutory specification of the specific group or groups administering the tax provision and the administrative procedure to be followed are summarized in this section.

Penalty Provision: This section summarizes the penalties provided by statute in the event the property owner does not fulfill prescribed requirements. For example, an owner of a landmark property assessed at current use may be fined if he or she demolishes the landmark or does not allow public access.

Source: The statutory survey was conducted by Jessica Winslow, Alan Neaigus, and James J. Németh of the Center for Urban Policy Research. It is also based in part on research materials provided by the International Association of Assessing Officers.

APPENDIX TWO

LANDMARK PROPERTIES AND THE PROPERTY TAX: ANNOTATED BIBLIOGRAPHY

Advisory Council on Historic Preservation. *The Contribution of Historic Preservation to Urban Revitalization.* Washington, D.C. U.S. Government Printing Office, January 1979. Report prepared by Booz, Allen and Hamilton, Inc.

This study investigates the effect of historic preservation activities in Alexandria (Virginia), Galveston (Texas), Savannah (Georgia), and Seattle (Washington). Included in the analysis is an examination of the physical, economic, and social changes occurring within historic neighborhoods in each of these cities. According to the study, historic designation and attendant preservation activities provide many benefits including saving important properties from demolition, assuring compatible new construction and land uses, and providing a concentrated area of interest to attract tourists and metropolitan-area visitors. Designation also has the beneficial effect of strengthening property values—an impact documented by comparing the selling prices of buildings located within versus outside the historic districts.

Almy, Richard R. "Considerations in Creating Property Tax Relief for Historic Preservation." In Gregory Andrews ed., *Tax Incentives for Historic Preservation.* Washington, D.C.: The Preservation Press, 1980, pp. 125-30.

Special property-tax programs are considered as a means of alleviating some of the economic pressures confronting the owners of landmarks.

Almy examines numerous such approaches including providing exemption or special rehabilitation incentives.* Recurring problems and issues in the assessment of historic properties are considered, such as valuing land at its highest and best use rather than current use; appraising historic buildings at replacement rather than reproduction cost; and defining depreciation in an appropriate manner. The author recommends adoption of legislation providing special property-tax relief for historic properties and implementation of assessment practices sensitive to landmark's special character.

Almy, Richard R. "Property Taxation and the Preservation of Historic Properties." *Research and Information Series.* International Association of Assessing Officers, August 1977.

A significant discussion of landmark properties and the property tax. Includes a selected bibliography and useful statutory appendix.

Andrews, Gregory, editor. *Tax Incentives for Historic Preservation.* Washington, D.C.: Preservation Press, 1980. See individual article citations in this bibliography.

Baker, R. Lisle. "State Tax Innovations in the Conservation Field." In Gregory Andrews, editor. *Tax Incentives for Historic Preservation.* Washington, D.C.: The Preservation Press, 1980.

Strategies to assist the conservation of historic properties are discussed, including special property-tax provisions such as assessment at current use and property-tax reduction.

The author considers several issues associated with the property-tax strategies, including local fiscal impact, equity considerations, federal tax implications, and legal restraints.

Booz, Allen and Hamilton Inc. *The Contribution of Historic Preservation.* See Advisory Council on Historic Preservation.

Buchana, Robert R. "Is There a Special Value for Antique Buildings?" *Appraisal Institute Magazine* 12, no. 3 (Fall 1968): 37-42.

---

*For the sake of consistency, this annotated bibliography utilizes the landmark-property-tax program terminology presented in Appendix one.

This article discusses the difficulty of valuing "antique buildings" if the appraiser rigidly follows the three standard approaches of cost, market, and income. The uniqueness of early building methods and materials makes it questionable to use the cost approach. Market comparisons may also be problematical since it is difficult to identify appropriate "comps." Income calculations may also be more complicated if, for example, the antique building has fallen into a lesser use, that does not represent adequate market utilization.

Confronted with these problems, appraisers often consider only the land and not the improvement value of antique properties. Buchana argues that this approach is shortsighted and recommends that appraisers should determine the use to which the historic structure may be put if restored. The article notes that there are no easy rules of thumb for appraising antique buildings and indicates that each property will have to be evaluated on an individual basis.

Cloud, Jack M. "Appraisal of Historic Homes." *The Real Estate Appraiser* (September-October 1976), pp. 44-47.

Difficulties of appraising historic homes are highlighted. To illustrate, appraisal assumes that the improvements on land are depreciating assets. In the historic context, however, the home represents "heritage" and therefore is not assumed to lose value.

The article then suggests three approaches to ascertaining value. The three techniques are modifications of the traditional cost, market, and income approaches.

A modified-cost methodology is recommended factoring the following considerations: (1) cost on a unit basis of an equally "historically desirable" dwelling in approximately the same physical condition (including site); (2) the average unit cost of an acceptable renovation and/or restoration; (3) less the estimated incurable physical deterioration; (4) plus the value of land and site improvements.

A second strategy is to use a modified market approach. Value is determined by adjusting recent, nearby, "arm's-length" sales. This approach is commonly used in appraisal, but implementation in the historical context requires a number of special emphases. First, the temporal definition of "recent" sales would have to be extended for the appraiser to obtain enough "comps" of historic homes. (This extension is required because there are relatively few sales of historic properties.) Second, and for similar reasons, the appraiser will have to consider "comps" over a larger geographical area. Third, the appraiser must be careful to examine only arm's-length transfers—donations of properties to private historical societies would therefore not be included. Fourth, the appraiser must carefully adjust the "comps" for "historical value." Historical value encompasses such considerations as type of architecture, historical significance of the owner/builder, and so on. Fifth, the "comps" will have to be adjusted by considering required restoration/renovation costs as well as the amount and value of land in each transaction.

A third strategy for determining the value of the historic homes is to use an income approach. The article cautions that utilizing this method is "basically dangerous" since it is often based on hypothetical situations that may or may not be possible or probable.

Costonis, John J. *Space Adrift: Saving Urban Landmarks Through the Chicago Plan*. Urbana: University of Illinois Press, 1974.

This monograph analyzes the transfer of development rights as a mechanism for preserving historic properties. As part of its overall analysis, it considers the impact of landmark restrictions on property value as well as the assessment of landmarks for tax purposes.

Chapter three discusses the cost of historic preservation restrictions—a measure termed "damages." Damages is determined by subtracting a landmark's present value from its fair-market value in the absence of designation. These "before and after" values are estimated by the income approach of appraisal. Other traditional appraisal methods are not so applicable. Applying the cost technique is problematical for it requires precise estimates of physical decline and functional obsolescense—factors inherently difficult to define in a landmark situation. Low sales frequency of landmarks often renders the market approach inappropriate.

Appendix four examines the relationship between landmarks and the property tax. It examines both the principles and practice of real-estate taxation, notes how and when landmarks may be penalized by prejudical assessment, and discusses "intergovernmental agreement" and other strategies for improving the equity of landmark's assessment/taxation.

Economics Research Associates. *Economic Impact of the Multiple Resource Nomination to the National Register of Historic Places of the St. Louis Central Business District*. Report prepared for the St. Louis Community Development Agency. Boston: Economics Research Associates, 1980.

The ERA study examines the economic effect of designating the St. Louis central business district by (1) considering the impact of comparable designation activity in Seattle (Pioneer Square), New Orleans (Vieux Carre), Savannah (Historic District), and other jurisdictions; and (2) evaluating the anticipated effect of historic status on numerous prototypical buildings located in the St. Louis CBD. The consultants conclude that designating the St. Louis CBD would have both positive and negative economic impacts and that the overall effect would depend on such variables as (1) the applicability/continuation of federal landmark income-tax incentives; (2) the type/extent of designation; and (3) future demand for CBD locations.

Dolman, John P. "Incremental Elements of Market Value Due to Historical Significance." *The Appraisal Journal* (July 1980), pp. 338-53.

Distinctions are made between properties with antique, architectural, or historical value. Procedures for determining historical value are illustrated by a case-study appraisal of Val-Kill, Eleanor Roosevelt's home in Hyde Park, New York.

Gilbert, Frank B. "When Urban Landmarks Commissions Come to the Assessor." In International Association of Assessing Officers, editor. *Property Tax Incentives for Preservation: Use-Value Assessment and the Preservation of Farmland, Open Space, and Historic Sites*. Chicago: International Association of Assessing Officers, 1975.

This article discusses the relationship of landmark designation and the assessment of historic properties. It cites numerous instances where owners of landmark properties in New York City claimed they were being overvalued by virtue of the fact that city assessors had not taken into account designation's redevelopment restrictions.

Gilbert stresses the need of landmark/historic district commissions to gain the confidence of local assessors so that, in his words, "a city's real estate tax program can reflect special landmark situations." The author discusses how the New York City Landmarks Preservation Commission acted in such a capacity.

In a brief comment on the Gilbert article, Carol Westfall, former president of the Chicago Landmarks Preservation Council, indicates that numerous Chicago landmark owners appealed their property-tax assessments on the basis of their building's landmark status. Westfall, like Gilbert, stresses the need for assessors to take into account the factor of historic designation in their day-to-day valuation activities.

Goldstein, M. Robert and Michael J. "Valuation of Historic Property." *New York Law Journal* (December 31, 1979), p. 1.

The authors discuss how and when property age and historical significance affect property value and cite leading court cases that have considered these interrelationships.

Of the three traditional approaches to the valuation of real property, the market technique is considered the most applicable to landmarks, provided that the factors of building age, condition, history, livability, etc. are considered. Historic designation's effect on property value is also discussed: designation will increase value where a landmark is already at its highest and best use; when value depends on removal, destruction, or substantial changes in a structure, designation will often negatively affect value.

Gordon, Roy L. "Valuing Historically Significant Properties." *The Appraisal Journal* 10, no. 2 (April 1974): 200-09.

This article discusses the applicability of traditional appraisal methods to valuing historic properties. According to the author, a sales technique employing suitable "comps" is usually the most appropriate procedure, provided adjustments are made for variations in building size, location, and neighborhood influences. Other issues relating to site comparability, income potential, and depreciation are also considered.

Hershman, Mendes. "Critical Legal Issues in Historic Preservation." *The Urban Lawyer* 12, no. 1,(Winter 1980), 19-30.

The author examines the findings and implications of the "landmark" United States Supreme Court decision, *Penn Central* v. *New York*. State and local supports for historic preservation are also noted including various property-tax incentives such as exemption and rehabilitation abatement/reduction. The author also considers the consequences of private historic preservation agreements.

Higgins, J. Warren. "Certified Historic Structures: Trap and Tax Shelter." *The Real Estate Appraiser and Analyst* (September-October 1978).

This article discusses numerous provisions of the Tax Reform Act of 1976. It concludes that landmark-rehabilitation incentive measures provided by the 1976 act should be considered in estimating the value of affected buildings.

"Landmark Preservation Laws: Compensation for Temporary Taking." *University of Chicago Law Review* 35 (1968): 362-75.

The author briefly considers the valuation of a temporary taking, such as occurs in establishing an historic easement. Reference is made to a "before and after" valuation procedure applied by the courts.

Latimer, Truett. "Government Assistance in Preservation Financing: The State Sector." In *Economic Benefits of Preserving Old Buildings*. (Washington, D.C.: Preservation Press, 1976.)

Truett surveys state activities to assist historic preservation financing. State landmark-property-tax programs are discussed, with specific attention paid to measures found in Alaska, Connecticut, Idaho, New Hampshire, New Mexico, and Oregon.

Maisenhelder, Howard. "Historical Value or Hysterical Value." *Valuation* 17, no. 1 (1970).

Maisenhelder criticizes appraisers who, as a matter of practice, increase the value of all historic properties by 20 percent. The author stresses the need to avoid unfounded generalizations; landmarks must be carefully appraised on a case-by-case basis if assignment of "hysterical value" is to be avoided.

Mann, Mary E. "Valuation of Historic Properties." In Eugene C. Cowan, editor. *Historic Preservation and the Law*. Washington, D.C., National Trust for Historic Preservation, 1978, p. viii.-2.

This article considers special property-tax measures for historic buildings, including tax exemption, rehabilitation refund/assessment/abatement, and assessment at current use. The author is opposed to tax exemptions, stating they erode the tax base and are not keyed to need. Support is voiced, however, for property-tax relief in the case of hardship.

Problems in assessing landmarks are examined, such as the inherent difficulty of determining the impact of designation "until someone actually attempts to make a specific use of the landmark property." Legislation articulating how historic properties should be treated by assessors is recommended.

McGee, Joseph H. "State and Local Taxation, Current Practices, Procedures and Effects." In Gregory Andrews, editor. *Tax Incentives for Historic Preservation*. Washington, D.C.: The Preservation Press, 1980, p.102-107.

The author discusses property-tax measures to encourage historic preservation. Instead of the usual practice of assessing real property at fair-market value, or "highest and best use," a number of alternative procedures are suggested, such as assessment at current use and incorporating in the assessment the effects of easements and other factors. Reference is made to statutory provisions stipulating special landmark assessment in California, District of Columbia, and other jurisdictions.

Morris, Eugene J. "Appraisals of Realty for Taxation." In Eugene Cowan, editor. *Historic Preservation and the Law*. Washington, D.C.: National Trust for Historic Preservation, 1978, p. viii-3.

This article presents an excellent analysis of the landmark-assessment issues. Morris first overviews the property-tax system in New York City and then summarizes problems of assessing New York City landmarks, such as the inherent difficulty of valuing the landmark's land separately from improvements. The author notes the variable effect of designation on property value and the need for assessors to be sensitive to these differing consequences. Optimism is voiced that the problem of assessing landmarks will ultimately be resolved in much the same manner as other vexing assessment issues, such as the valuation of properties subject to rent controls, have been dealt with.

National Trust for Historic Preservation. "Values of Residential Properties in Urban Historic Districts: Georgetown, Washington, D.C. and Other Selected Districts." *Information: From the National Trust for Historic Preservation*. Washington, D.C.: Preservation Press, 1977. Study authored by John B. Rackham.

This research paper compares property values in a historic district (Georgetown in Washington, D.C.) to those outside this neighborhood. Property values in Society Hill (Philadelphia) and other historic districts are also briefly noted. Side-by-side comparison indicates that historic status increases property value. In the words of the study, "The imposition of historic district controls in an area, complemented by the general recognition that they have been appropriately placed, results in the following pattern of residential property demand and value: available quality housing in reasonable condition within the district is marketed readily at increasing price levels; existing housing in poorer condition is acquired—often by developers—and renovated; and land for building sites, if available, is obtained and improved in conformance with architectural controls."

Assessment/property-tax implications resulting from the property-value appreciation within the historic neighborhoods are also considered. Various assessment strategies to alleviate inequitable landmark-property taxation are reviewed, such as assessment at current use. The District of Columbia's efforts in this regard are highlighted.

Nelson, John C. "Public Actions to Accommodate Changes in Property Values." In Eugene Cowan, editor. *Historic Preservation and the Law*. Washington, D.C.: National Trust for Historic Preservation, 1978, p.viii-5.

Nelson addresses the question of designation's impact on property value and also suggests various mechanisms to offset possible adverse economic consequences including (1) transfer of development air rights, (2) abatement of real-estate taxes, (3) grants-in-aid, (4) low-interest loans, and (5) modifying zoning, building, or other codes.

Powers, Lonnie A. "Tax Incentives for Historic Preservation A Survey, Case Studies and Analysis." *The Urban Lawyer* 12, no. 1 (Winter 1980): 103-37.

Numerous landmark-property-tax strategies are examined, and prototypical programs in Maryland, Oregon, and the District of Columbia are reviewed. The author concludes that the landmark-property-tax provisions have yielded mixed results as far as their usage by owners and impacts on encouraging rehabilitation.

Powers, Lonnie A. "State Historic Preservation Tax Statutes: Three Case Studies." In Gregory Andrews, editor. *Tax Incentives for Historic Preservation*. Washington, D.C.: The Preservation Press, 1980, pp. 108-24.

Landmark-property-tax measures in Oregon, Maryland, and the District of Columbia are compared and evaluated. Oregon's rehabilitation assessment has been applied to about 200 landmarks. The Maryland and District of Columbia provisions, in contrast, have experienced minimal utilization. Powers discusses the programmatic and other factors explaining these variations in usage. Copies of the Oregon and District of Columbia statutes are appended to the article.

Rackham, John B. "Values of Residential Properties." See *National Trust for Historic Preservation*.

Ragas, Wade R. and Ivan J. Miestchovich, Jr. "Historic Properties and Tax Incentives." *The Real Estate Appraiser and Analyst* (May-June 1980), pp. 9-14.

The authors consider Section 2124 of the 1976 Tax Reform Act and other federal income-tax provisions enacted to encourage the rehabilitation of historic properties. They conclude that the new incentives increase the profitability of landmark ownership and therefore should be considered in appraising landmarks.

Reynolds, Judith and Anthony. "Factors Affecting Valuation of Historic Properties." *Information: From the National Trust for Historic Preservation.* Washington, D.C.: Preservation Press, 1976.

This paper presents an appraisal process for valuing landmarks. It notes the importance of proceeding in a step-by-step process that includes definition of the appraisal problem, identification of the property's environment and physical and historical characteristics, examination of alternative uses, including the actual use, collection of data, and estimating value through one or more of accepted appraisal approaches.

The paper stresses the importance of considering the "variable characteristics" of the landmark, including site features, improvement level/type, historical significance, as well as the "qualifications" for highest and best use. These characteristics must be examined on a case-by-case basis. In the words of the authors: the "highest and best use of a property with significant historical association or character, if the property is located in a complementary environment and its physical integrity is high, may include preservation or restoration; for historical properties of lesser significance, the highest and best use may be preservation through adaptive use such as conversion of a dwelling to a law office; finally, if the aspects of physical integrity, functional utility and environment are insufficient to warrant preservation, then the highest economic use may be demolition of the structure."

Reynolds, Judith. "Preservation Easements." *The Appraisal Journal* (July 1976), pp. 355-60.

Reynolds reviews procedures for analyzing the effect of the donation/sale of preservation easements. She recommends that appraisers first consider the highest and best use in the before-easement case and then determine the highest and best use after the easement has been established. The difference between these "before and after" figures is the value impact attributable to the easement. The author highlights numerous related issues, such as how easements should be treated by assessors, and why different types of easements can exert varying effects.

"State Preservation Laws." *Wake Forest Law Review* 12 (1976): 112.

Numerous property-tax programs for historic preservation are reviewed, including reduction in North Carolina, and rehabilitation abatement in Maryland and New Mexico.

Scribner, David, Jr. "Historic Districts as an Economic Asset to Cities." *The Real Estate Appraiser* (May-June 1976), pp. 7-12.

This article examines how historic districts in major urban areas are delineated and also considers the impact of designation on city revitalization. It notes that the property values of buildings within historic areas are higher than sister structures located outside of such neighborhoods. In the Old Town area of Virginia, landmarks are worth approximately 2.5 times comparable buildings located just beyond the boundaries of this historic district. In Capitol Hill in Washington, D.C., values are four times greater; in the Federal Hill area in Baltimore, values are 7.5 times higher. The author argues that the linkage between property value and historic designation should be recognized by appraisers, and recommends that appraisers rethink some of their rules of thumb that are inapplicable in landmark situations.

Shlaes, Jared. "Transferable Development Rights: Impact on Real Property Tax Assessments." International Association of Assessing Officers, editor. *Property Tax Incentives for Preservation: Use-Value Assessment and the Preservation of Farmland, Open Space, and Historic Sites.* Chicago: International Association of Assessing Officers, 1975.

Shlaes discusses the impact of the transfer of development rights, referred to as TDR, on property-tax assessment. Transferor districts— those areas selling TDR rights—should experience a reduction in their assessments. In contrast, transferee districts—those areas receiving the added TDR rights—should experience an increased assessment. In theory, the reduction in the transferor districts and the increase in transferee districts should be approximately equal, but Shlaes notes that in practice this equilibrium may not be achieved.

Shlaes and Company. *Property Tax Incentives for Landmark Preservation: Draft Program for Use in Chicago and Cook County, Illinois.* Report prepared for Commission on Chicago Historical and Architectural Landmarks. Chicago: Shlaes and Company, August 1977.

One of the first and most comprehensive analyses of the statutory and programmatic state-of-the-art of landmark properties and the property tax. The study commences by classifying the landmark assessment/taxation approaches followed by California, Oregon, North Carolina, Virginia, and numerous other states. Field-level implementation of the landmark-property-tax programs in these jurisdictions is also highlighted. This national perspective is followed by examination of how landmark buildings are and should be treated by Cook County assessors. Appended to the study are copies of key landmark-property-tax statutes.

Stipe, Robert E. "State and Local Tax Incentives for Historic Preservation." In Gregory Andrews, editor. *Tax Incentives for Historic Preservation.* Washington, D.C.: The Preservation Press, 1980.

Several types of landmark-property-tax programs are described, including assessment at current use and special incentives for rehabilitation. Programs in Maryland, North Carolina, New Mexico, District of Columbia, Oregon, California, and Connecticut are discussed. The author notes the relatively low usage of these measures and attributes this to various reasons ranging from philosophical opposition to the provisions as a "backdoor approach" to practical limitations such as stringent eligibility criteria that disqualify many landmarks. The author concludes by considering some of the issues and inherent limitations of providing property-tax relief for landmarks.

Warsawer, Harold N. "Appraising Post-Revolutionary Homes." *The Appraisal Journal* (July 1976), pp. 344-54.

This article discusses the appraisal of nine Revolutionary-era homes in Manhattan by means of a comparable sales technique. While sales of exactly comparable properties could not be obtained, sales of equivalent homes were identified and analyzed. Selling prices of the equivalent buildings were adjusted, taking into account numerous factors, such as structure size, presence of special amenities (i.e., fireplaces), historic significance of the different properties, as well as the extent/cost of remodeling undertaken in each case.

"Use of Tax Incentives for Historic Preservation." *Connecticut Law Review* 8 (1976): 334.

Various forms of landmark-property-tax measures are discussed, including exemption, reduction, assessment at current use, and assessment to reflect encumbrances.